The Future of Social Security Policy

Current debates concerning the future of social security provision in advanced capitalist states have raised the issue of a Citizens' Basic Income (CBI) as a possible reform package: a proposal based on the principles of individuality, universality and unconditionality which would ensure a minimum income guaranteed for all members of society. Implementing a CBI would consequently entail radical reform of existing patterns of welfare delivery and would bring into question the institutionalised relationship between work and welfare.

Ailsa McKay's book makes a unique and positive contribution to the CBI literature by examining the proposal from a feminist economics perspective. Gender concerns are central to any debate on the future of social security policy, in that state intervention in the field of income redistribution has differential impacts on men and women. By drawing attention to the potential a CBI has in promoting equal rights of freedom for men and women this book serves to open up the debate to incorporate a more realistic and inclusive vision of the nature of modern socio-economic relationships.

Ailsa McKay is Senior Lecturer in Economics at Glasgow Caledonian University.

Routledge frontiers of political economy

The Future of Social Security Policy

Women, work and a Citizens' Basic Income

Ailsa McKay

Routledge
Taylor & Francis Group

LONDON AND NEW YORK

First published 2005
by Routledge
2 Park Square, Milton Park, Abingdon, Oxon, OX14 4RN

Simultaneously published in the USA and Canada
by Routledge
270 Madison Ave, New York NY 10016

Routledge is an imprint of the Taylor & Francis Group

Transferred to Digital Printing 2009

© 2005 Ailsa McKay

Typeset in Baskerville by Wearset Ltd, Boldon, Tyne and Wear

British Library Cataloguing in Publication Data
A catalogue record for this book is available from the British Library

Library of Congress Cataloguing in Publication Data
A catalog record for this book has been requested

ISBN10: 0-415-34436-0 (hbk)
ISBN10: 0-415-54764-4 (pbk)

ISBN13: 978-0-415-34436-4 (hbk)
ISBN13: 978-0-415-54764-2 (pbk)

Publisher's Note
The publisher has gone to great lengths to ensure the quality of this
reprint but points out that some imperfections in the original
may be apparent.

For Rory, Annie and Jim

Contents

Acknowledgements

My initial interest in the general area of social security policy materialised in a previous life when I was employed as a welfare rights adviser. I therefore owe a debt of gratitude to both colleagues and users of the service for the contributions they made in developing my awareness of the complexities and inefficiencies of current measures and the need for more informed discussion on future reform proposals. However, my academic pursuit of the CBI proposal would not have been possible without the encouragement of Professor Chris Pierson. This book is based on my Ph.D. thesis and Chris's supervision throughout the course of researching, writing and presenting my thesis was invaluable. I would also like to thank various colleagues at Glasgow Caledonian University for their continued support over the years. In particular, I extend thanks to Emily Thomson for her 'sisterhood' and Gordon Morlan for sharing his technical expertise. I am grateful to family and friends for their encouragement, patience, numerous bottles of wine and good food (often left considerately at the doorstep), over a considerable period of time. I am particularly grateful to Morag and Jim for their sustained efforts in thinking, reading and talking about it all. However, I would like to dedicate a special thanks to Annie Cameron, who never really understood why and how but was proud of me nonetheless. I only wish she had stayed around long enough to witness a final outcome. Finally my thoughts are with Rory and Annie. A big thanks to both of you for 'being there' and 'not being there' when appropriate, and of course to Jim for his role in making that happen. This book is dedicated to them.

Glossary

BA	Benefits Agency
BIG	Basic Income Guarantee
CBI	Citizens' Basic Income
CB	Child Benefit
CTB	Council Tax Benefit
CTC	Child Tax Credit
CSJ	Commission on Social Justice
DfEE	Department for Education and Employment
DSS	Department of Social Security
DWP	Department of Work and Pensions
EU	European Union
EC	European Community
ES	Employment Services
GDP	Gross Domestic Product
HB	Housing Benefit
IS	Income Support
ILM	Intermediate Labour Market
JSA	Job Seekers Allowance
MTR	Marginal Tax Rates
NIT	Negative Income Tax
NIC	National Insurance Contribution
OECD	Organisation for Economic Co-operation and Development
RMI	Revenue Minimum d'Insertion
UUB	Unconditional Universal Benefit
UHB	Universal Hourly Benefit
VAT	Value Added Tax
WFTC	Working Families Tax Credit
WTC	Working Tax Credit

1 Introduction
Social security reform – a possible strategy

Introduction

The overall purpose of this book is to draw attention to the confining nature of mainstream economic theorising in the policy process and to outline how a feminist economic perspective could contribute to the development of a more inclusive and realistic understanding of state welfare arrangements. The main subject of the book is an exploration of the Citizens' Basic Income (CBI) proposal and how it presents as an invaluable opportunity to reshape the future of social security provision in advanced capitalist states. The proposal itself involves the granting of a universal and unconditional minimum income guarantee and has evolved in recent decades as a possible reform package that would address effectively the dual and often conflicting objectives of social justice and economic efficiency. However, the CBI proposal remains a theoretical concept in that no advanced capitalist state has implemented a universal, unconditional minimum income guarantee.

Within a global context, the reform of social security policy is currently high on the political agenda. This is due mainly to the significant level of public resources dedicated to state-supported income maintenance programmes combined with growing concern over the persistence of widespread poverty and the related problem of social exclusion. Furthermore, concern regarding gender-based inequalities, particularly those directly associated with the operation of modern labour markets, is receiving greater attention in terms of public policy interventions. The 'social justice' case for the promotion of gender equality has been strengthened by a heightened awareness regarding the negative consequences of gender-based inequalities on overall economic performance. The concept of 'gender mainstreaming' is now considered a principal driving force in the design, implementation and monitoring of all public policies and programmes. The systematic integration of a gender equality perspective into every aspect of policy-making, implied by the concept of gender mainstreaming, is thus considered an important issue across Europe, both at an institutional and a national government level.

Although the CBI proposal has evolved in recent decades as a possible reform package that effectively would provide the foundations for transforming the nature of state welfare provision in line with a 'gender mainstreaming' strategy, the existing literature is devoid of this perspective. Arguments in favour of a CBI have been presented from a range of academic perspectives and there is a growing body of literature focused on evaluating the concept of a universal unconditional income guarantee with reference to the dynamics of modern socio-economic conditions. However, in line with current debates on the future of social security policy, the existing CBI literature is characterised by an emphasis on 'paid work'. That is, debates regarding the effects an unconditional income grant would have on individual behaviour have been dominated by analysis of its impact on existing patterns of formal labour market participation. Although the workings of the formal labour market is accepted as an extremely relevant factor in the design of any state-supported income maintenance programme, the prioritising of such above all else is indicative of a biased approach. That is, the focus on the world of paid work demonstrates a gender bias in that the life experiences of many women are largely ignored. Gender concerns are central to any debate on the future of social security policy in that state intervention in the field of income redistribution has differential impacts on men and women. This is due to the very crucial role that gender plays in determining individual behaviour and the failure to adequately account for such implies that current welfare reform agendas are 'gender blind'.

It will be argued that this 'gender blindness' is the direct result of an analytical approach to study that treats gender issues as 'add-ons' rather than an integral feature of the research process. It is in this respect that parallels can be drawn with the structures and processes associated with mainstream economic analysis. With reference to welfare reform debates, the claim is made that the emphasis on preserving a traditional productivist work-and-pay relationship, evident in the CBI literature, follows from an immutable acceptance of the governing principles associated with neoclassical economic theory in the research process. Gender concerns have remained at the periphery, and any attempts to include women have been made without altering the analytical framework. Conjectures regarding individual responses have been hypothesised within a model based on assumptions applied exclusively to all members of society. Such theorising follows the same pattern as the practice of economics as an academic discipline and as such fails adequately to address issues relating to gender inequalities. In terms of policy responses, this leads to a focus on 'acting' upon inequalities as they are identified or arise rather than 'transforming' the processes and structures that create and sustain such inequalities. Subsequently, the advantages of the CBI proposal in promoting the equal citizenship rights of women are not adequately considered and in many instances are misunderstood.

The aim of this book, then, is to develop a feminist economics perspective on social security reform with a particular emphasis on the CBI proposal. Evidence of the continually dominant influence of mainstream economic theorising in the analytical process will be presented. It will be argued that this represents a biased and exclusive perspective and, when applied, results in policy designed in accordance with a view of how the world *should* operate. Thus, the *subjective* nature of the neo-classical approach is exposed and the subsequent influence of value judgements is made explicit. From a feminist economics perspective, attempts to incorporate gender concerns within such an inherently biased analytical framework are limiting. The practice of including issues and concerns specific to women, previously neglected, may serve to enrich the discipline by ensuring that the subject matter studied is a more accurate reflection of real world economic phenomena. However, if in studying this broader subject matter the methods and analytical processes associated with the dominant neo-classical approach remain unaltered, the practice of 'doing economics' will fail to provide us with a framework for developing an understanding of the actual nature of such 'real world economic phenomena'. Accounting for the social construction of gender divisions and the influence this has on individual choice is key in developing an understanding of both the causes and consequences of gender-based inequalities. In terms of welfare reform it is therefore considered crucial that feminist economic theory is embraced, as much of what policy is trying to address results from socially constructed inequalities. Rather than 'add women and stir', a feminist economics perspective facilitates transparency in the policy process, effectively by adapting the existing analytical framework to account for the very different social experiences of men and women in market-based economies. Given the current mainstreaming agenda, adopting an approach that serves to *transform* the research process to ensure the systematic integration of gender as a primary influencing variable is considered desirable and indeed necessary.

This introductory chapter will outline the main aspects of the CBI proposal within the context of providing a foundation for transforming the nature of state welfare provision. In presenting the case for adopting a feminist political economy approach in arguing for a CBI, the purpose is to demonstrate why this is considered a necessary next step in current welfare reform debates.

Arguing for a Citizens' Basic Income

> The current debate between advocates and opponents of the introduction of a basic income, of a grant unconditionally paid to every adult citizen, constitutes, in my view, one of the most important controversies about the future of European welfare states.
>
> (Van Parijs, 1992c: 215)

A CBI is often viewed as an agenda for the reform of social security. However, the radical nature of the proposal implies a new perspective on the role of the state as a provider of welfare, a rethinking of the traditional work-and-pay relationship and a very different position on the rights and obligations of citizenship in modern state welfare regimes. For these reasons, a CBI should be viewed as a reform package that provides the framework for developing a new conceptual basis for the modern welfare state, rather than as an alternative proposal to existing social security measures. Understanding a CBI within these terms allows for clear links to be made with the proposal and the various 'crisis' theories, which currently dominate debates on the future of the modern welfare state. This in turn facilitates an understanding of how the CBI proposal impacts on the numerous welfare functions of the state and how it indirectly promotes rights of citizenship other than those related to income security.

A CBI will be clarified and distinguished from similar but distinct proposals. It will become evident that the concept itself is simple and appeals to a wide range of very different political and economic ideologies. The argument to be made is that the introduction of a basic income for all would not only address the social problem of poverty but would also satisfy the debate between the dual and often conflicting objectives of economic efficiency and equity. A CBI would promote labour market flexibility and at the same time erode the existing disincentives to work which currently arise from the interaction of the tax and benefit system. Furthermore, a CBI would promote gender justice and is a policy option that does not discriminate in favour of a predetermined set of normative values regarding living arrangements. Rather a CBI would provide the foundations for a system of state welfare provision that allows individuals to make independent choices about the way they live. For all of these reasons a CBI should not be viewed as a proposal for the reform of social security but as a philosophy which serves to justify the modern welfare state.

Within current debates on the future of state-supported income maintenance schemes the CBI proposal regularly emerges as an extreme option involving a radical transformation of existing social security and income tax arrangements (see for example Hills, 1993). The introduction of a CBI would not merely imply tinkering with existing systems in response to identified inadequacies or inefficiencies. The concept itself involves the acceptance of a whole new range of justifying principles regarding the nature of state-supported income maintenance. The existing literature witnesses varied and convincing attempts at identifying and analysing such justifying principles (see for example Van Parijs, 1992a). Despite these attempts the CBI proposal remains a theoretical 'pipedream' yet to be translated into reality. Powerful and convincing arguments are postulated from both supporters and critics alike. The main objections raised are expressed in terms of financial cost and the negative economic impact such a scheme would have on work incentives. The common link emerging from these criticisms is that the issue itself is misunderstood and the debate tends to centre on the idea of social security reform. Implicit within the CBI proposal is the acceptance of the interdependence of economic performance and social policy which in turn sets the stage for the building of new political alliances regarding the function of modern welfare states. A CBI is not merely an alternative to existing social security provision but rather a philosophy aimed at enhancing individual freedom and promoting social justice.

It is difficult to escape the normative issues arising when attempting to justify such a philosophy. Also, as the acceptance of a CBI would render any current system of state income maintenance redundant, it is attractive to view any such reform in terms of an either/or scenario. However, by adhering to positive economic analysis, critics of a CBI fail to recognise some of the more crucial long-term benefits to be gained. The contribution made by applying the tools of economic analysis to the study of social security policy is worthwhile in itself, but in terms of policy formation, it is a partial analysis. To fully appreciate and understand the nature of social security measures the debate must progress beyond the realms of determining an efficient allocation of resources and incorporate questions of social justice, citizenship rights and individual autonomy. Moreover, the process of resource allocation must recognise the influence of institutions and the state rather than relying solely upon the analysis of market interactions. It is claimed therefore that the theoretical basis for a CBI would be better served by appealing to a feminist political economy framework.

A feminist political economy

Analysing the CBI proposal within a feminist political economy framework involves developing an approach to study which views the world in terms of its inherent set of complex social and economic interactions. Furthermore, these interactions should be viewed with consideration to the dynamics of socio-economic conditions. Developing such an approach allows for the recognition of the limitations of exclusive theorising premised on a homogeneous and universal particular. Models of the body politic and the economy which are based on axioms determined by the theories, methods and institutions associated with the capitalist development of the Western world dominate the realm of social theorising. This 'Western scientific world view or mind-set' (Harding, 1991: 3) effectively acts in constraining new modes of thought. The generation of new theories, which are both descriptive and prescriptive, becomes a technically difficult thing to do when attempted within a community dominated by a monolithic or determinist discourse. In considering the future dominance of the capitalist economy, Gibson-Graham draws attention to the ways in which the discourse of capitalist hegemony limits our ability to articulate policy change:

> For if capitalism's identity is even partially immobile or fixed,... if it is the site of an inevitability like the logics of profitability or accumulation, then it will necessarily be seen to operate as a constraint or a limit ... We see this today in both mainstream and left discussions of social and economic policy, where we are told that we may have democracy, or a pared-down welfare state, or prosperity, but only in the context of the [global capitalist] economy and what it will permit.
>
> (Gibson-Graham, 1996: 14)

Analysing all social, political and economic processes within the specific boundaries of capitalist relationships serves to distort our view of the world. By accepting the immutable force of the capital accumulation process; the desire for profits; the supremacy of market-based interactions in determining the efficient allocation of resources and the rational choice model of both individual and collective action, we effectively categorise all human activity in an either/or scenario. That is, all interactions that can be explained within the confines of the model of the capitalist economy are positive, simply because they can be explained and therefore understood. This facilitates the descriptive and prescriptive processes of social theorising. Those actions or relationships which do not fit the model, and therefore are not understood, are subordinate to the norm and in a binary sense become negative. This type of theorising not only limits our understanding of the world but also informs our thinking on policy developments and limits the terms of reference for conceptualising new, or even existing, human relationships.

The CBI concept is considered to be a radical approach to welfare reform in that it implies a radical departure from existing institutional arrangements. The process of developing theoretical justifications for such a policy will eventually hit a stumbling block if this process takes place within the parameters outlined above. In order to get over this hurdle, the constraints imposed by accepting a singular and closed conceptualisation of the economy must be removed. Capitalism has developed as a view of how modern society does, and should operate, almost to the exclusion of all other views. However, although capitalist structures of power, control and ownership could be identified as the defining features of many social and economic interactions, they are not representative of all forms of relationships. Attempts to offer new explanations must first recognise that the dominance of the capitalist identity results from the social construction of ideas and it is those ideas that effectively act as a constraining force.

It will be argued that the issue of welfare reform would be better understood if the approach to study initiated a critique of the monolithic discourse of capitalist relations. The privileging of a set of specific ideals over all others is a form of bias which influences the research agenda and subsequent policy prescriptions. It is essential that this bias be identified within the research process, to allow for the construction of a more objective approach to study. In attempting to do so it is fruitful to draw upon a feminist approach, particularly within the traditionally male-dominated academic discipline of economics. Feminist economists have criticised their discipline for focusing exclusively on the analysis of choice, specifically the choices of independent rational economic actors aiming to maximise their own welfare with reference to scarce resources. This limiting definition of economics leads to the critique that:

> economists have not paid sufficient attention to relationships between men and women or parents and children, and that as a result, they have failed to provide a convincing analysis of economic development, political conflict, or social welfare.
>
> (Folbre, 1994: 4)

Accepting this critique opens the door to a new, more inclusive, economics. Feminist economists, faced with the task of incorporating what appear to be intangible factors, such as human and social relationships, into an almost impenetrable academic discipline, must first examine why and how the study of economics has come to be dominated by such narrow and limiting assumptions.

In their critique of contemporary orthodox economics, feminist economists have drawn upon feminist scholarship concerning the social construction of gender and the social construction of academic disciplines. In exploring the hypothesis that contemporary economics has been heavily influenced by preconceived notions about what is considered worthy of study, and what is considered to be the most appropriate method of study, feminist economists have concluded that there is a determining link between their discipline and socially constructed gender categories. By making this link, feminist economists not only reinforce the claim that economics is socially constructed, but also shed light on the bias inherent within the discipline by identifying the polarisation of gender associations. The understanding of gender in terms of the 'masculine' (equals hard, strong, separate, scientific), and 'feminine' (equals soft, weak, connected, intuitive or emotional) dualism has been applied to the study of economics. A positive connection with all that is masculine and a negative connection with all that is feminine have subsequently influenced how the discipline of economics is understood.

The privileging of the masculine model has not however occurred by accident. In discussing the development of the discipline, Ferber and Nelson argue that if we begin by rejecting the suggestion

> that the ideals and definition of economics have been given to humankind through divine intervention ... [and] ... instead recognise that the discipline we call economics has been developed by

particular human actors, it is hard to see how it could fail to be critically influenced by the limitations implicit in human cognition and by the social, cultural, economic, and political milieu in which it was created.

(1993: 1)

Economics as an academic discipline has traditionally, and continues to be, dominated by men (see for example Palmer, 1995; Hewitson, 1999: 40–41). Accepting the claim made by Ferber and Nelson regarding the influence on the discipline by the 'limitations implicit in human cognition', it could be argued that male economists would define the discipline in terms of what they understand:

> The subject of the economist's model world is an individual who is self-interested, autonomous, rational, and whose active choices are the focus of interest, as opposed to one who would be social, other-interested, dependent, emotional, and directed by an intrinsic nature. In many ways, this description resonates with the economist's self-image as well.
>
> (Nelson, 1996: 22–23)

Economics has at its core the study of human behaviour and therefore it is a social science. However in their strive for accreditation in a hierarchical academic community, economists have persisted in applying the tools of rigorous scientific analysis to their chosen fields of study, almost to the exclusion of all other methods. Quantitative approaches are favoured over qualitative methods and formal mathematical models are given supreme status over informal descriptive measures. This facilitates the economists ability to abstract, simplify, measure, and subsequently analyse, a subject matter which appears on the surface incredibly complex and difficult to predict. For Nelson,

> Economics, as a human endeavour, reflects human limitations in understanding a reality that is always beyond our grasp. Economics, as a social endeavour, reflects some points of view, favoured by the group that makes the rules for the discipline, and neglects others.
>
> (1996: 23)

Economics, then, as an academic discipline is socially constructed and dominated by a particular, and limited, conception of human interactions. Furthermore, this dominant view is believed to incorporate a gender bias in that the discipline is constructed by men, studied by men and presents policy prescriptions which benefit men. Thus, as Hewitson argues, the 'knowledge' of the economics discipline is in doubt in that 'the context of discovery may be biased because of male domination, and furthermore, male domination may also affect the context of justification'(Hewitson, 1999: 40). The gender imbalance within the profession is therefore a cause for concern, not only with reference to equity considerations in terms of employment practices, but also because it serves effectively to exclude issues relevant to women from the research agenda. Although the 'absence or invisibility of women is a problem which characterises many disciplinary frameworks' (Hewitson, 1999: 46), the absence of women at all levels within the economics profession presents a particular problem for a discipline with such a wide social remit. Feminist economists endeavour to remedy this problem and to reorient the discipline in a more gender neutral direction.

This does not mean that feminist economists 'seek to excise all of the values traditionally associated with science', but rather they wish to draw attention to, and remove 'the biases that may arise from an unexamined emphasis on masculinity' (Ferber and Nelson, 1993: 11). Their task, then, is not to refute all that is associated with a 'masculine' economics and to replace it with a new 'feminine' economics. Such an approach would be criticised for illustrating a gender bias in favour of women, an equally limiting and narrow approach to that which exists now. The goal is to practice a more objective science. However, objective in this sense does not mean value or interest free, since this would be almost impossible to achieve in a research community and, more importantly, the promotion of certain values and interests is an integral component of the research process. It is argued that a greater degree of objectivity would be achieved by developing an approach to the discipline which incorporates a range of values and interests representative of the population, rather than focusing on the particular at the exclusion of alternatives. This would allow for the inclusion of methods and topics previously ignored in the practice of economics, subsequently broadening the horizons of the discipline and improving the tools of economic analysis. Feminist economics is therefore not to be understood as 'women doing economics' but rather it should be regarded as a method of inquiry serving to shape the discipline of economics into a more useful and informative mechanism for understanding the complexities of human activity. In an editorial written for the first issue of the journal *Feminist Economics* launched in 1995, Diana Strassman confirms this as the strategy of feminist enquiry:

> By challenging the merits of narrowly situated economic theories and research agendas reinforcing the interests of adult men, feminists have therefore sought to enhance the visibility and perceived importance of the wide range of policy initiatives advocated and debated by feminists in economics and elsewhere. Whether engaged in discussing welfare reform, childcare, family planning, economic development, structural adjustment, domestic abuse, sexual harassment, discrimination, affirmative action, pay equity, family leave, or the feminisation of

poverty, feminists have initiated a sweeping debate on economic policy issues vital to the economic well being of the majority of humans. In so doing feminists have begun to challenge an economic practice that for too long has served the interests of a restricted and unrepresentative group of people.

(Strassman, 1995: 4)

Drawing upon this strategy facilitates the development of a feminist political economy. Traditional approaches to analysing, and explaining, structures of power, ownership, control and collective identities are criticised from a feminist perspective for being incomplete and inconsistent. The overriding emphasis on rational self-interested economic agents making informed, free choices, and the uni-dimensional nature of class struggle, which effectively form the basis of contemporary theories of political economy, are limited assumptions. That is, such assumptions fail to adequately account for the life experiences of many individuals and women in particular. To paint a more complete picture a new approach is required that accepts the insights to be gained from traditional theories but also broadens the realms of inquiry to include the influence of social institutions. Nancy Folbre, in stating a case for developing a feminist political economy, draws attention to the omissions in traditional theories:

> Feminist scholarship documents the ways in which groups based on gender, age, and sexual preference have forged their collective identities and pursued their collective interests. The evidence of persistent struggle is embedded in the historical silt of formal rules that have denied women, children and homosexuals rights over person and property and limited their ability to accumulate assets. Less tangible, but no less central, has been the reproduction of cultural norms and personal preferences that have legitimated adult male heterosexual authority. None of these mechanisms of hierarchical constraint has ever been limited to the family, but they have remained largely invisible to those who placed the family outside the domain of political economy.
>
> (1994: 48)

Opening the doors to a new method of inquiry represents a starting point for deconstructing particular ideals and beliefs regarding the functioning of modern capitalist economies. Research which is premised on a set of given assumptions modelled in a different era for the primary purpose of explaining, and indeed justifying, a particular political and economic structure is criticised for illustrating a bias in favour of that structure. A feminist political economy provides a theoretical framework for dismantling the obstacle imposed by the capitalist identity and breaking from old traditions in creating a new discourse of economic difference. Within this framework a central focus is the analysis of socially constructed structures of constraint, how such constraints are informed and influenced over time, and how they impact on both individual and collective action. It is argued that this approach leads to a broader and richer conceptualisation of socio-economic relationships. Consequently, applying this approach to the area of welfare reform, and the CBI proposal in particular, results in a more comprehensive understanding of the issues and opens the doors to new measures representing radical departures from the past.

Outline

In exploring the welfare reform agenda, with specific reference to income maintenance policy, the focus of Chapter 2 is to identify the purpose, nature and structure of income transfers in modern welfare states. An examination of the theoretical framework employed in justifying state-supported benefit systems will demonstrate the relevance of mainstream economic analysis. However, it will be argued that neo-classical economic theory has tended to dominate the study of income maintenance policy and has resulted in benefit structures designed to conform to a particular set of ideals regarding the function of income transfers in a market-based economy. This effectively serves to constrain reform debates by prioritising the objective of economic efficiency. Chapter 3 will build on this hypothesis by outlining the objectives and functions of income maintenance policy and the relationship between such measures and other areas of public policy. The distinction will be made between income maintenance policy and the concept of 'social security' for the purpose of demonstrating the broad range of objectives that can be associated with state action in the field of income redistribution. It will be argued that reform strategies should be assessed with reference to such objectives. The first step in the reform process should therefore involve an undertaking to explore the nature and functions of state-supported income transfer schemes. Such an undertaking will serve to illustrate the prevalence of traditional economic theory in the policy design process, and subsequently, in setting the reform agenda. To further substantiate this claim, Chapter 4 will provide an overview of contemporary social security policy in Britain. Recent developments in the operation and design of the British system can arguably be identified with an approach to policy founded on assumptions akin to those central to neo-classical economic theory. It will be argued that these influences are common to modern advanced capitalist welfare regimes, albeit to lesser or greater degrees. Chapter 5 will introduce a CBI as a policy response to the perceived crisis in state-supported welfare systems. An evaluation of the CBI proposal will be approached within a theoretical framework that draws upon a feminist political economy model. It will be argued that although gender issues are central to any debate on social security reform, the potential benefits of a CBI in terms of promoting gender justice have been sadly overlooked. It is claimed that this is due to a continued acceptance of the governing principles associated with neo-classical economic theory in the research process. Providing evidence of such serves to demonstrate the inherent tensions in introducing a radical approach to reform within a traditionalist and institutionalised approach to policy analysis. Chapter 6 will trace the historical development of minimum income guarantee proposals outlining their relationship to traditional debates on economic efficiency, and more contemporary debates on citizenship rights, particularly the issue of social exclusion. The purpose behind tracing the development of the CBI concept is to provide evidence of the continuing emphasis on preserving a traditional productivist work-and-pay relationship within the literature. This focus is criticised for illustrating a gender bias in that the life experiences of women are largely ignored. The CBI proposal remains firmly grounded in theoretical discussion with little prospect of transformation into policy, despite evidence tracing the variations of proposal as far back as the onset of modern capitalist development. The remainder of the book will argue that this situation can only be remedied by widening the parameters of analysis. Chapter 7 will explore contemporary arguments in favour of a CBI, which have been framed in response to the crisis in welfare hypothesis. This will demonstrate the limitations in the debate thus far. It will be argued that the existing literature fails adequately to address issues relating to gender inequalities. Chapter 8 will develop a feminist economics perspective on the CBI proposal. This will entail deconstructing the traditional work/non-work polarisation in the same way that feminist economists have attempted to deconstruct the masculine/feminine distinction that has been applied in their discipline to the detriment of the understanding of economics. The application of feminist economic theory in the analysis of income maintenance policy serves to refine our understanding of the CBI proposal. Furthermore, a feminist economics perspective contributes positively to the debate on social security reform by providing a further, convincing, theoretical justification for a CBI on the grounds of promoting gender justice.

2   Justifying income transfers

Introduction

> In the standard paradigm of orthodox economics resource endow-
> ments determine personal wealth and personal income distribution.
> These endowments are taken as "given" exogenous variables, at least
> to economists. Consequently remedies for inequalities in the distribu-
> tion of wealth and income fall largely outside the purview of the posit-
> ive science of neo-classical economics and can only be justified on
> normative non-economic grounds.
>
> (Burkitt and Hutchison, 1994: 19)

> Income transfer programs are a fundamental component of the
> welfare state in most, if not all, advanced western societies. We know
> this from the proportion of government budgets devoted to such pro-
> grams; from their primary role in the establishment and subsequent
> development of the welfare state; and from the universal impact
> which social security and taxation have on the economic well-being of
> families and individuals.
>
> (Mitchell, 1991: 1)

Why are income transfer programmes deemed necessary? What is the function of state-supported income maintenance programmes and how do
these programmes interact with other areas of state welfare provision?
What types of programmes can modern welfare states continue to financially sustain given the changing nature of the economy and in particular
the structure of contemporary labour markets? Is there continued political
will to support the public provision of income maintenance programmes
and if so should these programmes be universal or selective? Have the
problems that programmes are designed to address been adequately identified and is there a mechanism to ensure that effective monitoring and
evaluation takes place? Does existing income maintenance policy meet the
conditions implied by the current emphasis on mainstreaming gender in
all areas of public policy? These questions are undeniably central to the

reform debate on the future of income maintenance policy. However, what appears to be missing from that debate is an informed discussion focusing on what is understood by the concept of income maintenance.

The provision of individual financial security is a principal function of the modern welfare state. How such security is provided, the adequacy of coverage, and the actual levels of payments made, vary considerably from country to country. Diversity in design is largely a result of variations in the perceived or even stated goals of income transfer programmes. In turn the goals or objectives of policy will be informed by ideological dogma. However, differences in systems apart, state-supported income maintenance programmes are an orthodox feature of the modern economy. Furthermore, the development of such programmes occurred within a climate of political consensus regarding the crucial role of the state in securing and promoting social welfare. Throughout the post-war era interventionist policies were generally accepted as an integral feature of modern capitalist development. As a consequence any talk of income maintenance policy reform was undertaken against a background of the need to support and maintain existing capitalist economic and social relations. Recent political, economic and social developments have led to a breakdown in the 'post-war consensus' and subsequent erosion of support for the mixed economy of welfare. Current debates are therefore no longer dominated by the overarching theme of 'state welfare' but rather are characterised by the search for alternative structures believed to be more appropriate in meeting the exigencies of global, competitive economies. The emphasis has switched from tinkering with the design of systems to questioning the whole apparatus of modern welfare state activity and income maintenance policy has not escaped attention. However, it is argued that the reform process itself has continued with the traditions of the past in that it has been prefaced, and hence informed, by the practice of prioritising the needs of a specific set of capitalist structures.

Current debates on the future of income maintenance policy have been maintained within a framework of fixed parameters relating to the role of income transfer programmes in the overall functioning of the modern economy. This in itself is a value judgement and serves to limit our understanding of income maintenance policy. What is required is an approach to study that effectively recognises the inherent biases within current debates and facilitates the development of a more inclusive framework for analysing policy. This chapter will set out the research agenda by examining the purpose, nature and structure of income transfers in modern welfare states. This will allow for criticism of the narrowly conceived notion that publicly provided cash benefits exist primarily to relieve poverty. Initially it will be argued that the theoretical framework employed to provide justification for benefit systems will depend upon how those systems are defined. Restricted definitions result in the adoption of limiting theoretical arguments. In turn this leads to rigidity in the reform process.

The chapter begins by summarising the predominant theoretical arguments employed in justifying income maintenance programmes. The need for state intervention in the transfer of incomes between individuals, or groups of individuals, has long been argued for on the grounds of economic efficiency. Drawing upon traditional economic theory, such arguments have proved convincing in justifying state-supported benefit systems and have benefited from a general level of consensus amongst the academic community and policy makers alike. However, the tendency for conventional economic arguments to dominate the theoretical background has resulted in benefit structures designed to conform to a particular set of ideals and beliefs regarding the nature of human behaviour. It will also be argued that the practice of analysing income maintenance policy has been dominated by adhering to a traditional political economy framework, thereby emphasising preconceived notions about the direct relationship between policy and overall economic performance. State-financed and delivered income maintenance programmes will obviously impact on the functioning of both the macro and micro economy. However, stressing the significance of such in the analytical framework serves to overshadow the multiplicity of functions associated with income maintenance policy. Identifying those functions allows for a broader conceptual understanding of the nature of policy and provides the foundation for developing a more comprehensive analytical framework. This process contributes positively to the reform debate by illustrating that policy options remain constrained by narrowly-defined objectives. Removing those constraints would enable an expansion of the boundaries of the current debate to include a broader range of choices for the future.

Despite the above noted observations, it is worth restating that the relevance of economics in the study of income maintenance policy is not to be denied. What is in question, however, is the merit bestowed upon a particular way of doing economics. A continued and virtually exclusive attachment to the assumptions and models associated with the neo-classical school of thought has meant that the practice of doing economics has become synonymous with the application of neo-classical theory. Any attempt to move the reform debate forward would therefore benefit from a process of identifying how neo-classical thought is applied in the field of income maintenance policy and thus distinguishing such from alternative approaches. This will lay the foundations for developing a feminist economics perspective in the study of income transfer programmes in that it would provide evidence of the compelling influence of neo-classical economics in the design of systems. Furthermore, this would confirm the accusations made by feminist economists that their discipline has been effectively hijacked by the practice of privileging a set of ideals and norms pertaining to human interactions, which in itself is indicative of an approach constrained by value judgements. The reform of existing structures of income maintenance systems must therefore begin with an undertaking to investigate and, subsequently, question the leverage of traditional economic theory in the design process.

Justifying the benefit system – a question of economics?

As a component of public policy, income transfer programmes are subject to scrutiny with specific reference to economic efficiency, administrative feasibility and political acceptability. Furthermore, due to the direct impact such programmes have on individual welfare, questions of social justice, gender equality and citizenship rights must also be addressed. What is less clear is how these questions should be prioritised and this tends to be where most of the controversy arises regarding future policy direction. Questions of setting and prioritising objectives are essentially normative and therefore will be informed by the value judgements of policy makers. It is difficult to escape such judgements in any policy analysis. What is essential, however, is that they are identified and recognised as potent contributory factors in the reform process. That is, value positions should be made explicit, thereby ensuring the transparency of the influence of various institutional structures in the analytical process. Thus the positivist position, upheld by mainstream economists, is brought into question. Claims to objectivity are really more about value 'blindness' in the sense that an assumed set of ideals permeate the research process unquestioned and invisible. Adopting a feminist economics approach would serve to switch the focus from 'blind' to 'neutral' by ensuring that the influence of value structures are identified at the outset, and adhered to where appropriate.

Historically, the development of income transfer programmes has been associated with high employment levels and sustained periods of economic growth:

> Specifically, the welfare state was seen as strengthening economic performance because of two widely shared perceptions: the stabilising effect of social transfers on the economic cycle and the positive contribution of social insurance to workers adjusting to economic change.
>
> (Buti *et al.*, 1998: 17)

More recently the dynamics of the international economic environment have led to a breakdown in the general consensus regarding the integral feature of income maintenance policy in the efficient functioning of the modern economy. Persistent high rates of unemployment, combined with various demographic changes, evident throughout the economies of the advanced western world, have placed new pressures on the public purse. Spiralling costs, coupled with a general slowing down in rates of economic growth, have raised concerns in many industrialised countries over the future sustainability of the modern welfare state. In response, most member states of the EU have been forced to review their respective welfare systems. Reform packages have been introduced within an atmosphere of caution and restraint. The emphasis has been on curbing further expenditure growth and limiting the dependence on deficit funding. In turn, economists have increasingly found that the financing and delivery of publicly provided welfare services is an area deserving of their attention:

> The economics of the Welfare State is now centre stage, entering debates about the macro-economy and the wealth of nations. Reform of the Welfare State is seen as one of the key policy issues of the 1990s.
>
> (Atkinson, 1995a: 1)

Within the reform debate attention has primarily focused on the design and operation of income transfer programmes. This is due in the main to the direct impact such programmes have on fiscal policy, the functioning of the labour market and costs to employers. Although priority has been given mainly to measures designed to cut spending, or at least to reduce the rate of growth in spending, questions of economic efficiency have increasingly come to dominate the debate on the future of state-supported income transfer programmes.

Markets, efficiency and income transfers: the neo-classical approach

Conventionally, the study of economics has been dominated by the rational justification of policy options with reference to the goal of efficiency. The process of analysing and evaluating public policy within the economics profession generally focuses on questions of economic efficiency and policy effectiveness. That is, a particular policy is deemed acceptable if the social costs are minimised whilst the social benefits are maximised and the subsequent reallocation of resources will contribute positively to the overall welfare of society. Economists who study income transfer programmes generally start from the premise that state-supported income maintenance schemes are justified in terms of market failure. Simply put, this means that where the market fails to provide adequate incomes, or appropriate insurance against loss of income, there exists a rationale for state intervention to promote overall social welfare. For economists, the maximisation of social welfare will depend upon achieving both allocative and distributive efficiency in all sectors of the economy. Economists are therefore mainly concerned with analysing, and subsequently setting out, the necessary conditions for efficiency. However, it is important to note that this statement is a generalisation and should not be taken to imply that the process of economic analysis is exclusively driven by efficiency considerations. Nor is it to be assumed that all economists (and indeed economics *per se*) are to be associated with a defining unified methodology. What is being argued is that modern mainstream economics has come to be identified with a particular approach and within this approach the efficiency/inefficiency dichotomy has dominated the domain of policy analysis. Presenting a valid critique of this position requires a basic understanding of the principal assumptions inherent within mainstream, or what is referred to in the profession as 'neo-classical', economic thought. The following section, therefore, represents a summary of the main elements of neo-classical economic analysis traditionally employed in the study of state supported and/or regulated income transfer schemes.

The theoretical background: a non-technical overview

The study of economics is primarily concerned with the problem of scarcity. The resources available to society are limited in supply whereas our material wants are unlimited. Hence the prevailing view of the human condition, within the discipline, is that our wants are always outstripped by our desire to fulfil them. Both production and consumption decisions have to be made as to which desires should be met and which should be left unfilled. The consumption of various goods and services in order to satisfy our wants yields positive economic benefits. Likewise, the more goods and services produced and available for consumption increases the amount of benefits to be enjoyed overall. However, any choice involves a cost in terms of the best alternative forgone and economists refer to this as the opportunity cost. For example the cost of spending more money on state provided income maintenance programmes may involve sacrifices in terms of increased spending on government funded retraining schemes, hence the opportunity cost of employing more resources in the provision of income maintenance is the reduction in resources available for retraining. The government in this situation could be said to be making a trade off between investing in skills for the future and state-financed income security in the present. The outcome of such a decision will depend upon the overall objectives of the government which will almost certainly be determined by political ideology. However, orthodox economists have been preoccupied with the practice of building a theoretical framework, divorced from the influences of political processes, with which to analyse, evaluate and predict the outcome of alternative uses of our scarce resources:

> The methodology of neo-classical economics rests on two basic building blocks. The first is the idea that the economy is an analytically separate realm of society that can be understood in terms of its own internal dynamics. Economists are perfectly aware that economic behaviour is influenced by politics and culture, but they see these as exogenous factors that can safely be bracketed as one develops a framework that focuses on purely economic factors.
>
> (Block, 1990: 21)

By applying objective scientific analysis to the study of human behaviour, economics as a social science attempts to build simplified models of the economy and in turn, through a process of deductive methodology, it provides us with a tool for predicting and evaluating the outcome of various consumption and production decisions. Such a process is viewed as necessary in that divorcing themselves from the 'normative' issues arising in questions of policy options, economists attempt to contribute in a 'positive' way only. The overarching approach to economics then is the positive, or rather scientific, analysis of choice in the resource allocation process for the purpose of providing direction as to the optimal utilisation of scarce resources with reference to the objective of maximising social welfare. If economics, as an academic discipline, is to be ascribed with a subject matter, accepting this description of the dominant economic approach means that arguably it can be identified as the scientific study of choice.

It follows that the methodological underpinnings of the neo-classical tradition dictate that certain assumptions are made about the conduct of a wide variety of economic agents. At this point the student of economic theory is introduced to the concepts of rationality, self-interest, marginality and the overall objective of utility maximisation in the study of individual decision making. The hypothesis on which the conventional economic theory of human behaviour is based is that an individual, when faced with competing choices, will choose that course of action yielding the most economic benefit. The individual will gather all the necessary information required to make the appropriate choice and will always and everywhere attempt to maximise personal satisfaction or utility. Human behaviour, then, within the realms of economic theory, is determined by rational utility-maximising economic agents. However, individuals do not only make choices as consumers but also as producers and as policy makers. Subsequently the assumption of rational utility-maximising behaviour is applied to firms as well as to governments. It follows then, that if costs are incurred in the form of opportunity costs and benefits are received, the appropriate course of action for any decision-maker is to weigh up all relevant costs and benefits, selecting the outcome where benefits are maximised and costs are minimised.

Individual preferences aside, economists seek to ascertain how individuals reveal the values they assign to the associated costs and benefits of their actions. The choices made by rational utility-maximising economic agents are, in practice, marginal choices. That is, the majority of decisions are made on a 'more or less' as opposed to an 'all or nothing' basis. Resources will be allocated to those activities with marginal values which are greater than their respective marginal costs. The assertion is made that as consumption of a particular commodity increases, the marginal benefits accruing to the individual will decrease. Subsequently the more an individual has of a certain item the lower its marginal value will be to him or her, and substitutions will be made for products with a higher marginal value. Resources are therefore allocated on a marginal basis and substitution will cease when the marginal value, or utility gained, is equal to the marginal cost, or the price, for all goods or services consumed in any given time period.

This is a highly simplified version of utility theory. In reality the study of consumption choices requires a more complex approach incorporating issues such as: influences other than price which inform consumer preferences; imperfect knowledge in the market place; how prices are set; and how values are assigned in the absence of any market price. However, by following a path of wholly abstract and logical reasoning the methodology of traditional economic theory facilitates the development of axioms or rather 'laws' which govern the study of human behaviour. The approach is highly individualistic and reduces the complex nature of a whole range of human interactions into a few simple and unifying theories. For example:

> The implication that *MV* equals price implies the so called "law of demand": *The higher the personal cost of obtaining any entity, the less will be acquired in any period of time.* It also implies that the prices voluntarily paid by individuals to gain an increment of a good, or receivable to compensate for the loss of a good, provides an observable measure of *MV*.[1]
>
> (Culyer, 1983: 14)

Developing a theory, which explains the process of individual resource allocation, proves invaluable in evaluating the impact of a whole range of public policies on individual behaviour. For instance the use of government taxes or subsidies principally act to alter the market-determined prices of both consumption and production goods and services. Any change in price subsequently will alter the marginal cost:marginal benefit ratio faced by individuals in a given time period and will, therefore, result in a reallocation of resources. Consider an increase in price brought about by the imposition of a tax. The marginal cost to the consumer has increased and, if no other factors have changed to influence the subjective marginal value attributed to the good or service by the individual, then marginal cost is now greater than marginal benefit. The rational economic agent will act to decrease consumption thereby ensuring that, given the law of diminishing marginal utility, the marginal value increases. Changes in consumption patterns will cease when the marginal cost to the individual is once again equated with the marginal benefit gained. Accepting that consumer and producer choices are determined by appealing to the theory of marginal utility provides economists with a hypothetical framework for predicting the outcomes of policies that artificially distort market prices.

With reference to income transfer programmes, this abstract approach is utilised to explain individual choices in allocating their time between work and leisure. Traditional neo-classical labour supply theory is derived directly from marginal utility theory. It seeks to explain the behaviour of individuals with reference to their respective labour supply decisions, given the constraints imposed by a fixed number of hours available for allocation and market-determined wage rates, which effectively allows for calculations to be made about the prices of work and leisure. The theory assumes that individuals are faced with an either/or scenario when allocating their time use, in that the only choice open to them is to consume work time or leisure time. The work option provides material benefits and is necessary in modern capitalist societies for economic survival while the leisure option is pleasurable, yielding positive benefits other than those associated with meeting basic economic needs. The theory implies that rational economic actors will:

> ...seek to find the combination of the two which gives them the greatest overall satisfaction (or utility), and (once basic survival has been achieved) yield leisure to work if, and only if, an increase in income results.
>
> (McLaughlin, 1994: 146)

Premised on these few simple propositions, the traditional neo-classical theory of labour supply provides economists with a framework to analyse any individual's desire to work. The process of logical reasoning leads to the conclusion that individuals will only be prepared to work additional hours if the wage to be derived from that work is higher than the value attributed to the associated sacrifice in leisure time. It follows that any income derived from sources other than formal paid work will impact on labour supply decisions, *ceteris paribus*. With a given level of desired income the need to enter into paid work is diminished for any individual when income levels are maintained via state-supported income transfer programmes. Such programmes effectively alter the individual's budget constraint by raising the price of work relative to leisure. Assuming stable utility functions, individuals will react to the availability of unearned income from the state by choosing less work and more leisure, thereby generating entitlement to state benefits.

Although this is a very basic introduction to traditional neo-classical labour supply theory it proves sufficient to demonstrate the point that the process of purely abstract logical theorising, the dominating practice of traditional economists, results in the development of 'laws' which are then employed to predict the outcomes of policy. Furthermore, these 'laws' are increasingly drawn upon to inform policy design in the area of state welfare provision. This is mainly a product of the developing awareness of the relevance of economic analysis in the study of social expenditure plans. However, it can also be argued that the case for widening the remit of applied economic theory is welcomed, and indeed, strengthened by the relative simplicity of the arguments. Abstract and unifying theories of human behaviour benefit from ease of understanding and hence translation. It follows that those charged with the responsibility of predicting the outcomes of possible reform packages, and/or evaluating the effectiveness of existing measures, are attracted by an analytical framework which presents a single integrative theory for analysing an individual's decision making processes when faced with competing choices.

Much of the contemporary discussion on the future of income transfer programmes has found credence by appealing to orthodox economic theory. Debates on selectivity and targeting, as opposed to universality, have primarily focused on questions of economic efficiency with specific reference to the impact the benefit system has on individual work incentives:

> The strength of the view that social security provision is inherently problematic for reasons of disincentives ... finds its rational appeal in, and seeks legitimacy from, neo-classical economic theory.
>
> (McLaughlin, 1994: 145–146)

The incentive/disincentive question has plagued current debates on state-supported income transfer programmes and the emphasis has been justified by appealing to the logic of neo-classical labour supply theory. The central tenet is that any form of income support on offer from the state carries with it the possibility that individual labour market activity will alter for the purpose of eligibility for benefits. This in turn will have a negative impact on overall economic welfare:

> In orthodox economic theory benefits allow an unemployed person to choose to enjoy leisure rather than return to work. While this might maximise that individual's well being, it lowers social output below what it might have been in the absence of such benefits. A wedge is driven between individual utility maximising outcomes and socially efficient outcomes. Incentive problems may be created not just for the unemployed person but also for their spouse if benefits depend on the income of the family. If one partner works then the other may lose all rights to benefits.
>
> (Johnson, 1994: 164)

Thus, any form of cash benefit will diminish individual work effort with obvious negative consequences for overall economic performance. The acceptance of this hypothesis will inform the ultimate design of the benefit system. For example: generous cash benefits will be argued to have unacceptable adverse incentive effects; income tested programmes should operate to ensure that the income gained from paid work is always positive, thereby avoiding the disincentive effects of high marginal income tax rates; entitlement conditions for universal or contingent benefits should be set in such a way as to avoid impacting on an individual's willingness to earn and/or save; and the cost effectiveness arguments for assessing benefit entitlement on a family income basis as opposed to individual income should not be offset by the disincentive effects such benefits have on all household members.

Designing the tax and benefit system with these factors in mind raises questions about the trade-off between the redistributional impact of income transfer programmes in alleviating individual economic insecurity and the overall impact on economic efficiency. For economists, the central concern is about net gains to society and accordingly any policy which involves a reallocation of resources from one individual, or groups of individuals, to another must be considered in terms of the potential contribution made to social welfare as a whole. For these reasons income transfer programmes are considered with specific reference to the macro economic environment, alongside the micro economic issues regarding the impact that measures have on individual labour market activity. For economists, then, the key aspect of any examination of state intervention in the area of income redistribution is to determine the effect such activity has on the functioning of capitalist economic structures, with particular reference to the world of paid work.

This approach to policy analysis produces limiting arguments in deter-mining the actual design of systems. Furthermore, the acceptance, and indeed, privileging of the capitalist model of economic organisation inherent within the traditional economics approach to social policy pro-duces equally limiting theoretical justifications for publicly-supported income redistribution schemes. An essential feature of traditional eco-nomic theory is the acceptance of a range of correctable imperfections in the workings of a market economy. That is, the belief is held that the operation of the free market will not always lead to a socially optimal allo-cation and/or distribution of resources due to the existence of unavoid-able market failures. The prices assigned to goods and services in the market place will not always reflect their true respective values mainly due to the imperfect knowledge of producers and consumers and imperfect competition amongst both buyers and sellers. Natural tendencies towards monopoly production, powerful forms of collective action and time lags in the market signalling mechanism are intrinsic features of the free market and will lead to the distortion of market prices. Government intervention can rectify such failures by providing information (legislating on specific safety and quality standards); controlling and monitoring monopoly power (setting up various regulatory bodies); and actively supporting the flexibility of markets (establishing agencies that provide information on job availability).

However, in addition to these failures, the free market in certain situ-ations proves wholly ineffective in achieving socially optimal price and output levels. The nature of many goods and services make it difficult, if not impossible, for them to be traded in a perfectly competitive market. Consider for example situations where the private production/consumption calculations of individual economic agents do not account for the social benefits to be derived, or the social costs incurred, as a result of their independent activities. This will result in levels of production or consumption that are not socially efficient and therefore represent a welfare loss to society. The consumption of vaccinations against infectious diseases is a frequently cited example demonstrating the outcomes of the existence of 'externalities' in market transactions. Assuming that individual consumption decisions are based on a utility-maximising rule then the individual, in choosing the amount of vaccinations to consume, will settle at the level where the marginal *private* costs incurred are equated with the marginal *private* benefits gained. By accepting that the consumption of vaccinations by any individual yields positive benefits for society as a whole, and that the market-determined price for any particular vaccination does not incorporate this societal benefit, it can be concluded that there will be a disparity between rates of marginal private benefit and marginal social benefit at any given level of consumption. It follows that the consumption patterns of independent individual rational utility-maximising agents will not realise these external benefits to society, resulting in under-consumption. In order to raise consumption and hence output levels, some mechanism has to be found to internalise the social benefits of vaccinations. In this instance state intervention is justified, for the purposes of assisting the market in reaching a socially efficient equilibrium level of output. The form of intervention will depend upon the extent of the external benefits to be realised. Subsidies will act to lower the market price for individuals, therefore increasing levels of demand. However, if the intention is to enforce a minimum level of consumption, some form of regulation could be employed, for example compulsory retirement insurance. In both cases the desired outcome of increasing consumption levels and, therefore, production levels is achieved whilst at the same time the fundamental principles of market allocation are retained.

Closely related to the problems associated with externalities are those raised by public goods. Such goods display certain characteristics, which render them inappropriate for production and allocation in a free market. Economists distinguish between pure public goods and semi-public goods with the difference being determined by the extent to which goods exhibit non-rivalry in consumption and non-excludability. Some goods when produced make it impossible to exclude others from consumption, giving rise to the *free-rider* problem and, in certain instances, the consumption activities of some will not impinge on the amount left for consumption by others. Very few 'pure' public goods exist, but if the potential for non-excludability and/or non-rivalry exists the market will generally not serve as an efficient means of production and, in many instances, the good or service will not be produced at all. In these cases the most appropriate form of intervention is public production, thus ensuring the maximisation of social benefits and a mechanism for imposing relevant charges on users.

State intervention is therefore justified in a number of instances and in a variety of ways with the prime purpose of correcting market failures, thereby ensuring the survival of the market mechanism as the primary means of allocating society's scarce resources. As previously stated, within traditional economic theory, justification for state intervention in the redistribution of incomes is founded on the principles of correctable market failures, particularly those relating to externalities and information problems. Individuals seeking to insure themselves against all possible contingent risks may find that the insurance market fails to supply the product they demand. This is primarily the result of asymmetric information; that is, the consumer has more information than the supplier. The market therefore fails to produce an efficient level of output which is directly attributable to the problems of *adverse selection* and *moral hazard*:

> The former arises where the purchaser is able to conceal from the carrier[2] the fact that he is a high risk, e.g. in medical insurance, where it may be possible for people to conceal facts about their health. Moral hazard (slightly to oversimplify) occurs when the customer can costly manipulate the probability of the insured event without the supplier's knowledge.
>
> (Barr, 1993: 118)

These problems make it difficult, if not impossible, for insurance companies to distinguish between high risk and low risk clients and, therefore, render them unable to calculate the relevant premiums. If premiums are calculated on an average risk the tendency will be for low-risk individuals to opt out with obvious negative consequences in terms of the pooling of risks formula. Adverse selection means that private insurance markets will either fail to provide insurance at all or will prove to be inefficient in meeting consumer demand. Furthermore, if insured individuals can influence the probability of the risk they are protected against, there exists an incentive to capitalise on insurance and not to take preventative action. The result is overconsumption of insurance:

> ...people might drive less carefully if they are insured, or buy fewer fire extinguishers, since insurance reduces the cost to the insured individual of those unwelcome events ... moral hazard does not make insurance impossible but causes inefficiency, in that people take less care than if they had to bear the full loss themselves.
>
> (Barr, 1993: 121–122)

Depending on the nature of the event or risk insured, it may also lead to overconsumption of certain goods and services:

> In the case of medical care, for instance, if an insurance company pays all medical costs, neither patient nor doctor is constrained by the patient's ability to pay. The marginal private cost of health care is zero for both doctor and patient, even though social cost is positive. The results of this form of moral hazard are twofold: because of the divergence between private and social costs, consumption of health care (and consequently the insurance payout) is larger than is efficient; and there is an upward bias in insurance premiums.
>
> (ibid.: 122)

The suppliers of insurance companies can adopt various measures to counteract the effects of asymmetric information. These include regulatory devices. For example: the employment of insurance inspectors to determine the validity of claims or requiring medical examinations prior to accepting a potential client; or incentive mechanisms such as rewarding infrequent claims through the offer of lower premiums. Although such measures serve to reduce the effects of adverse selection and moral hazard in the market for insurance, they do not fully address the problem of information failures. Furthermore, inefficiencies will persist due to the problems associated with externalities.

For an efficient equilibrium to be attained in the private market for insurance, some form of control mechanism is required on the demand side of the equation as well as the supply side. The demand for insurance requires that the rational maximising individual derives utility from the consumption of insurance. Assuming that the rational individual is risk-averse then it follows that satisfaction is derived from the knowledge that risk itself is abated. Thus the value assigned to certainty is equivalent to the price of insurance. However, individuals may be unwilling to purchase insurance in certain circumstances because the private costs outweigh the private benefits (consider the multiplicity of effects of informational problems discussed above). The specific problem of externalities can be identified when the process of adverse selection imposes external costs on low-risk individuals, causing them to opt out or underinsure. Furthermore, non-insurance gives rise to the 'third-party payment problem which will generally create a divergence between private costs and social costs' (Barr, 1993:124). In such instances the costs arising from an eventuality will be borne by the individual alone. In many situations this can be said to be an efficient outcome in that it is based on the rational choices of a utility-maximising economic agent who has independently calculated that the benefits of certainty are not sufficient to merit the associated costs of the particular risk. Inefficiency, however, arises when the costs of non-insurance on the part of any single individual are borne by additional parties. An obvious example is the costs associated with car accidents. Quite often costs are imposed on other road users in terms of damage and/or personal injury. These costs are not included in the independent calculations of the non-insured individual as they are external and the operation of the free market will provide no mechanism for ensuring that they are fully met by the responsible party. Not all external costs are readily identifiable when considering the unwillingness of individuals to consume insurance:

> The most obvious example of such a problem would be myopia when considering pension provision. It may well be that 25-year-old individuals would not make any voluntary provision for their retirement, but that they would regret their failure to do so when they reached retirement age.
>
> (Dilnot and Walker, 1989: 5)

The costs to the individual in this scenario are clear in that they will be without a secured income upon retiring from the formal labour market and, assuming that they have no alternative resources to draw upon, the risk of poverty is subsequently heightened. Less clear is how the independent actions of these 25-year-old individuals impose costs on others. The sight of old people dying of starvation on the streets is an unpleasant one and will cause disutility to those witnessing such scenes. Accepting then that the utility functions of many individuals will determine that they are motivated to alleviate the plight of the poor and their dependants (or at least to clean up the streets) demonstrates the existence of external costs. Voluntarism in insurance markets, then, implies that the total costs to society of many eventualities will not be fully accounted for. This type of inefficiency can be addressed by making insurance compulsory, in particular insurance to cover the external costs imposed on third parties.

However, such regulation assumes efficiency in the supply of private insurance. As previously argued, the potential for informational problems with regard to some insurable risks means that this is not always the case. The question then becomes one of finding an appropriate mechanism for addressing simultaneous market failures on both the demand and supply sides of the equation. Private markets for unemployment, sickness, maternity and retirement insurance demonstrate the existence of both externalities and asymmetric information (albeit to differing degrees) and as such will not achieve a socially optimal equilibrium. Private insurance for these contingencies will not be provided in sufficient quantities and, for some individuals, will not be available at all, nor will all individuals voluntarily consume it due to differences in independent assessments of risk. State intervention is therefore justified by appealing to economic efficiency arguments.

The economic benefits of interventionist policies are best illustrated with the example of unemployment insurance. Combining the practice of compulsory membership with public provision forms the basis of national insurance schemes. With regard to unemployment, such schemes are designed to protect all individuals in a society from the economic costs associated with job loss. The probability of unemployment is higher for some individuals than others. Furthermore, unemployment is an inherent feature of modern capitalist economies and, therefore, to a greater or lesser degree is often out of the individual's control. The exogenous nature of unemployment combined with its unpredictability renders the calculation of risk, both on the part of the supplier and of the purchaser, subject to imperfect information. The private market thus fails, resulting in efficiency arguments for state intervention.

Although equipped with an analytical framework for justifying state involvement in the market for unemployment insurance, little has been said about the actual nature of that involvement beyond compulsory membership and public provision. Questions remain regarding issues such as benefit levels, the conditions and duration of eligibility, contribution rates and additional payments for those individuals experiencing extra costs. Debates focusing on such issues will be determined by the stated objectives of policy and are therefore mainly normative in nature. That is, the relative merits of the options available will be judged in accordance with a range of possible social objectives, economic efficiency being only one such consideration. For example, income transfer programmes may be supported by appealing to the potential they have for promoting equity. An efficient allocation of resources does not guarantee an equitable distribution of resources and in fact the efficient operation of a free market may actually require unequal outcomes. Mechanisms which redistribute resources from the rich to the poor can be viewed as a way of alleviating the worst aspects of free market allocation, but whether or not this is a desirable outcome will depend upon the impact such mechanisms have on the primary goal of economic efficiency. In terms of justifying state involvement in income transfer programmes, policy does not have to be redistributive in order to promote efficiency, but it may be the case that equity is pursued as an indirect consequence of efficiency considerations. In stating the theoretical case for social insurance schemes, Barr raises both efficiency and equity arguments:

> The efficiency arguments rest on externalities, justifying compulsion, and technical (mainly information) failures on the supply side of the insurance market, justifying provision of the major benefits.... If we ignore consumption externalities, the main equity arguments are (a) that the poor may feel less stigmatised by insurance, and (b) that if insurance is publicly provided for efficiency reasons, it can then be used as a redistributive device. These arguments are compelling.
>
> (Barr, 1993: 200–201)

However he goes on to warn against confusion regarding the purpose of social insurance:

> There are good reasons for thinking of it both as a technical instrument for dealing with market failure *and* as a redistributive device. But the two cases are argued on very different grounds and should be carefully distinguished.
>
> (ibid.: 202)

Social insurance schemes can therefore be *justified* on the grounds of economic efficiency but the extent to which they are redistributive will be a matter of policy design and will depend upon how objectives are prioritised.

This distinction is crucial when considering the policy reform debate. The emphasis within the traditional economics approach is on providing the theoretical justification for state intervention of any kind and the overarching emphasis on efficiency will ultimately influence the form policy takes. Although other objectives may be considered, this will take place within an efficiency/inefficiency dichotomy, with specific reference to the operation of the market economy. In considering the design of income maintenance policy, the application of mainstream economic analysis implies that state intervention is justified in terms of particular market failures and should operate so as to alleviate the worst aspects of unequal outcomes (only when such outcomes have efficiency implications) arising from the workings of the free market. However, equal attention should be given to the potential for state-supported schemes to create perverse incentives, discussed earlier. That is, systems should be designed so as not to adversely impact on individual incentives to save and earn, thus not posing a threat to the continued efficient workings of capitalist-defined economic arrangements. In discussing the adverse incentive effects of both income-based and contingent-based benefits, Dilnot and Walker identify some possible problems:

> ...financial support tested against income may cause a disincentive effect to the extent that income may be under the recipient's control via his or her labour supply decisions ... provision for the elderly may cause individuals to save less during their working life. Similarly, income support for the unemployed may cause unemployed individuals to search less intensively for a new job and/or demand a higher paying new job; while employed individuals may take less care over behaviour that may lead to their dismissal – poor timekeeping for example. The same type of phenomenon may also be associated with income support contingent on sickness: compulsory sickness insurance may reduce self insuring behaviour such as eating a healthy diet.
>
> (1989: 7)

Thus supporters of the traditional economics approach to income maintenance systems would favour systems which: provide minimal amounts of
support; target benefits to those identified as being most in need over universal provision; and impose restrictive eligibility conditions designed to
promote self help and lessen welfare dependency. In their economic
analysis of social insurance schemes, Creedy and Disney draw attention to
the relevance of theory in the design process:

> ...the problem of moral hazard has usually preoccupied the debates
> on state support, whether in the form of the old Poor Law (which
> relied on "less eligibility" and on close monitoring by the use of the
> workhouse), or in more modern forms of social insurance. Thus the
> payment of unemployment benefit has usually been linked with a
> "work test", involving the use of labour exchanges, and individuals are
> disqualified from receiving benefits for a certain period if they are dis-
> missed from their previous employment, leave voluntarily, or are on
> strike.
>
> (1985: 17)

The application of traditional methods of economic analysis to the study
of income transfer programmes, therefore, provides policy makers with
powerful and convincing theoretical justifications for state intervention,
and an analytical framework for judging the efficacy of different design
packages.

Historically, design of income transfer systems, at least in Britain, has
been primarily influenced by the underlying philosophy of orthodox economic theory. It can be argued that the emphasis on the individual,
encapsulated within the traditional economics approach, is clearly visible
in the British system of income transfers. Although other influences can
be identified, the dominant legacy has been one of safety-net type provision and self-help (Thane, 1996: 279). This has been accompanied by an
overwhelming preference for supporting the role of the labour market in
determining and allocating incomes:

> The Beveridge Plan was the culmination of measures to relieve tem-
> porarily occurring poverty due to transitional "flaws" in the economic
> system. From the Elizabethan Poor Laws through the National Insur-
> ance Act of 1911 to the measures advocated by Beveridge in 1942, the
> explicit assumption was that incomes are chiefly derived from employ-
> ment.
>
> (Burkitt and Hutchinson, 1994: 19–20)

An examination of policy initiatives undertaken in recent decades provides evidence that the reform process has been driven by a desire to eliminate adverse incentives from income transfer programmes, particularly

those relating to labour supply (see for example Hemming, 1984: ch 5; Lister, 1991; McLaughlin, 1994; HM Treasury, 1995). Measures introduced have resulted in the increased use of means-tested benefits, reductions in the real levels of benefits and a diversion of resources from out of work benefits to programmes which supplement in-work incomes. The over-riding purpose of such measures has been to reduce the replacement ratios of incomes in and out of work and to promote the efficient targeting of resources. The case for greater targeting is strengthened by global economic change and the consequential fiscal constraints experienced by national governments.

The British experience with income maintenance policy demonstrates the fundamental influences of traditional economic theory. However, as previously argued, not all economists adhere to the traditional approach and, although the British experience is not unique, income transfer systems throughout the capitalist world are not homogeneous. Differences in tradition, culture and political processes all contribute to diversity in design and the prioritising of objectives. The argument made at this point is that applying the tools of economic analysis proves useful in the study of state interventionist policies, particularly with regard to efficiency considerations. Common financial constraints coupled with the problems of escalating unemployment rates have led to an increasing emphasis on efficiency in all modern welfare states. Justifying real reductions in expenditure and promoting active labour market participation are therefore crucial elements in the policy reform debate. It then becomes obvious how increasing deference is bestowed upon an analytical framework that presents income transfers as a function of capitalist models of organisation, particularly with reference to the world of work.

However, it would be erroneous to accept this case scenario as implying that the future for state-supported income transfer schemes is bleak. The relevance of neo-classical theory in explaining the nature of income maintenance policy is not to be denied, but nor should it be assumed that it necessarily entails even greater targeting and a move towards residual safety-net type provision. Consider for example the arguments surrounding the adverse incentive effects of benefits. Assuming that an individual is secure in the knowledge that they are insured against ill health does not automatically lead to the conclusion that they will 'enjoy' poor health, and hence be lax in their actions to promote good health. That is, certain behavioural assumptions can simply not be made without first having prior knowledge of individual preferences. The process of traditional economic theorising ignores these preferences, beyond the overarching principle of rationality and utility-maximising behaviour, thus the practice of simplification leads to erroneous results.

Most of the research aimed at demonstrating the disincentive arguments contained within the neo-classical model have tended to focus on labour supply issues:

Most economic work into the disincentive effects of benefits has not sought to demonstrate the existence of this effect (which is already assumed and intrinsic to subsequent modelling) but rather to estimate the size of the effect of social security provision on unemployment levels and durations.

(McLaughlin, 1994: 146)

However, as McLaughlin goes on to claim, despite substantial research in this area the findings have proved inconclusive and therefore 'some economists have questioned the validity of the assumptions underlying this kind of modelling – that is, questioning the existence, rather than the size of a benefit-induced disincentive' (op. cit.). In the varied criticisms attention has been drawn to a variety of factors, other than those associated with benefit levels, such as prevailing labour market conditions and social norms, which may influence individual choices with regard to formal labour market participation. Furthermore:

. . . financial incentives for the unemployed to take a job should not be summarized solely in terms of the nominal levels of income available in and out of work. Also of potential significance is the income risk which arises from making the transition into work, and which provides a disincentive to labour force participation for risk-averse individuals. There is a possible "employment lottery", not just an "employment trap".

(Jenkins and Millar, 1989: 149)

On aggregate, the results of a large number of empirical studies indicate that both the level and structure of benefits combine to create possible disincentives to work, but the extent to which such occurs is not as substantial as neo-classical theory would suggest. The degree of generalisation assumed within the traditional model does not account for possible divergences between groups, or even within groups of individuals, in terms of their work behaviour. In fact Dilnot and Kell argue that the majority of research into the disincentive effects of income transfers have focused solely on the labour market decisions of men, and they accurately state that the results should not be taken to imply that the behaviour of women would follow the same path (1989: 153). In their study of the labour supply decisions of women married to unemployed men they found that the observed work patterns of such women proved 'consistent with the incentives implied by the tax and benefit system' (ibid.). However they went on to state that:

We are at pains to emphasise that other factors may lie behind our results. In particular, it seems highly plausible that women married to unemployed men will be less likely to work because they have low education and skill levels (like their husbands), and because they live in areas of the country where there is a low demand for all types of labour, male and female. Sorting out the relevant importance of these and other explanations for the observed work behaviour of married women requires a detailed and carefully estimated econometric model of female labour supply, which is the longer run aim of our research.

(ibid.: 153–154)

From the above quote it is clear that the traditional economists' preference for making simplified and generalised assertions based on limited observations is continued. The assumption of 'low levels of education and skills' plus residence in unemployment blackspots is taken to apply to all individuals who are out of work. However in this study at least it is recognised that further research is required in order to assess the 'relevant importance' of these factors and to identify any alternative explanations.

Gender relations in the economy present in the above study as an obvious 'alternative explanation'. Failing to take account of such in any analysis of the disincentive/incentive effects of income transfers will not provide an accurate picture of the overall impact on the functioning of the economy. That is, accounting for gender in the policy design and evaluation process does not necessarily imply that policy makers must divert their attention from a near exclusive focus on efficiency-based objectives to now consider the promotion of gender equity. Although this is considered a worthwhile end result in itself and will be discussed in later chapters, the case to be made at this point is that the practice of justifying income transfers within a neo-classical economics framework may lead to policy that will not have the desired effect. The tools and analytical processes associated with mainstream economic theorising do not readily accommodate the treatment of gender differences. Thus, policy designed, delivered and evaluated within such a framework will be gender blind. Consider, for instance, the emphasis placed on the disincentives aspect of income transfers with specific reference to the world of paid work. Gender differences play a crucial role in determining access to and location within the formal labour market. Given the gendered nature of caring activities, women may find that the principle factor informing their labour market behaviour is not an evaluation of incomes in and out of work but the availability of adequate and affordable child care. Policies designed to promote paid work will remain inefficient in that they will have a negligible impact on the labour market participation of many women unless they are combined with measures to improve 'the availability and affordability of child care and child benefits in a gender-neutral, non stigmatised way' (MacDonald, 1998:16). In assessing the gender implications of recent reforms to social security policy within the UK, Fran Bennett makes reference to the shift away from treating women as 'dependants' of their male partners and the subsequent focus on 'individualisation' within the benefit system (2002: 564–565). Bennett goes on to identify such as a key feature of the government's overall agenda of 'expanding the boundaries of the groups of benefit recipients for whom paid employment is considered the most appropriate activity' (ibid.: 565). Such a move should be applauded from a gender perspective in that it serves to secure individual rights to benefits. However, it would appear that the rationale is to be found in the drive to promote labour market activity rather than by appealing to the goal of gender equity. Whatever the justification, the increased emphasis on individualisation, at least with reference to social security policy aimed at the working age population, has the potential to promote more gender-equitable outcomes. The crucial point here is that this potential will never be realised if gender concerns are neglected in the analytical process. As Bennett argues:

> Many commentators ... have noted the need for a clear gender analysis to accompany this increased emphasis on individualisation, to ensure that this is not detrimental to the interests of (some) women. In particular, they have emphasised the need to focus on questions about the quality and quantity of care provision for both children and adults – in terms of infrastructure and of the gendered division of labour – and about labour market conditions, especially the continuing gender pay gap, job segregation and the lack of training for women workers.
>
> (ibid.: 565)

With specific reference to policy developments in the UK, the lack of gender awareness evidenced by recent reform measures is arguably the direct result of an analytical approach that fails adequately to account for gender differences. Despite the shift towards a focus on individuals, at least with reference to labour market activation measures, the use of categories such as the 'family' or 'household' continue to dominate the operational nature of social security policy in the UK. For Bennett:

> ...these words suggest a view of the "couple" or family as an undifferentiated whole – rather than as a unit made up of individuals who share many things, but whose experiences in the labour market and the couple/family will also be different, in part because of their sex. Using this alternative, gendered perspective, it would be more likely to be made clear that it is usually individuals rather than couples who "earn" (and who will often earn different amounts depending in part on whether they are men or women) and that under the current UK tax system, it is not "families" but individuals who pay income tax.
>
> (ibid.: 562)

However, as Bennett argues, this failure of the UK government to follow through on previous commitments to approach the welfare reform agenda in a gender sensitive way reflects 'a particular conceptualisation of the major issues facing the UK and the government's policy priorities' (ibid.: 563). That is, the overall objective is to promote paid work for all but the focus on 'households' is driven by the perceived notion that families living in households where no-one is working are at a greater risk of poverty. This reasoning justifies prioritising the goal of reducing the number of 'workless' households and subsequently developing policies that are not gender sensitive but rather assume an homogeneous unit. The gender blind nature of such an approach runs contrary to the goal of promoting employment opportunities for all, and as Bennett points out, is not in line with targets developed at a European level encouraging all member states to act on ensuring 'that a certain percentage of the workforce – and more specifically of women – is in paid employment' (ibid.: 563). Given that women experience different sets of constraints from men, particularly with reference to accessing paid employment, policies may be ineffective if they are framed within an analytical construct dominated by the financial incentives/disincentives dichotomy and universally applied to the identified target group. That is, although such policies may serve to promote paid work for many individuals, the failure adequately to account for the very different needs of many unemployed women implies that the overall impact will contribute further to existing gender inequalities, at least with reference to the labour market participation rates. Furthermore, if such policies are designed in such a way as to incorporate an element of compulsion, the risk of poverty may actually be exacerbated for many women who find themselves 'forced' into low paid, insecure jobs whilst simultaneously meeting the associated financial demands of formal child care expenses.

Thus, social security policy designed and delivered with specific reference to the goal of promoting work incentives which fails to incorporate gender as an influencing variable will ultimately act in reinforcing traditional gender inequalities. As Macdonald argues:

> Social security provisions are increasingly evaluated in terms of the incentives/disincentives they create, and the possible market distortions they introduce. However, women are disadvantaged by the market and its underlying social norms as it now operates ... When work incentives are discussed, the realities of women's labour market opportunities and their care responsibilities must be taken into account.
>
> (1998: 16, 20)

Evaluating social security policy through a gender lens thus provides evidence that claims of gender neutrality associated with the practice and application of mainstream economic analysis are misleading. Gender relations are key in determining the actual impact of social security systems and the neglect of such throughout the policy process will result in a lack of recognition regarding both the nature and consequences of gender-differentiated outcomes. A gender sensitive analysis of social security would allow for a more accurate evaluation of the whole range of policy related outcomes. Furthermore, it would serve to indicate where gender neutrality could more accurately be described as gender bias. That is, the increasing emphasis within the reform agenda on cost effectiveness and promoting efficiency gains, or at least limiting any losses, within a market economy assumes a particular perspective on the nature of human behaviour. Implicit within this perspective is the notion that individuals will respond in similar ways to measures aimed at promoting economic independence. Within this context, the incentives/disincentives dichotomy is employed to illustrate the negative impact of generous social security measures, thus justifying the practice of targeting benefits to the poorest and implementing a range of policies aimed at promoting active labour market participation. Arguably, this approach is indicative of bias in that it favours those who can more readily access an independent income. Given women's relative disadvantaged position within the labour market, combined with their greater responsibilities for reproductive and care work, policies which involve a retrenchment of state support and an increased reliance on the market will inadvertently promote the strategic interests of men over those of women. With reference to the standard evaluation criteria of efficiency, policy designed within this gender-biased analytical framework will result in outcomes that negatively impact on overall economic performance. From a feminist economics perspective, it is considered crucial that evidence of any bias informing the policy process is made explicit and that any potential efficiency gains are understood within the context of any potential efficiency losses. Adopting a feminist economics perspective in the study of social security policy would therefore necessitate the systematic integration of gender concerns throughout the policy process. With this in mind it is crucial that the analytical framework employed in justifying state involvement in the area of income maintenance takes adequate account of gender differences.

The case made then is that, even from within the discipline itself, the predicted outcomes arising from the application of traditional economic theory to policy analysis are to be treated with caution. Although it is recognised that the overall methodological framework can provide valuable insights into the nature of economic transactions, the potential for criticism arises when the traditional model is oversimplified and solely applied. However, the relevance of neo-classical theory in analysing the relative efficiencies of particular policy outcomes should not be dismissed. With a given set of capitalist-based structures and a concurrent need to economise on the use of public resources, the tools of orthodox economic theory can be applied successfully in attempts to define and promote overall economic efficiency. Furthermore, the influence such an approach has had on both the formulation of objectives and the resulting policy design in the field of income maintenance cannot be denied, either in a historical or contemporary sense.

Due to the implications that state intervention in the transfer of incomes has for altering the allocation and distribution of resources, it follows that the study of income transfer programmes is very much a question of economics. Income inequalities can pose a threat to the goal of economic efficiency, particularly if they arise as a result of market failure. Returning to the opening quote, it can thus be argued that 'remedies for inequalities in the distribution of wealth and income' do indeed fall within 'the positive science of neo-classical economics'. The question then becomes: is the positive science of neo-classical economics an appropriate tool for explaining and predicting the outcomes of a range of policy options? With regard to income maintenance policy this question would appear to have a positive answer for those who adhere to the view that future policy direction requires an even greater targeting of resources alongside active measures to promote work incentives. As Hill argues:

> ...an important feature of the economics approach has been its strong emphasis upon the targeting of social security policies. Advocates from this school of thought have therefore become very involved in examining ways of integrating taxation and benefits and ways of developing means-tests. By contrast to those influenced by the social administration approach, who have argued that general entitlements to benefit contribute to social solidarity, minimize stigma and maximize take-up of help by poor people, this group of students of the social security system have tended to emphasize what they see as the inefficiency of universal benefit systems.
>
> (1990: 8–9)

He goes on to criticise the core assumptions of the traditional economics approach, focusing on what he refers to as the 'naivety' in presupposing the superiority of efficiency considerations in the policy making process:

> The flaw in the approach to rationality used by this group of students of the social security system lies in a belief that policies operate exactly in the way in which they are intended to operate, and in the belief that citizens all behave as "rational economic individuals" fully informed about the options available to them and able and willing to make calculations about the forms of behaviour that will benefit them most efficiently.
>
> (ibid.: 9)

Dissent can therefore be identified from both within and outside the discipline. This chapter has drawn attention, on a preliminary level, to the nature of that dissent. However, the purpose of this book is not to provide a general critique of neo-classical economic theory. Rather the arguments raised have sought to demonstrate the practical relevance of the economics approach to the study of income transfer programmes whilst at the same time clarifying the problems associated with accepting the superiority of a particular set of beliefs and ideals regarding the nature of economic organisation. That is, by initially viewing the workings of the economy in terms of a capitalist framework, the traditional economics approach lacks validity in the claim that it represents a positive scientific approach. The starting point itself is normative in nature in that it incorporates a vision of the 'good society'. It follows that any policy analysis will be informed by this vision and therefore undertaken within a framework of a given set of values regarding what 'ought' to be.

Consequently, any reform process will remain constrained by this approach. Questions regarding the future of income maintenance policy must therefore begin with an explicit recognition of this constraining boundary. By illustrating that the objectives of policy are implied within the traditional economics model, the limiting and constraining nature of this approach has been identified. The implications for income maintenance policy, in particular, are that with a fixed framework employed in the setting of objectives the resulting debates on policy design are too narrow. Atkinson's arguments, in his examination of the theoretical case for targeting, exemplify the problems associated with adopting a limiting framework:

> ...although politically fashionable, calls for greater targeting, need to be treated with caution. The argument in favour has to be made explicit and critically examined. Behind such policy recommendations lie views with regard to (a) the objectives of policy, (b) the range of instruments available to attain those objectives, and (c) the constraints under which policy has to operate (economic, political and social). All too often policy debate is based on implicit assumptions about the nature of objectives. It is tacitly assumed that the sole objective of policy is the reduction of poverty, whereas the typical social security programme in Western countries has a multiplicity of objectives. Even if the alleviation of poverty were the over-riding concern, the relative efficiency of different policies would depend on the precise way in which poverty is measured and on the "sharpness" with which the poverty objective is defined.
>
> (1995a: 223–224)

For traditional economists the debates surrounding policy objectives are essentially normative and therefore not within their domain. However, it is evident that the application of economic analysis to income maintenance policy is an important, if not crucial, element of the reform process, not least because of the significant function state-supported income transfer programmes perform in the modern economy. Furthermore, scarcity in resources is a given and therefore questions of efficiency can not be ignored. With regard to income transfer programmes, on a macro level, efficiency considerations focus on the proportion of public spending dedicated to the welfare services, and on a micro level, questions of efficiency involve examining the effectiveness of existing and/or alternative programmes, given the government's overall objectives, alongside an analysis of the distribution of total resources between programmes (Barr, 1993: 8). An analysis of income transfer programmes must therefore take account of the role such programmes play in the overall functioning of the welfare state: how programmes evolve and the various factors that inform the resulting design; the effects policies have on individual behaviour and on the workings of the economy as a whole; and finally how efficient (bearing in mind the dual aspect of the efficiency criteria) policies are in achieving the range of predetermined objectives. However, the methods employed by the narrowly defined traditional economics approach are limiting. The near exclusive focus on efficiency tends to leave questions of equity unresolved and prioritising objectives within a dominant framework of social welfare maximisation overshadows issues of social justice.

State-supported income transfer schemes impact, both in a negative and positive way, on individual resource capabilities. As such, the operation of such schemes have important social as well as economic implications. In market-based economies the relative command over resources assumed by any one individual will in turn determine a whole range of social interactions for that individual. For these reasons income maintenance policy must be viewed in terms of the differences it makes to peoples lives and not just those implied by the relief of absolute poverty. By assuming that state intervention in the redistribution of incomes is primarily a response to identified market failures these issues are ignored. As Dilnot and Walker argue: 'Far too often, social security policy is discussed without a serious consideration of why we have a social security system and what we want it to achieve' (1989: 5).

They go on to claim that although all income transfers (at least in Britain) can, in principle, be justified in terms of market failure in the resource allocation process, and/or in terms of the related objective of achieving a socially optimal level of distribution:

> What appears to be lacking is an adequate consideration of which objectives should have priority, and of whether the current mix of benefit regimes is likely to achieve these objectives most effectively.
>
> (ibid.: 6)

Conclusion

The technical aspects of traditional economic theory prove enlightening when applied to an examination of the relative successes of governments and/or the market in achieving various goals. However, the overwhelming emphasis on economic efficiency is in itself a value judgement and serves to diminish the importance of debates on alternative goals. In a traditional sense, applying the tools of economic analysis to the study of income maintenance policy means that questions of choice, efficiency and optimality in the resource allocation process take precedence over questions of justice or fairness. Allowing the reform debate to progress beyond the current confining parameters requires an approach to study that incorporates a multiplicity of objectives and recognises the multi-disciplinary nature of public policy analysis. Any serious consideration of the range of policy options available must accept as a starting point that design is a function of predetermined policy goals. It is crucial then that these goals are made explicit and remain transparent throughout the reform process.

Identifying the biases inherent within the traditional economics approach to income maintenance policy has explained the rationale for concentrating on the direct relationship between policy and the formal labour market. However, accepting this as a criticism does not justify a full-scale rejection of this approach but rather indicates that any future application of the theory should bear the reasons for such concentration in mind. Whether it is considered desirable to remove this bias, thus opening up the debate to other influences, depends on the view taken regarding the purpose of income transfers. Attempts at resolving this issue require an inquiry into the actual nature of income maintenance policy and an examination of the range of possible outcomes. This in turn facilitates the development of a broader conceptual understanding of policy objectives and thus paves the way for a more informed discussion on possible reform packages. That is, understanding income maintenance measures in terms of their wider remit in promoting 'social security' is considered an essential first step in the reform process. However, as long as the superficial application of neo-classical economic theory continues to dominate policy debates, this step will be a difficult one to take. Overcoming this hurdle can be viewed as part of a feminist economics agenda. The following chapter therefore sets out to redress the criticism that social security policy is all too often discussed without due consideration given to the questions of why we have a system and what is it we want it to achieve.

3 Social security or income maintenance policy?

A question of definitions

Introduction

Cash transfer programmes are usually classified within the area of state welfare provision known as 'social security'. The purpose of this chapter is to explore the use of the term 'social security' as it is used in relation to modern welfare state activity and to set it apart from actual income maintenance policy. The rationale for doing so is to demonstrate the relevance of differences in policy goals in setting the agenda for reform debates. It has already been argued that the assumed objectives of policy serve to inform the resulting policy design. It follows that limited conceptions of objectives will result in equally limiting discussions regarding policy options. An attempt to open up the reform debate to include a wider range of choices, therefore, requires that the nature of objectives be fully understood.

Emphasising the part that assumed objectives have played in the forming of policy is representative of initiating a feminist economics approach. That is, the purpose is to demonstrate the dominant influence neo-classical theory has had, and continues to have, in the design of income maintenance policy. As argued in the previous chapter, in any traditional economic analysis, the orthodox approach is initially to assume the prevalence of a particular set of structures which form the basis of all economic and social interactions. Within neo-classical theory, the structures assumed, and accepted as all embracing, are those associated with a capitalist model of economic organisation. From this starting point, the goal of economic efficiency emerges as superior over all other possible policy objectives. This is not to say that objectives such as equity or justice are considered irrelevant. Rather, within a given framework of scarce resources, freedom of choice and market-based transactions, the strive for efficiency is considered essential in ensuring economic prosperity. Thus, it is assumed that once efficiency in the production, allocation and distribution processes is achieved, the focus can then turn to questions relating to a range of further objectives. The practice of ranking objectives in this manner serves to limit policy options.

As indicated in the preceding chapter, the significance of efficiency considerations in the design process should not be denied. However, what is in question, with regard to the future direction of income maintenance measures, is the prioritising of efficiency above all else. Furthermore, the concept of efficiency itself is a particular one in that it is generally assumed to refer to the goal of maximising benefits and minimising costs, in all economic and social exchanges. However, the range of costs and benefits included tends to be those which can be easily measured in quantifiable forms. It is argued that this practice will continue as long as the analytical framework employed is that associated with an adherence to traditional economic theorising. One way of reversing this trend is to begin by questioning the validity of such a framework: that is what a feminist economics perspective sets out to achieve. Rather than embarking on the reform process with a predefined set of objectives in place, a more informative approach would involve examining the actual nature of policy in terms of what it can and will do. Once this has been established decisions can than be made on the relative merits of particular policy options on the basis of their impact on stated objectives. Thus, the practice of making value judgements regarding objectives is still very much a part of the process, but it is now more transparent in the debate. That is, objectives do not dictate the terms of policy options but rather serve to influence decisions regarding which policy to adopt. This is a turn-around in terms of approaches in that it involves starting from a base of examining what income transfers actually do rather than setting out with an agenda of what we would like them to do.

It follows, then, that adopting this different approach allows for a broader range of policy options to be introduced to the analysis. In terms of the reform process this represents an important move forward in that the debate is no longer constrained by an unyielding attachment to particular and narrowly-construed considerations of economic efficiency. Applying this approach to the study of income maintenance reform, therefore, requires that the various policy tools available and/or currently employed are initially identified and subsequently examined in terms of their operating structures and possible outcomes. By doing so it will become clear that income maintenance policy can promote a wide range of objectives and serve as a potent feature in the operation of modern capitalist economies. Furthermore, it will underpin the ensuing discussion on the advantages of a CBI in that the focus on the variety of objectives indicates the merits of a CBI when compared with existing schemes. That is, the analytical approach adopted serves to refine our understanding of the operational nature of income maintenance policy, which aids in the process of realising the full potential of a CBI. However, such an investigation into the nature, purpose and outcomes of income transfers will also serve to shed light on conventional practices regarding the design and implementation of income maintenance policy, thereby providing evidence of a continual focus on narrowly defined economic outcomes.

Are income transfers primarily a mechanism for maintaining the incomes of those individuals deemed to have insufficient resources, or are they to be considered as part of a range of measures designed to promote the 'social security' of all citizens? Answers to this question will be largely informed by ideological considerations. However, drawing the distinction and identifying the dual purpose of state intervention in this area allows for a broader conceptual understanding of the multiplicity of policy objectives. This chapter begins therefore by exploring the use of the term 'social security' in an attempt to establish a working definition of the concept. The second section will examine the actual design of social security policy, identifying the dominant factors influencing policy formation within an historical context. A further section will outline the functions and objectives of social security policy alongside illustrative examples of current policy. Attention will also be drawn to any evidence of gender bias in the design and operation of existing measures and how such measures reflect particular assumptions about gender relations in modern capitalist economies. The conclusion will be drawn that contemporary policy developments, and the subsequent reform agenda, continue to be predominately informed by the governing principles associated with a neo-classical approach to social welfare issues.

Defining social security

> The concept of income maintenance refers to the provision of transfer incomes by the central or local state, to a wide range of people, who are unlikely to be able to obtain adequate incomes in other ways.
>
> (Hill, 1996: 61)

> Social security is not only a form of income maintenance; it also constitutes a major element of the provision of welfare within many countries, and, no less important, a significant aspect of their economic structure.
>
> (Spicker, 1993: 103)

Attempting a definition of social security is problematic in that the expression itself has come to be associated with various forms of state welfare policy and not just with those associated with direct cash transfers. In the British context the expression 'social security' is used to refer to the 'whole range of state income maintenance policies' (Hill, 1990:1). However, in America 'social security' refers to the system of social insurance and the term 'welfare' is used to denote state-supported means-tested benefits (Hill, 1996: 61). Throughout the European Union the coverage and definition of what constitutes 'social security' varies considerably, although when used it normally includes the public provision of health care (see for example Keithley, 1991). Studies of social security policy involving international comparisons normally make use of figures relating to 'social protection' (see for example DSS, 1993b). This term refers to the public provision of contributory and means-tested benefits; health care; compulsory occupational pensions; and personal social services.[1] The International Labour Organisation (ILO) have stated that the term 'social security' can:

> ...basically be taken to mean the protection which society provides for its members, through a series of public measures, against the economic and social distress that otherwise would be caused by the stoppage or substantial reduction of earnings resulting from sickness, maternity, employment injury, unemployment, invalidity, old age and death; the provision of medical care; and the provision of subsidies for families with children.
>
> (ILO, 1984: 2)

This definition of social security includes benefits in kind as well as cash benefits and therefore encompasses those public measures included in the category 'social protection' mentioned above. However, the ILO appear to adopt an even wider concept of social security when discussing the origins of the term itself:

> The term "social security" was first officially used in the title of the United States legislation – the Social Security Act of 1935 – even though this Act initiated programs to meet the risks of old age, death, disability and unemployment only. It appeared again in an Act passed in New Zealand in 1938 which brought together a number of existing and new social security benefits. It was used in 1941 in the wartime document known as the Atlantic Charter. The ILO was quick to adopt the term, impressed by its value *as a simple and arresting expression of one of the deepest and most widespread aspirations of people all around the world.* (own emphasis)
>
> (ibid.: 3)

In this context the term 'social security' implies an ideological goal of ensuring and maintaining the protection of all citizens from economic insecurity and recognising the importance of the desire of all citizens to be secure in the knowledge that such public protection exists. The term social security, therefore, can be associated with a set of ideological objectives as opposed to the narrower definition which refers to actual income maintenance policy.

Accepting this wider definition of social security has important implications when analysing policy:

There are many policies that may be employed to improve the degree of such *(social)* security, including asset redistribution, labour market interventions, agricultural reform, food programs and public works.

(Atkinson, 1989b: 99)

Social security policy hence encompasses a whole range of public policies, which contribute positively to social welfare, and any policy analysis would involve examining any form of government activity in the provision of welfare. Furthermore, policy evaluation would entail reference to the overall objective of providing 'social security' in an ideological sense and determining the success or otherwise of the particular policy, which in turn would inform future reform proposals. The subject of analysis will therefore be determined by how the concept of 'social security' is used.

For the purpose of this book the term 'social security' is viewed as distinct from social security policy, which is used to refer to state-supported schemes providing financial assistance in times of need. The practical focus will be on social security policy. That is, the definition accepted is the narrower concept, which is normally associated with direct income maintenance policies or cash transfer schemes. Adopting this definition allows for a thorough examination of one specific policy area, income maintenance policy, the central focus of the book. Furthermore, in the British experience the term is normally used in this context. However, the approach adopted in this study draws upon the broader concept of 'social security'. Direct cash transfer programmes do not operate in isolation but rather inter-relate with other areas of government policy and have both direct and indirect effects on overall economic activity. For example, methods of financing will influence the government's fiscal stance; levels of benefit will influence patterns of consumer spending and both the type and level of support may influence work incentives, which will have an impact on labour market activity. It follows that any policy analysis must take these effects into account which implies that social security policy should be viewed in terms of its impact on the structure of the economy as a whole:

> In particular, there is a wide range of ways in which social security interacts with taxation policies. Policies which provide relief from taxation under certain circumstances – for example, relief from taxation of mortgage interest payments or pension contributions – have an important impact on individual incomes and therefore cannot be considered entirely separately from the more direct income maintenance policies.
>
> (Hill, 1990: 2)

Considering these impacts and the role that they play in the functioning of both the social security system and the economy in general requires an understanding of the objectives of government policy. The transfer of incomes within groups is the main source of finance for modern state welfare provision and has come to play an increasingly important role in economic and social policy. Considering the significant amount of public resources dedicated to programmes and the central role social security plays in modern welfare states, evaluating state-supported income maintenance schemes in isolation is a partial analysis. This analysis will therefore focus on the operation, function and design of social security policy in the narrow sense, that is income maintenance policy, but will also incorporate the broader concept by examining the wider objectives of such policies and how they interact with related areas of government policy.

Defining income maintenance policy

In practice, the welfare state of almost every industrialised country is based on a mix of different kinds of benefit. Benefits can be classified according to their *purpose* or according to the *basis* on which they are awarded. In terms of purpose, some benefits are designed to provide an income during periods of our life when we cannot rely on earnings. Others are designed to help meet additional costs faced by some groups of people at every income level (e.g. child benefit), while others are designed to relieve poverty (e.g. income support). In terms of the basis of payment, some benefits are based on national insurance contributions; others are means-tested; a third group are neither means-tested nor contributions based.

(CSJ, 1993: 1)

In addition to direct cash benefits provided by the state, income maintenance programmes also involve the employment of various tax allowances and/or reliefs, which effectively act as a form of income supplement. Furthermore, various forms of private schemes exist which contribute to individual income by either insuring individuals against contingent risks such as ill-health, or by serving to 'income smooth' across the lifecycle such as private or occupational pension schemes, employer based insurance arrangements or private life insurance policies. Although provided within the private sector, such schemes are intrinsically linked to government policy. This can be either through the support of public finance via subsidies or individual tax relief; through government legislation which dictates the types of arrangements that can be entered into; and/or through the state's role in regulating such schemes to prevent abuse by either provider or beneficiary (Hill, 1990: 3; CSJ, 1993: 2). Finally, individual incomes are affected by government activity in the housing market; the public provision of free or highly subsidised health care and education; and government policy in the field of employment. All of these factors along with the role of private provision and the operation of the tax system are important considerations when examining the design of income maintenance schemes. However, the purpose of this section is to identify the principles of justification for income maintenance policy and how these principles influence the type of policy adopted. The primary focus then is to identify the *purpose* and *basis* of publicly operated direct cash transfer mechanisms.

Income maintenance, offered by the private sector or related government policy in the form of subsidies, benefits in kind and taxation measures, affects primarily patterns of income distribution which indirectly influence individual incomes. However, the intrinsic purpose of the aforementioned activities is not direct income maintenance per se, but rather the outcomes of policy merge with the outcomes associated with the more direct forms of cash transfer mechanisms, that is income redistribution. When examining the effectiveness of direct income maintenance policies in relation to the goal of income redistribution it is therefore essential that the effects of those indirect measures mentioned above are taken into account. However, this section of the analysis is concerned with: identifying the justifying principles for the public provision of direct income maintenance; explaining how such principles inform the basis of delivery and finance; and outlining the various functions of income transfer programmes.

The rationale for state-supported income transfer payments covers a range of objectives that can be categorised under four main headings:

1. Poor relief

State-supported income maintenance provides people with financial assistance in times of need and therefore is often directly associated with the social problem of poverty (see for example Alcock, 1987; Brown and Payne, 1994: ch 2; Atkinson, 1989b; Deacon, 1995; Spicker, 1993). However, cash transfer mechanisms can also be employed to enable individuals to spread their income over the lifecycle and to insure against financially risky situations such as unemployment or ill health. The actual design of policy will determine whether the intention is to relieve poverty, defined in its narrowest sense as being without an income, or to prevent poverty by influencing consumption behaviour.

2. Reductions in inequality

Both cash benefits and tax reliefs or allowances have redistributive effects and therefore it is possible to associate such policy with the goal of equality, or rather with the goal of reducing income *inequalities* (Barr and Coulter, 1995: 274–275; Mitchell, 1991: 11).

3. Promoting social solidarity

Beneficiaries of cash benefits may not be poor and likewise all of those who contribute to the funding of those benefits may not be rich. State provision of benefits to the elderly and those with young families acknowledge the fact that various stages in the lifecycle are more financially demanding. This example of policies aimed at preventing poverty and promoting economic security also reflects the '...way in which social security systems enforce solidarity between generations' (Spicker, 1993: 106). Child Benefit (CB) in Britain, which is tax-funded, exemplifies this notion of solidarity in that people in work without children contribute to a scheme which provides guaranteed financial support, regardless of other means, to families.

4. Supporting the market economy

The design and delivery of income maintenance measures can play a crucial role in supporting, and thus preserving, the political and economic structures associated with advanced capitalism (see for example Hill, 1990: 3; Piven and Cloward, 1993; Dean, 1991). Linking income maintenance policy with particular patterns of behaviour assumes a set of social relationships compatible with market-based economies and industrial progress. Policies which emphasise labour market participation and encourage, or even reinforce, particular family structures, typifies the function of social security in producing behaviour which conforms to 'dominant norms' (Spicker, 1993: 106).

The relative weightings attached to the aforementioned objectives will determine the actual design of income maintenance policy. That is, the perceived purpose of the policy will influence the actual basis of delivery and finance. However, before any analysis of the link between the objectives and the design of policy can be made it is essential to lay out the options currently available for the transfer of incomes from the state to individuals. In developing a taxonomy of approaches to the public provision of income maintenance, Hill lists the following options:

1   Approaches involving entitlement if specific demographic, social or health status criteria are fulfilled, without reference to contribution conditions or means-tests.
2   Approaches involving previous contribution conditions, such as social insurance.
3   Approaches involving means-tests, such as social assistance.
4   Approaches providing relief from taxation – notably because of commitments to dependants or contributions to private income maintenance schemes.

(1996: 75)

The first three approaches are associated with the award and payment of cash benefits. Tax expenditures, such as specific tax reliefs or personal tax allowances, are *implicit transfers* in that they do not involve an actual cash payment but rather a reduction in tax liability (Barr, 1993: 170). This is reflected by the fact that in Britain, unlike cash benefits, the proportion of public money allocated to these implicit transfers does not appear in the government's official figures on public spending. As with all tax expenditure, these forms of transfer are an 'invisible item in government accounts' in that they are viewed as negative revenue due to the reductions they make in income tax receipts (ibid.: 182).[2] However this is not an indication that tax expenditures are an 'invisible' element of income maintenance policy.

Income tax reliefs or allowances play a crucial role in the operation of income maintenance policy in two particular ways. The tax system is used to promote various forms of savings with the intention of reducing overall government spending in the future, for instance the practice of applying tax reliefs to 'tax approved' pension plans. Income tax allowances, on the other hand, effectively complement cash benefits designed to provide financial assistance to those on low incomes. The actual structure of taxes and benefits and how these interact primarily determine incomes in and out of work. Individuals on the margins of social security and income tax will experience high Marginal Tax Rates (MTRs); that is, the proportion of increased gross income that is lost through a combination of benefit withdrawal and increased income tax liability. High rates of benefit withdrawal, combined with low wages and low tax thresholds serve to effectively trap people in situations of welfare dependency.

Increasingly in Britain the use of tax credits is being employed as a key component of New Labour's 'making work pay' agenda. Tax credits act in supplementing income from work by deducting a given amount from an individuals tax liability, thus reducing the amount of tax due and in certain circumstances involve a refund, paid through the tax system. The shift from benefits to tax credits, in Britain, is driven by the perceived notion that 'taxes are positively associated with paid work while benefits are negatively associated with dependency' (Millar, 2003b: 129). Tax credits will thus act in reducing the stigma of claiming benefits to support income from work by establishing a delivery mechanism that is more closely linked with an individual's actual employment. The greater use of the conventional income tax system as opposed to benefits is consistent with the governments overall agenda of significantly shifting the balance from *Welfare* to *Work* in the design and delivery of income maintenance policy. Although administered through the tax system, the provision of income support via various tax credits, alongside tax allowances or reliefs, is a fundamental component of state-supported income transfer measures. It is crucial then that such mechanisms are considered when analysing the design and operation of explicit transfers, that is state funded and provided cash benefits.

The three approaches to the payment of cash benefits, identified by Hill above, form the basis of explicit transfer mechanisms within modern welfare states (see Eardley *et al.*, 1996: 2; Brown and Payne, 1994: 21–23; Atkinson, 1989b: 100). Payments can be categorised as either universal or non-contributory contingency-based benefits, contributory benefits or means-tested benefits. In practice a social security programme can employ any single approach or any combination of the three. The actual design of policy will be a direct result of policy makers' relative preferences, which will be indirectly influenced by the prevailing political, economic and social environment. Decisions regarding policy design will therefore be influenced predominately by normative issues such as perceptions regarding which categories of individuals should or ought to be supported and which life situations are more financially risky than others. Attempts to form arguments of justification for state-income maintenance policy must, however, consider the rationale for claim as well as the rationale for payment. Before going on to outline the actual structure of the three approaches it is essential that the claiming rationale is understood. Accepting this duality of purpose allows for a more positive approach to be applied in analysing policy.

Rainwater *et al.* identify three principles of the modern welfare state upon which individuals make income claims against the state and upon which the state in turn makes the necessary claims on individuals and business in order to finance their social welfare commitments (1986: 126). They assert that:

> ... the history of the welfare state is a history of the differential reliance upon the three principles of contribution for specific contingent-risks, universal citizen rights, and need (with the endless subtleties of meaning in each principle) in order to make the welfare state acceptable to different groups in society.
>
> (Op. cit.)

They go on to claim that these three principles determine the nature of claims, which in turn determines the patterns of delivery and the financing arrangements of actual cash transfers. Table 3.1 establishes a framework of principle, basis and purpose of income maintenance policy options, identifying examples of actual benefits operating in Britain that conform to the typology.

The three approaches to cash payments can be readily identified within the table, and within this framework, the actual purpose of policy is directly associated with the claiming principle. Justifying policy in terms of recognising the responsibility of the state to maintain the incomes of those citizens who find themselves experiencing financial difficulties is not only a partial analysis, but can be criticised for relying too heavily on value judgements regarding the role of the state. By linking explicitly the basis

Table 3.1 A typology of approaches to income maintenance policy

Principle	Benefit basis	Purpose of benefit
Contributory	Social insurance	To compensate for lost earnings e.g. Job Seekers Allowance-contributory (JSA)
Individual need	Means testing or social assistance	To specifically relieve poverty and provide a safety net of provision which no individual should fall through e.g. Income Support (IS)
Universal citizenship rights	Categorical, conditional or unconditional benefits	To promote common citizenship by helping to meet additional costs specific categories of people are faced with e.g. Child Benefit (CB)

of benefit structures with their purpose, a more comprehensive understanding of social security policy evolves.

Contributory/social insurance

Social insurance is based on the principle that benefits are a form of return for contributions paid whilst in paid work. Individuals insure themselves against loss of income, which can be either temporary or permanent, by contributing to a state-supported insurance fund. The basis of entitlement is past contribution records, that is evidence of paid social security contributions by both employee and employer, and benefits can be either wage-related (Bismarkian)[3] or flat rate and uniform (Beveridgian). Social or national insurance implies a pooling of risks and avoids the problems of adverse selection. Workers are protected against contingencies, such as sickness, old age or unemployment, which might interrupt their income. The purpose of social insurance is to provide social protection and to aid economic stability for individuals when their capacity to earn is threatened by either circumstances beyond their control or by a foreseeable contingency such as retirement.

The main advantages of social insurance schemes are that they incorporate a notion of 'rights' to benefits and in theory they can be designed to ensure that they are largely self financing. However, social insurance is limited in its ability to provide social protection for all citizens. The eligibility criteria involves a test of contributions and so a test of previous work experience. This effectively excludes large numbers of individuals who may require social protection but fail to meet the qualifying conditions, for example young people with limited work histories, women with significant gaps in their employment or those with earnings below the contribution threshold (Spicker, 1993: 137; Rowlingson, 2003: 24). Consequently this approach to income maintenance policy demonstrates the principle of universality only when the contribution condition is satisfied. It does not aid those individuals who have never had an income to lose or never will have an income from which they can make sufficient contributions. National insurance is 'essentially an approach geared to the average needs of the working population as society interprets these at any given time' (Brown and Payne, 1994: 23). In this instance normative issues arise in the analysis in that the decision to implement social insurance policies may be influenced by the opinions of policy makers on the structure of society and their resulting interpretations of 'need'. This is a crucial consideration when discussing reform options and the effectiveness of social insurance measures. However the point made at this juncture is simply that social insurance is based on the contributory principle and the purpose is to deal positively with contingent risks.

Individual need/means testing or social assistance

The positive analytical framework of associating the claiming principle of individual need with income tested benefits can be questioned in that conceptual definitions of 'human need' are highly controversial and subjective (see for example Doyal and Gough, 1991). However by assuming that individual need is 'individually determined' (Rainwater *et al.*, 1986: 127), the rationale for claiming income or means-tested benefits is expressly linked with the principle of need without having to consider the various interpretations of what constitutes human need.

Means-tested benefits often exist alongside social insurance programmes and serve to fill the gaps in coverage. Benefits are conditional in that they are awarded on the basis of a test of existing income or capital. Recipients are deemed to be lacking access to sufficient economic resources. Entitlement criteria require categorising individuals as poor or being in need of assistance and therefore means-tested benefits are associated with the principle of targeting resources. Mean-tested schemes represent a 'safety-net' income that theoretically no-one should fall through. Social assistance or means-tested benefits are therefore often associated with the provision of a minimum income guarantee. In practice, systems differ in their level of generosity and qualifying conditions. However, common to all means-tested schemes is the identification and agreement of a minimum level of income guarantee and the requirement to categorise individuals as poor or being in need of assistance. Benefits which involve a means test are, therefore, associated with the principle of vertical redistribution in that resources are targeted towards those identified as being most in need and, if financed via a progressive tax mechanism, the result is a transfer of resources from the rich to the poor.

The main criticisms of means-tested benefits are that they stigmatise the poor; they involve establishing an explicit poverty line and, depending upon the system of delivery, they can be complex and difficult to administer. Furthermore any system of aid which is subject to a test of existing economic resources requires investigation into individual circumstances in order to determine eligibility. Such necessary intrusion serves to weaken any kind of notion of a 'right' to a minimum income and promotes further stigmatisation of the needy. This can serve to put claimants off from applying, making low take-up rates an inherent feature of means testing. Depending upon the nature of the system and the specific rules governing receipt, the distinction between actual resources and access to resources can become blurred. Problems arise regarding the classification of diverse individual circumstances and the dynamics of social living. Government departments assigned the task of administering the means test can interpret the rules at their discretion which will inevitably result in inequalities in treatment. Means testing can therefore be criticised in terms of its ability to relieve poverty, reduce inequalities and promote social cohesion. The minimum income guarantee is not a right within such systems in that it 'is not based on either past contribution or universal entitlement, but on political discretion' (Rainwater *et al.*, 1986: 131).

Universal citizenship rights/categorical benefits

The third principle justifying state-supported cash benefits is that which enshrines the notion of universal citizenship rights. Social insurance is limited in coverage and therefore will only promote the citizenship rights of those afforded access to the labour market. Means testing does not advance the rights of citizenship in that systems are discretionary, stigmatising and may not reach effectively the intended target group. Reliance on either mechanism, or a combination of both, will not automatically ensure comprehensive cover and hence will advance the citizenship rights of some but at the same time deny those of others. Beneficiaries will not always be easily identified in that different groups of individuals will benefit at different stages throughout their lifecycle. These individuals will not benefit by way of being citizens but rather as members of a predefined group, that is categorised as 'workers' or 'poor'. Claims for income assistance from the state may legitimately be made by individuals outwith these categories.

When discussing social security policy, universalism implies universal entitlement. That is, benefits are available to everyone with no qualifying test such as paid contributions or the demonstration of need. A programme of universal benefits would involve the granting of benefit to every resident of the country, financed from general taxation. The link between contribution and receipt is indirect in that although citizens contribute to the programme through their individual tax liability, payment of taxes is not a condition of entitlement and subsequently there is no barrier to entitlement for non-taxpayers. Universal programmes are therefore based on the notion of common citizenship and the principle of government responsibility in securing independent income guarantees. Universalism is hence associated with comprehensive coverage and ease of delivery.

The rationale for universal entitlement is quite distinct from that for contributory entitlement. The Beveridge model of social insurance[4] based on flat rate benefits, flat rate contributions and universal coverage encapsulates a particular principle of universalism. Such a scheme can be claimed to promote 'equality of status' in that all 'citizens are endowed with similar rights, irrespective of class or market position' (Esping-Anderson, 1991: 25). The principle of universal coverage was the principal reason the scheme benefited from widespread public support.[5] The concept of universality, however, was in essence a 'myth' as many people were excluded from the scheme due to insufficient contributions or the fact that specific client groups were simply not eligible for benefits (Ginsburg, 1992: 144; Alcock, 1987: ch 6). Benefit entitlement linked to contributions meant that only those who participated in the formal labour market would be in a position to contribute to the scheme and hence social insurance would be unavailable to individuals not afforded access to the labour market. This included groups such as disabled people, children, pensioners, the unemployable and married women dependent on the financial support of their working husbands. The Beveridge model of social insurance can thus be said to display the characteristic of selective egalitarian universalism in that once the contribution condition was satisfied all recipients were treated equally. Furthermore the universality inherent within the Beveridge scheme explicitly promoted the citizenship rights of the male worker. Unpaid work was not recognised in terms of access to social insurance and women were assumed to be financially dependent upon their male partners. Women who did engage in paid work were deemed to relinquish their rights to benefit upon marriage and to subsequently rely upon their husband's contributions and hence entitlements.

Considering those schemes where the principle of universalism is adopted as a justification for social security provision outwith the social insurance model, entitlement is not based on citizenship alone. The payment of a universal grant (often referred to as a demogrant) to every citizen of a society is not yet a reality but many current schemes provide categorical universalism. That is, certain benefits are universal in the sense that they are paid to all members of a particular demographic category with no qualifying test other than belonging to the selected category. Benefits are paid regardless of income or contribution but recipients must belong to the stipulated category.

Benefits illustrating a degree of universality are disability benefits which have no qualifying test of eligibility other than satisfying the predefined disability criteria. The principle of universalism witnessed by these benefits is similar to that discussed above with regard to universal social insurance in that it is a form of selective universalism. Qualifying criteria are determined by perceptions of the needs associated with varying degrees of disability and therefore presuppose a normative judgement on what constitutes 'disability'. Entitlement is not automatic but must be supported by actual evidence of the specified disability. Subsequently, as with means-tested benefits, there is scope for discretion and benefits may not actually reach the targeted group. Where ill health is concerned, individual circumstances are diverse and volatile so delivery becomes complex and affects take-up rates. For these reasons it can be concluded that non-contributory, non-means-tested benefits are universal in the sense that once in receipt all claimants are treated equally but inequalities arise in determining entitlement, undermining the principle of universality.

Benefits paid for children and to the elderly are currently the closest approximation to a universal system of social security. However, arguments for these benefits involve factors other than the advancement of universal citizenship rights. First, age-based categorical universal benefits are easy to administer in that the target group is readily identifiable and remains stable over a period of time. Second, both benefits for children and the elderly are expressions of social solidarity, in that recognition is made of the social responsibility for child-rearing and the care of the elderly. No stigma is attached to receipt, and benefits are financed via general taxation; therefore they are perceived as being redistributive over the lifecycle and from those without children to those with. Implicit within such schemes is the acknowledgement of the higher costs associated with children and old age and the responsibility of society to meet part of those costs. Such benefits are associated with high take-up rates and administrative simplicity, and are deemed to be effective in reaching the intended beneficiaries. However, universal schemes are costly and, as the primary redistributive effects are horizontal rather than vertical, universal tax financed benefits do not address directly the problem of income inequalities.

Income maintenance programmes can be justified with reference to the three claiming principles which will determine the actual structure of cash transfer mechanisms. The main differences in structure are the financing and delivery arrangements. Furthermore the purpose of these benefit structures is identified within a framework of public provision of financial assistance. As previously stated all three approaches can be adopted and are not mutually exclusive in implementation. However, financial assistance may be considered the primary function of income maintenance policy but, as stated above, social security policy performs a broader role in the workings of the economy.

The objectives of social security policy

> There is a sense in which, although they do not rhyme (like "love and marriage"), poverty and social security go together like a "horse and carriage". Not only does one drive the other, but they are formed or designed so as to fit one another. There is a peculiarly intimate relationship between the kind of poverty that is still experienced in advanced western societies and the social security systems through which we claim to relieve or prevent such poverty.
>
> (Dean, 1991: 1)

Social security measures can be identified with a broad range of objectives. The four broad categories, previously outlined, cover those objectives directly associated with direct cash transfer mechanisms. However, when considering social security in its wider context the objectives of policy are more extensive and less tangible in terms of definitive categories. In order to develop a richer understanding of the role social security plays in the overall functioning of the economy, the objectives and related functions of social security measures must be analysed within a broader conceptual framework.

In a study comparing the incidences and outcomes of social security transfers and income tax in operation in ten countries, Mitchell, at the outset, makes the following observation:

> In the first instance, all the countries in this study have income transfer policies which are aimed at ensuring that a minimum standard of income is enjoyed by all. In this context it is reasonable to assume, as a first approximation, that this indicates a desire to ensure that poverty is avoided or alleviated.
>
> (1991: 11)

However, for Spicker:

> Social security is not "about" the relief of poverty, and it is difficult even to claim that the relief of poverty is the primary objective; in some countries the relief of poverty has had a relatively minor role and in general the claims of social protection, compensation and provision for special needs seem at least as strong. If poverty remains a major concern for social security systems, it is not least that many kinds of objective associated with social security systems are obstructed by its persistence.
>
> (1993: 116)

In common with Dean, Spicker sees an intrinsic relationship between poverty and social security policy. He appears to be claiming that poverty, or rather the 'persistence' of poverty, serves to hinder the operation of social security measures in the goal of promoting social welfare. Although incidences of poverty can be directly attributable to insufficient money incomes, prolonged experiences of poverty can have as much to do with lack of access to resources other than income. Inadequate housing, health care and education facilities are all identifiable contributing factors to the spiralling effects of poverty. Policy aimed at addressing these issues may indirectly impact positively on resolving the social problem of poverty. However, policies designed with the singular aim of providing a 'safety-net' of income to alleviate poverty effectively will address one issue to the exclusion of all others. Minimum income guarantees operating in isolation will have a modest impact on improving the socio-economic conditions of those individuals living in poverty. Income maintenance may therefore be *about* the relief of poverty, understood in the narrow sense of being without a money income, but social security policy has a wider remit. This important distinction is exemplified in the differing rationales for the French and British systems of social security:

> The term "Social Security" in Britain refers to all government transfers provided by the Department of Social Security (DSS), no matter how they are funded or delivered. In France, only those schemes funded by hypothecated taxes – contributions paid by employers and employees are called *securité social*... the more precise use of the term in France accompanies a stronger commitment to the contributory principle than in Britain.
>
> (Evans *et al.*, 1995: 3)

This stronger commitment is representative of differing perceptions regarding the objectives of policy. In the British context, both in a historical and contemporary sense, the alleviation of poverty is generally considered the main focus of social security policy and thus the design of systems was based on providing a minimum subsistence level of income. However, in France, social security policy is considered within a wider framework:

> Indeed discussion of poverty in France is currently seen as a multidimensional phenomenon, a cumulative condition of social, environmental, employment and familial handicaps. Policy therefore must not only take into account the need for income for subsistence but also the social and economic and familial ties of all who are poor or who are threatened with poverty. In place of a direct policy concern for poverty there is an appreciation of social exclusion.
>
> (ibid.: 16)

This demonstrable difference in policy objectives has important implications when considering the CBI model for reform. The focus on poverty results in an emphasis on economic issues, whereas the broader focus on exclusion allows for a simultaneous widening of the debate relating to policy outcomes.

As stated in Chapter 1, the objective of equity is a fundamental consideration in justifying state intervention in the transfer of incomes. Variations in the design of social security policy emerge partly as a result of differences in commitment to considerations of equity. Social security schemes financed from insurance contributions or tax revenue effectively redistribute resources form one sector of the population to another. Theoretically all four approaches to income maintenance, previously identified, can promote both vertical and horizontal equity: vertical, in the sense that cash benefits may redistribute income from rich to poor thereby reducing income inequalities; and horizontal, in that benefits paid should reflect relevant factors which contribute to additional costs of living such as age, family size, or disability, but not irrelevant factors such as gender or race (Barr, 1993: 10). In practice the contribution made by social security measures in reducing income inequalities will be determined by the actual delivery and financing arrangements adopted. Inequality will only effectively be reduced in a vertical sense if benefits are financed through a progressive tax system or a progressive social insurance scheme. Claiming procedures and how the receipt of benefits affects entitlement to other forms of public or private support will influence take-up rates. Policy directed at alleviating the worst aspects of poverty and targeted at those individuals or households identified as being most in need may not actually reach the predefined population group due to low take-up rates. Furthermore, the practice of discretion in the award of benefits may actually contribute positively to inequality in that certain categories of claimants may be treated more favourably than others.

Attempts to relieve poverty and reduce income inequalities are not the sole functions of social security policy and these objectives can be tackled by measures other than those relating to direct income maintenance. State policy in the fields of housing, employment, health, education and transport all have a direct impact on resource redistribution and overall relative standards of living. For Alcock, 'Once the issue of inequality, rather than poverty, is addressed then the question of the economic structure of power and resources becomes central to analysis' (1987: 10). The whole range of state activity in the economy which primarily relates to resource allocation can in fact create or even preserve income inequalities and, in turn, indirectly cause poverty. Measures intended to support the poor, designed with this principal function in mind, which do not take account of the causes of income inequality, may fail in terms of the stated goal by not targeting the actual source of the problem. Although incidences of poverty can be used as an indicator for measuring the success or otherwise of income maintenance policies, to singularly link social security policy with poverty is a limited approach. Identifying the various functions social security policy can perform will illustrate the role that cash transfers play in the operation of modern welfare states and will provide a framework with which to analyse the motivating factors influencing design.

In his introductory observations on social security policy, Hill states that:

> Social security measures are generally perceived as required because market-related economic processes generate inequalities, with consequences in terms of individual deprivation which are deemed to be politically unacceptable, either because of the threat they pose for social order or because of political movements and ideologies which demand remedial measures.
>
> (1990: 3)

For the purpose of this analysis the use of 'perceived' in Hill's statement is of particular interest. The question immediately posed is, 'perceived' by whom? For Hill it would appear that the issue of 'individual deprivation', or poverty, is of concern to those who wish to preserve the existing political and economic structures of society and also to those who view poverty as an unacceptable feature of modern capitalist society because of their particular ideological beliefs. The conclusion drawn is that justification for cash transfer mechanisms can be sought within a twin pronged argument. State-supported poor relief is acceptable to those who adhere to the principles of market-based economies since such policies are considered essential to the efficient workings of the market. However, government action to remedy poverty is also viewed as a crucial function of the modern state by those who not only recognise the inherent failings of market structures but also question the priority given to existing economic structures. Support from this viewpoint is derived from a desire to 'remedy' the situation, rather than merely 'support' the existing capitalist order. The social problem of poverty, which stems from the process of distribution in capitalist economies, provides both functional and ideologically-based justifications for state-supported income maintenance schemes. Divergence in schemes will result from conflicting desires to either alleviate poverty or to prevent it. The common motivating force for all income maintenance policy, though, is recognition of the need for state involvement in supporting the less-well-off members of society.

Poverty, although widely experienced in its harshest form throughout history, only became a 'public' concern with the advent of capitalism:

> Poverty in feudal society was not a "social problem" in so far that it was an ascribed status to which the greater part of the population was born and from which it could neither in theory nor practice escape. With the collapse of feudalism and the development of capitalism in its various stages, poverty as a problem emerged, representing on the

one hand the failure of the labouring classes to give full effect to their economic emancipation, or on the other hand the failure of the market economy to ensure the efficient (and/or humane) reproduction of labour power.

(Dean, 1991: 69)

The transition from feudal society to industrial society brought with it a whole new range of social relations. The activities of subsistence economies were fundamentally altered by the introduction of money and market exchanges. With the development of industrial capitalism 'commodity production and consumption came to gain precedence over production for self' (Gorz, 1994: 53). For Esping-Anderson this process of 'commodification' applied equally to individuals:

In pre-capitalist societies, few workers were properly commodities in the sense that their survival was contingent upon the sale of their labour power. It is as markets become universal and hegemonic that the welfare of individuals comes to depend entirely on the cash nexus. Stripping society of the institutional layers that guaranteed social reproduction outside the labour contract meant that people were commodified.

(Esping-Anderson, 1991: 21)

In modern capitalist societies, then, money income is a primary source of individual welfare and many individuals, for whole sets of reasons, may find themselves deprived of access to such incomes at various points in time. As a consequence, those individuals will find themselves in poverty, unless of course they can rely upon financial support from sources other than private markets. The existence of poverty is thus an inherent feature of capitalist society:

In subsistence economies everyone works; the labour force is synonymous with the population. But capitalism makes labour conditional on market demand, with the result that some amount of unemployment becomes a permanent feature of the economy.

(Piven and Cloward, 1993: 5)

Commodified, then, individuals, or rather individual labour, becomes subject to the workings of competitive markets. Fluctuations in demand and supply will determine relative prices and resources will only be employed when demand and prices dictate. As Alcock states this leads to a situation where:

...at any given time there may be many workers who are ill-suited to labour because of age or disability or who are not required for labour because the forces of production are already at full capacity or because the products produced cannot be sold in a competitive market. These workers in effect constitute a reserve army of labour, some more likely to be chosen than others, who can be employed by capital if circumstances encourage profits but who will otherwise remain outside the wage relationship.

(1987: 11)

State provision of financial assistance to those individuals unable to secure a money income via market exchanges is effectively a response to the problem of poverty, caused by unemployment and the consequences of unequal distributions of power and wealth, essential features of capitalist development. The distribution of cash benefits compensates individuals for a lack of financial resources and equips those individuals with an income, which they can dispose of as they choose. This facilitates further rounds of consumption and production and so the process of capital accumulation and development continues. As previously stated, whether the distribution of cash benefits to sustain incomes constitutes a measure to relieve poverty or to prevent it depends upon the actual design of systems, which depends largely upon ideological considerations. At this point in the analysis all that can be assumed is that state support for the poor, that is minimal subsistence level relief, is an essential ingredient for the survival of capitalist modes of production. Poor relief promotes the efficient workings of the market economy and is therefore an identifiable function of income maintenance policy. In fact in listing the aims of cash benefits, Barr indicates that the relief of poverty is an aim 'about which there is general agreement' (1993: 429).

Poor relief in itself serves the economic arrangements of capitalist systems but it is arguable that financial aid targeted at the poor also performs an important role in serving the broader political economy of capitalism. Concerned about the motives behind the expansion of support for the poor in the USA throughout the 1960s, Piven and Cloward undertook a study of relief programmes in order to substantiate their argument that relief was a 'secondary and supportive institution' within capitalist societies (Piven and Cloward, 1993: xv). Their groundbreaking work *Regulating the Poor*, first published in 1971, argued that:

...expansive relief policies are designed to mute civil disorder, and restrictive ones to reinforce work norms. In other words, relief policies are cyclical – liberal or restrictive depending on the problems of regulation in the larger society with which government must contend.

(1993: xv)

For Piven and Cloward, poor relief programmes have two main functions: 'maintaining civil order and enforcing work' and their study draws upon historical evidence relating to the development of poor relief, focusing mainly on the contemporary American public welfare system to illustrate their theory (ibid.:xvii). They conclude that expansive programmes are designed to maintain civil order and restrictive programmes serve to enforce work norms. Their insights as to the broader functions of public relief programmes are crucial to this analysis. They serve to reinforce the arguments made earlier about the role social security policy plays as a fiscal tool applied in regulating the economy and how patterns of development conform to the perceived needs of the development of capitalist political and economic structures. Of significant interest when discussing the overall objectives of income maintenance policy, is their assertion that the giving of relief is a means of controlling individual behaviour, particularly that related to formal labour market participation. Piven and Cloward accept the argument that 'all societies require productive contributions from most of their members, and that all societies develop mechanisms to ensure that those contributions will be made' (ibid.: xix). Although poor relief is recognised as such a mechanism within market-based economies, they go further to argue that:

> ...much more should be understood of this mechanism than merely that it reinforces work norms. It also goes far toward defining and enforcing the terms on which different classes of people are made to do different kinds of work; relief arrangements, in other words, have a great deal to do with maintaining social and economic inequities.
>
> (Op. cit.)

It can be concluded from Piven and Cloward's observations that the actual design of poor relief programmes is intended to support existing social relations and hence serve the political and economic base of capitalist society. Poor relief given in this sense is not associated with a reduction in inequality but rather should be viewed as attempts to alleviate poverty whilst at the same time promoting the economic relationships which generate such inequalities. Poverty prevention or elimination would necessitate:

> ...a change in the relative position of the poor and thus an attack on inequality via a fundamental shift in power and resources ... And if that inequality is to be reduced then intervention must be made into the economic structures which produce it – the pattern of wages and investment...
>
> (Alcock, 1987: 11)

This argument is of primary importance to the reform debate. Current income maintenance measures are both expressly and tacitly linked to traditional patterns of work-and-pay operative within capitalist modes of production. Persistent poverty, inequality in terms of access to resources and gender discrimination are associated outcomes of this relationship and future social security reform measures, targeted at altering any one, or a combination of these outcomes, must first question the economic structures that existing policy, directly or indirectly, serves.

In an attempt to apply Piven and Cloward's thesis to the British situation, Hartley Dean builds on their work, primarily focusing on the role social security plays in promoting what he refers to as 'extra good' behaviour (1991: 1–2). For Dean:

> The preoccupations of social security policy and the rules of the social security system are quite divorced from the causes of material inequality in society, but they are highly effective in identifying and marginalising the poor so that they appear as a "claiming class" or "underclass". Thus, social security has a disciplinary effect. Not only does it place constraints on claimants, but it structures the way in which claimants and non-claimants are made to identify themselves, to act and to think about each other.
>
> (1991: 9)

Dean develops the argument that relief giving mutes civil disorder and enforces work norms to include a further dimension, that of imposing 'individual self discipline and extra goodness' (ibid.: 2). He argues that although the objective of poor relief has remained a central focus of social security policy, what has evolved since the fifteenth century is a system of 'social control' (ibid.: ch 3). Dean describes the social security system in Britain as 'a vehicle for social control' and identifies 'the motive force or "engine" which drives that vehicle with the fundamental antagonism between capital and labour' (ibid.: 35). Taking the view that the package of benefits and services provided by the modern welfare state (the so-called 'social wage') have 'a direct effect in containing popular discontent and averting threats of social disorder', Dean contends that the 'social wage was one of several measures intended to improve capital accumulation by mitigating the hazards and excesses of an unplanned free market' (ibid.: 11–12). He argues that:

> The social wage was to be paid, not as a ransom, nor even out of beneficence, but with a view to regulating the potential of the working and non-working population as both producers and consumers.
>
> (ibid.: 13)

Dean goes on to assert that although the social wage serves the mutual interests of capital and labour, it also directly benefits the recipients by making a 'day to day contribution to real living standards' (ibid.: 13–14). However, he argues that the payment of the social wage is also a mechanism the state can employ to 'buy' social order in that it transcends the

individual antagonistic relations between labour and capital by influencing the price of labour, thereby serving to shift the focus from class
struggle in the market place to political struggle between citizen and state
(ibid.: 17–18). He concludes:

> The provision by the state of the social wage has the capacity to make
> the relationship between the individual citizen and the state appear as
> a matter of social policy, whereas the subjection of labour by capital
> cannot have that capacity. What is argued here is that it is only
> through the state that the domination of labour by capital may be
> translated into social control.
>
> (ibid.: 18)

Dean applies a similar argument to the idea of the 'social sanction' (ibid.:
20). Through a system of punishments and rewards, the state can deter or
enforce particular forms of individual behaviour and so promote social
discipline. Dean utilises Foucault's account of the reformatory prison as
the 'embodiment of disciplinary techniques' to develop an understanding
of the significance of social sanctions to social control:

> ...according to Foucault, the reformatory prison may not merely be
> regarded as the site of discrete forms of social sanction, since it has
> refined, developed and continues to exemplify the techniques of
> power (such as "surveillance" and "normalisation") which Foucault
> calls the "disciplines". Such techniques are exercised throughout our
> social institutions – in factories, schools and hospitals – as mechanisms
> of a continuous discipline by which all individuals (whether they be
> delinquents, workers, pupils or patients) may be distinguished and
> meticulously ordered.
>
> (ibid.: 22–23)

Dean argues that state administered sanctions are effective in the exercise
of social control because the 'disciplinary techniques' they embody are of
particular application in the 'differentiation, accommodation and supervision of individual behaviour' (ibid.: 23). When considering the role the
capitalist state plays in supporting and reproducing the social and economic relations of capitalist modes of production these disciplinary techniques become a powerful tool in institutionalising the whole process of
subjection and muting class struggle. This leads Dean to assert that in
modern capitalist states:

> What therefore passes as social policy must embody social control; not
> because welfare reformers are necessarily cynical and manipulative;
> nor even because they are gullible and naïve (although some doubt-
> less have been); but because the fundamental terrain upon which

reforms are fought for, the discourses of debate and the inherent limits to state action are all fashioned and constrained through the essential form of capitalist social relations; and because that essential form is one of exploitation, not co-operation.

(ibid.: 34)

Arrangements for the provision of financial assistance to the poor are therefore ancillary to the preservation of the capitalist economic and political order. In this sense, a primary function of poor relief is to institutionalise and maintain a particular set of social relations. Evaluating the success or otherwise of policy may not therefore necessitate a headcount of the poor but rather an assessment of how effective policy is in supporting the structures of modern market-based economies. Whilst the relief of poverty may be the most indisputable objective of social security policy, it is apparent from the above discussion that the motivation for relieving it may be driven by considerations other than those relating to benevolence or promoting social justice. The primary objective of social security policy is therefore less transparent than initially assumed. Further analysis is required to identify more clearly the actual functions of social security instruments.

Conceptualising social security arrangements solely in terms of cash transfers from the rich to the poor is a limited approach. Micro-analysis of this sort results in policy formation aimed at alleviating the worst aspects of poverty. The policy instruments available to promote 'social security' must be viewed in a wider macro environment:

> Social security is an instrument for social transformation and progress, and must be preserved, supported and developed as such. Furthermore, far from being an obstacle to economic progress as is all too often said, social security organised on firm and sound bases will promote such progress, since once men and women benefit from increased security and are free from anxiety for the morrow, they will naturally become more productive.
>
> (Francis Blanchard in the preface to ILO, 1984)

Social security arrangements play a pivotal role in the pursuit of economic growth and as such constitute a primary element of any modern welfare state. Fiscal measures employed to enhance income security in times of need not only affect those in direct receipt, but also contribute to the welfare of society in general. Social security must therefore be considered in light of the impact policy has on social welfare. Individual welfare is derived from many sources. The security of money income, either via the wage system, occupational pensions or public relief measures is of little use when other needs remain unmet. Access to adequate housing, health care, education, child-care facilities and the labour market are all crucial determinants of welfare. If social security is to mean public responsibility for the relief of need then the concept itself encompasses a whole range of issues which interrelate and respectively contribute to social welfare in a positive way.

If this broader view is taken, it follows that transferring cash from the rich to the poor is but one outcome of social security policy. Minimal poor relief may be legitimised in terms of equity and economic efficiency arguments; however, in considering the financing of relief, it becomes apparent that it is not only those with abundant resources who pay for security for the whole. Abel-Smith draws attention to the fact that the welfare state in modern societies has:

> ...provided a minimum of security – a right of access to free or nearly free health and welfare services, to a minimum number of years of free education, to minimum income in defined contingencies, and in many countries to subsidised housing. To a considerable extent all this is paid for by the transfer of income within groups, using property taxes, indirect taxes and social security contributions.
>
> (1985: 33)

He goes on to conclude that:

> ...to a large extent, the welfare state is a mechanism which redistributes income over life. But it also redistributes from those with no children to those with more than the average number, from those with secure employment to those with insecure employment, from those with short lives to those with long lives, from those with good health to those with poor health. While the lower income groups may have large families and less secure employment, it tends to be the higher income groups whose children continue longest in education and who retire earliest and draw their pensions for the greatest number of years.
>
> (ibid.: 33)

Identifying social security with poor relief is too narrow an approach to adopt when analysing policy. Beneficiaries of cash benefits may not be poor and likewise not all of those who contribute to the funding of those benefits are rich. Social security is about social protection. Consequently issues about delivery, finance and outcomes have more wide ranging consequences than the mere relief of the plight of the poor. Spicker identifies six main functions of social security which illustrates more precisely the nature of social security policy in terms of the state provision of welfare: 1) meeting needs, 2) remedying disadvantage, 3) maintaining circumstances, 4) the production of disadvantage, 5) changing behaviour, and 6) developing potential. (1993: 105–109). Examining each in turn provides a useful framework with which to appraise the social welfare function of social security and to identify the problems social security policies are intended to address.

The first three functions can be grouped under the heading 'fostering living standards and reducing inequality'. Establishing a minimum standard of living is a prerequisite for any strategy of poverty relief. Cash benefits providing minimum subsistence incomes can be viewed as a means of meeting the most basic needs of those who find themselves unable to secure money incomes from any other source. The system of Income Support (IS) in Britain provides such a safety net of provision which no-one should fall through. Poverty, however, should not be considered the sole indicator that needs are not being met. The need for economic security provides the rationale for benefits paid to individuals who are not necessarily identified as poor. Insurance-based benefits such as unemployment, sickness and retirement pensions protect individuals from unexpected or even unmanageable drops in income. Meeting needs is combined with the objective of maintaining circumstances and in so doing the system operates to safeguard individuals from those circumstances most likely to lead to poverty. The avoidance of poverty is further advanced by those benefits that promote income smoothing. State provision of benefits to the elderly and those with young families acknowledges the fact that various stages in the lifecycle are financially more expensive than others. This example of policies aimed at preventing poverty and promoting economic security also reflect 'the way in which social security systems enforce solidarity between generations' (Spicker, 1993: 106). CB, which is tax-funded, exemplifies this notion of solidarity in that people in work without children contribute to a scheme which provides guaranteed financial support, regardless of other means, to families. Contributors are not necessarily direct beneficiaries, and may never be throughout the course of their lifecycle providing they remain childless.

With the exception of this intergenerational solidarity aspect of social security provision, the arguments raised thus far regarding the functions of social security have concentrated on issues of economic efficiency. Policies aimed at the relief of poverty, income smoothing, and insuring against the risk of economic insecurity impact upon levels of economic activity. As such they act as important economic regulators which can be manipulated to bolster or dampen demand as required. Social security payments, however, are primarily redistributive and should be analysed with regard to equity. Spicker views the function of 'remedying disadvantage' as focusing on compensation at an individual level and at a social level it represents the promotion of equality (ibid.: 105). Disadvantaged groups, such as disabled people or the poor, are identified and compensated for their restricted access to resources. This compensation is met by those individuals with greater resources. This transfer of resources illustrates elements of both vertical and horizontal equity, as defined earlier.

The functions discussed above relate mainly to the clearly identified objectives of efficiency and equity. The final three functions identified by Spicker are not so easily compartmentalised. However, a common element is the function of promoting labour market participation and flexibility which in itself is an important component of economic efficiency. Historically, systems of poor relief in Britain have been contingent upon individuals conforming to social norms: the punitive nature of the work house test of the Poor Laws; the assumption of the male breadwinner in the Beveridge model of social insurance; and the 'actively seeking work' eligibility criteria for unemployment benefits are all examples of the 'production of disadvantage'. Systems are designed within a framework of punishments and rewards. In fact Spicker maintains that of all the welfare services:

> Social security is probably most vulnerable to this criticism in its emphasis on work and participation in the labour market and in its reinforcement of familial norms.
>
> (ibid.: 106)

Individual consumption behaviour can be altered by the provision of benefits which follows on logically from the function of maintaining circumstances. Benefits not only affect behaviour in the consumption of consumer goods and services but also directly influence the choice between work and leisure. The disincentive effects of social security payments have been discussed above and the topic will be revisited as it is a central focus in the CBI debate. At this point it is sufficient to comment on the ability to promote work incentives by manipulating benefit levels and/or restricting receipt. On the positive side, social security arrangements can indeed foster opportunity. Benefits which are linked to training schemes or education can develop individual potential and on a social level serve to enhance social integration.

Conclusion

The purpose of this chapter has been to establish a working definition of income maintenance policy and to set it apart from the concept of 'social security'. This is considered an essential first step in any undertaking to reform policy in light of modern demands. First, it is argued that it represents a turn around in terms of economic analysis and, second it provides the basis for demonstrating the broad range of objectives that can be associated with income transfer schemes. That is, the subject of income maintenance policy is approached from a perspective that initially sets out to examine what policy can actually achieve. This is viewed as distinct from more traditional economic approaches where the analytical agenda is dominated by the practice of evaluating existing policy, and/or options for the future, with almost exclusive reference to considerations of economic efficiency.

Distinguishing between policy and the ideological concept of social security serves to illustrate how the analytical process is shaped by assumed objectives regarding the role of the state as a provider of welfare. If social security is understood to refer to the range of measures adopted by the state to protect citizens against a set of specific economic and social risks, associated with the operation of capitalist-based structures, this will dictate the terms of reference in evaluating policy. It follows that if economic efficiency is assumed to be the ultimate aim, state intervention will be justified only if it renders efficiency gain, or, at least, does not lead to any efficiency losses. However, if social security is understood in a wider context, that is, in terms of an ideological objective to provide and/or promote an environment where each individual is afforded equal protection against economic insecurity, policy interventions are then assessed with reference to such a goal. The dominance of efficiency considerations in the evaluation process has thus been replaced by the value placed on the provision of social security. The point being made is that identifying and defining the terms employed is considered necessary for demonstrating the relevance of stated objectives in the subsequent analysis. It is argued that the transparency of objectives is an essential component in the policy process. The predominant focus on efficiency, inherent within traditional economic analysis, implies that policy will be primarily informed by such. However, this is not always expressly stated, but rather tacitly assumed, and thus can be said to hinder the reform process with a 'hidden' agenda. A more enlightened and informed approach involves examining the nature of policy, assessing the overall implementation consequences of such, and then deciding on suitability with reference to stated aims. Such an approach conforms with the principles of feminist economics.

Discussing the functions of social security has served to clarify the range of social problems that policy can be applied to, and the justifications for specific benefit payments. The particular aims and objectives of any social security strategy will depend largely upon the relative priorities given to the problems the system is designed to address. Outcomes will be influenced by the effects of government policy on the wider economic environment and therefore vigilance should be exercised in evaluating the success or otherwise of a particular policy. Strategies for reform should therefore be considered with these points in mind. However, much of the current debate on the future of social security has focused on issues of affordability. It is argued that the emphasis placed on costs is indicative of a narrow and confining approach to the reform process. Furthermore, it is an approach largely informed by the continued drive for economic efficiency, defined in terms of its rather limited neo-classical sense. Talk of crisis has been dominated by finance and a raised awareness of the economic and social marginalisation experienced by ever increasing numbers of individuals and groups of individuals in modern capitalist economies. Policy makers are faced with a constraining economic environment, coupled with a need to reform in light of modern demands. The trend has been to engage in cost cutting, while simultaneously putting in place measures to restore faith in the labour market as the main source of economic and social welfare. However, the efficacy of this particular reform strategy is questionable given the continued concerns raised regarding increasing incidences of poverty and social exclusion. Current trends do not represent any great departure from historical developments, nor do they appear to be rendering policy more effective in meeting the needs of those individuals that systems were designed to address. Furthermore, it is argued that the reform of systems continues to be driven by the perceived needs of capitalist-based structures of economic organisation, particularly those related to work and pay. This specific mind set is arguably the result of a lasting adherence to neo-classical economic theorising and serves as a restrictive boundary in the reform process. In support of such claims, the following chapter will provide an overview of contemporary social security policy in Britain, alongside an analysis of the dominant influences informing policy in recent decades. It will be argued that social security policy is primarily viewed as a support structure in the operation of formal labour markets and, as such, systems are designed with this purpose in mind. Thus policy outcomes are considered almost exclusively with reference to the world of paid work. From a feminist economics viewpoint this demonstrates a failure to fully appreciate the causes and consequences of material deprivation in modern society.

4 'Basic income' or 'basic income maintenance'

A micro-approach to policy

Introduction

Social security arrangements in Britain encompass a wide range of measures with varying delivery and entitlement structures. The system as a whole is incredibly complex and can be criticised in terms of its effectiveness in meeting modern social problems. Recent developments in the operation and design of the British system have witnessed gradual erosion of the notion of 'rights' to benefits and a subsequent favouring of schemes that serve to abate any tendency towards a culture of 'welfare dependency'. This has meant a shift in emphasis from insurance-based benefits to public assistance type means-tested forms of support, which are believed to be a more effective method of targeting those most in need. Such developments have occurred within a climate of caution and restraint regarding absolute levels of public expenditure. However, expenditure on social security is largely demand led, which makes overall control of spending levels difficult. Furthermore, the combined effects of increasing rates of long term unemployment; structural change in the labour market; the dynamics of modern family forms; and various demographic changes have contributed to growing levels of poverty and income inequalities. Thus, both the type and the scale of problems the social security system is designed to address have been rapidly changing in recent decades.

The purpose of this chapter is to provide a brief overview of contemporary developments in British social security policy and to identify the nature of the 'new' demands that existing systems are struggling to meet. Particular attention will be drawn to the discriminatory nature of current social security policy, which is attributed to the explicit relationship between income maintenance programmes, both past and present, and the formal labour market. Although the focus is on the British social security system, it will be argued that the British experience is not entirely distinct from developments elsewhere. However, the extent to which international comparisons are made is limited for the purpose of illustrating convergence as opposed to difference. The chapter concludes that policy developments in recent decades have been predominately informed by the type of microeconomic analysis typical of that which is central to neo-classical economic theory. That is, in terms of social security policy, the focus has been on adapting systems in accordance with the needs of modern labour markets. Discriminatory changes in social security legislation have occurred alongside active employment measures in attempts to ensure that the world of paid work is commonly accepted as the main source of economic and social welfare in modern capitalist economies. It is argued that this particular strategy is founded on basic assumptions about consumption behaviour and individual choice. It is in this sense that the approach can be criticised for its limiting and partial nature.

Understanding the nature of real world economic phenomena is a central feature of feminist economic analysis. It follows, therefore, that inequality is considered a topic worthy of study. In fact the 'remarkable development of feminist economics in recent years is informed by the recognition of inequities' (Sen, 1995: 51). For feminists then, economists should demonstrate a willingness to engage in poverty debates and, more importantly, should view the analysis of the different distributional implications of particular policy options as part of their mainstream agenda. Developing a feminist economics perspective in the study of social security policy therefore necessitates an undertaking to analyse the causes and consequences of poverty in contemporary society. In doing so it becomes apparent that there is a whole host of contributing factors in the determination of individual income levels. Furthermore, individual income, either in terms of amount or source, is not necessarily an accurate indication of an individual's welfare status or standard of living. It is clear then that an anti-poverty strategy, which is largely based on promoting labour market participation, may indeed only be addressing part of the problem. However, this is an unsurprising scenario, considering that such strategies have been framed within a narrowly conceived microeconomic analytical process.

The British social security system: evolution and design

The actual design of the present social security system in Britain draws upon the three justifying principles, outlined in the previous chapter, with the resulting differences in patterns of finance and methods of benefit delivery. Current British cash transfer mechanisms involve the use of contributory benefits, means-tested benefits and categorical universal benefits, albeit in varying degrees. In tracing the historical development of social security provision in Britain it has been possible to identify dominant strategies and clearly-defined objectives, at least to the period following the implementation of the Beveridge proposals. However, limitations and deficiencies emerged within the Beveridge plan soon after implementation both in terms of adequacy of benefit levels and comprehensiveness of coverage. Numerous additions and modifications were made to the Beveridge design, which ultimately rendered income maintenance policy in Britain piecemeal in terms of development and highly complex in terms of structure. Consequently it 'has become harder to describe it clearly and to discern any coherence in its principles' (Brown and Payne, 1994: 24).

A brief history

Most studies of contemporary social security policy in Britain accept the immediate post-war period as a starting point mainly because this period can be identified with the implementation of a major piece of legislation that transformed and rationalised existing social security measures. However, extensive state involvement in the provision of income maintenance to citizens was evident in Britain prior to the Second World War. The Poor Law, established in 1601, provided means-tested minimum subsistence local poor relief and the reforms enacted in the 1834 Act reasserted the principles of minimum relief, the means test and local finance and administration. However, at the same time the new Act introduced harsher tests of eligibility due to the increasing demands imposed upon the system by the process of industrialisation and accompanying population movements. A national system of means-tested pensions was introduced at the beginning of the last century with the 1908 Old Age Pensions Act. This illustrates the first major departure from the Poor Law in that a national non-contributory means test was introduced and furthermore the Act removed the statutory obligation of family members to contribute in meeting the needs of their less fortunate relatives (Atkinson, 1991: 123). National Insurance was introduced in the early decades of the last century with the enactment of the 1911 National Insurance Act which provided sickness and unemployment benefit for specific categories of workers. Although benefits were time limited and strict insurance principles were applied with regard to contributions paid and benefits received, the system represented the first form of a state-supported insurance scheme to be implemented in Britain. The onset of mass unemployment in the inter-war years resulted in high levels of public expenditure committed to meeting unemployment benefit claims. Furthermore, evidence was emerging regarding the inefficiencies of locally administered poor relief arising from problems raised by wide scale geographical disparities in levels of deprivation. Faced with the problem of escalating costs and a lack of control in containing those costs the solution was to centralise the state system of poor relief. The Unemployment Act of 1934 established the Unemployment Assistance Board which effectively replaced the Poor Law. The provision of a state-supported 'safety-net' for the unemployed and their families was now centrally administered and funded. Therefore, for the first time in Britain there was a national scheme of means-tested benefits which provided a uniform system of poor relief. By the end of the 1930s a state system of social security provision was well established in Britain.

The post-war years witnessed a shift in policy direction with the implementation of the proposals contained within the Beveridge Report, published in 1942. The basis of social security provision was now firmly established in the form of a compulsory social insurance scheme, which was believed to be the primary means by which to eliminate poverty once and for all. Beveridge, therefore is 'remembered, first and foremost as the proponent of social insurance as the appropriate means of providing a defence against Want' (Wilson and Wilson, 1993: 354). This belief was shared across the political spectrum and thus the immediate post-war period is characterised by political consensus with regard to the role of contributory-based benefits within a model of state social security provision.

Although the principle of social insurance was already evident in British social security policy, the Beveridge model extended membership of the national insurance scheme to the vast majority of the working population. A tripartite arrangement between employees, employers and the State would secure regular weekly contributions from each party, to be paid into a national insurance fund. Central to the scheme were the principles of uniformity and comprehensiveness:

> All would pay contributions, and all would be eligible for benefits that would cover them against loss of earnings due to sickness, old age, unemployment or any other anticipated contingency "from the cradle to the grave". Contributions would be flat rate, they would not vary with earnings. Benefits would also be flat rate, but they would be sufficient for subsistence: they would be enough to live on. More over, everyone who was receiving benefit would have established a right to that benefit through the payment of contributions, and so the amount they received would not depend upon their other resources or those of their families.
>
> (Deacon, 1995: 74–75)

In practice, however, a social security scheme that encompassed a direct link with formal labour market participation, necessitated by the contributory principle, could never be truly comprehensive, and more importantly, relied upon the continued commitment to the policy goal of full employment. Recognition of certain circumstances, where access to employment was either denied or limited for certain individuals, led to the justification for a policy of social assistance. Those individuals not covered by social insurance would be provided for via a package of means-tested benefits. Thus a system of social assistance would provide a 'safety net' of provision which would supplement the social insurance model and therefore ensure the principle of comprehensive coverage. Although the

Beveridge scheme was never implemented in its entirety (the main omissions and changes were due to financial considerations), the social security system established in post-war Britain was firmly based on the insurance principle with the subsequent institutionalisation of the notion of 'rights' to benefit. Means-tested benefits were initially introduced to˙ fill the gaps in coverage. However, as those gaps became more widespread the reliance on social assistance accelerated.

By the early 1960s the use of means testing within the social security system was growing – as opposed to diminishing – in importance, due to the identified inadequacies in terms of eliminating 'want' inherent within the Beveridge design for social insurance. Furthermore the Beveridge model was failing to meet the needs of modern society: the 'rediscovery of poverty'; growing numbers of elderly depending on benefits; emerging evidence of changing family structures away from the 'male bread-winner/dependent wife' model; and rising unemployment were all characteristic of the 1960s through to the late 1970s. Such developments had profound effects on the development of social security policy:

> In this period, therefore, the increasing cost of social security tended to limit government willingness to concede the comprehensive reforms demanded by those who sought to build on the Beveridge model. Cost considerations continually tempted governments to use "selective" rather than "universal" benefits to solve newly emergent problems – rent and rate rebates, the subsidy of lower wages through family income supplements, and extension of supplementary benefit to single-parent families.
>
> (Hill, 1990: 51)

Thus cost considerations have dominated the debate at least since the time of Beveridge and the resulting emphasis is on a set of social security measures that provide 'value for money'. The primacy of economic efficiency over social policy has served to focus the debate around the relative efficacy of means-tested versus non-means-tested benefits. In fact as Spicker indicates, since the implementation of the Beveridge proposals, social security policy in Britain 'has been built around the tension between universality and selectivity' (1993: 119).

However, questions of affordability have not been the sole factor influencing British social security policy in recent decades. Benefits distributed on a universal basis, regardless of the existing resources available to the recipients of such benefits, are criticised in terms of the stated objective of poor relief by those who support the selective targeting of benefits:

> If the major aim of the benefit system is to keep incomes above some minimum level, then it is rather ineffective in doing so. Not only does

low take-up mean that some people "slip through the net", but a high proportion of benefit expenditure provides income in excess of this minimum. If our principle objective is to boost low incomes to an acceptable level, this could be done much more cheaply, and/or we could afford to be considerably more generous to the poor, if payment to those who do not strictly "need" the money were curtailed.

(Dilnot et al., 1984: 55)

The logical argument which follows from such criticisms is that overall spending on social security could be reduced if all universal benefits were replaced by benefits targeted specifically at those identified as poor, which out of necessity would be means-tested. That is, if the aim of selective targeting is to relieve poverty, then:

> ... poverty must be established under a means-test before benefit can be received, and benefit is paid only at a subsistence level to meet presumed absolute needs. To pay benefits beyond this level, or to those who are not poor, would be "wasting" state support on those who do not "need" it.

(Alcock, 1987: 141)

The savings made from increased use of means testing could be used to enhance the targeted benefits and go some way to improving the efficiency of the system in addressing the social problem of poverty at neutral cost. Those who advocate the increased use of targeting are therefore clearly driven by cost considerations and support structural reforms to the benefit system in the name of economic efficiency.

The Thatcher administration, elected in 1979, formed a government committed to cutting public expenditure overall. Influenced by the arguments of the 'targeters', the Thatcher government set about replacing universalist principles with means testing wherever possible. Furthermore, in terms of social security policy, the relief of poverty, or put in Beveridge's terms 'the abolition of want', was no longer identified as the prime objective. In fact:

> One of the hallmarks of the Thatcher era was the fierce debate over the nature of poverty. The more apparent poverty became the more strongly its level and indeed its very existence were strongly denied ... Margaret Thatcher ... argued that to call people living on income support "poor" was to denigrate them. Instead the poor were often described as "dependent". Some people argued that poverty was caused not by low wages or unemployment but by long-term dependency on state support. Welfare itself generated poverty.

(Oppenheim, 1993: 11)

Thus the social problem of poverty, insofar as it existed, was believed to be a by-product of the social security system itself. In terms of policy goals, then, income maintenance measures should be redesigned so as to reduce the role of central government as a provider of welfare; to promote an ethos of individualism and self-help; to reverse the trend whereby generous social security benefits were acting to threaten work incentives; and to simplify the system where possible with an emphasis on curtailing incidences of fraud and abuse (see for example Lister, 1989). Policy developments throughout the 1980s and early 1990s were primarily informed by questions of cost containment and an accompanying emphasis on building a structure that encouraged the principle of self reliance.

Historically, therefore, the benefit system in Britain evolved primarily as a means of relieving poverty and policies were designed with this aim in mind (Spicker, 1993; Barr, 1993). However, consideration of the role social security plays in promoting a desired behavioural response among both actual and potential recipients has proved equally important:

> Traditionally the British social security system has not been overly generous in the amount of money it provides through benefit payments, not least because of a belief, inherited from the Poor Law days, that generous benefits will undermine paid work and low-paid work in particular.
>
> (Becker, 2003: 105)

Although the actual design of systems has witnessed various changes in emphasis since the seventeenth century, this overall objective of income maintenance has remained unaltered. At different stages in history, benefit payments have been viewed either as a 'gift' from the state; as a form of reward dependent upon the individual fulfilling a harsh work-test; as a return to the individual for investments made in a prior period of economic activity; or as a right of citizenship. Legislation regarding conditions of entitlement, rates of benefits and methods of payment has served to create a social security system built around an ethos of 'punishments and rewards'. Whatever the form cash assistance has taken, the ultimate purpose has always been to relieve the harsh realities of poverty. In promoting this cause, theoretical positions can be espoused as to whether the intention was to maintain population growth in line with agricultural production; to ensure a reserve army of labour to draw upon in boom periods; to prevent social disorder; or to meet a contractual obligation on the part of the modern state in terms of the rights of citizenship. The relative significance of such theoretical positions is crucial when examining the actual mechanisms employed in providing state-supported income maintenance as well as the outcomes of social security policy. However, starting from the premise that the relief of poverty has been the historical constant, albeit described in a modern context as the 'effective targeting of those most in need', and remains the primary motivating force inform-ing social security policy in Britain, it provides a foundation with which to critically evaluate the future of social security policy.

Contemporary developments and current design

> Reform of the social security and tax systems is at the heart of the Labour government's aspirations to combat social exclusion, to eradi-cate child poverty, to increase employment rates among all people of working age and to modernise the welfare state.
>
> (Millar, 2003a: 1)

The landslide victory of New Labour in the May 1997 general election indicated the possibility of a fresh approach to social security policy in Britain. Although New Labour's election promises contained few specifics about social security policy in particular, it was clear that there was a firm commitment to enact measures that would improve access to the labour market, thereby tackling poverty and reducing demands on the public purse:

> ...the focus on paid-work-as-welfare reflected concerns about tradi-tional progressive social security policy, especially in a context where containing public expenditure (and so ultimately taxation) was seen as central by the Government.
>
> (Brewer et al., 2002a: 5)

Although driven by a desire to cut public expenditure, the 'centrality of paid work' with respect to social security policy was indicative of a much wider aspiration. The reform of social security was to be considered in terms of an overall objective to transform the values and institutions of the welfare state in line with modern socio-economic conditions. This implied redefining the role of benefits and a subsequent recasting of the rights and responsibilities of both claimants and government to ensure the system was delivered in accordance with the needs of an internationally competitive market economy. The period from 1997 has thus witnessed major developments in the design and delivery of social security policy in Britain, the key features of which are summarised below.

Overall responsibility for the development and monitoring of the social security system rests with the Department of Work and Pensions (DWP). However, recent reforms have resulted in an increased role for the Inland Revenue, the most notable of which is the administration of the various new tax credits. The DWP, formed in June 2001, replaced the former Department of Social Security (DSS), as well as taking over some responsibilities which were previously the remit of the Department for Education and Employment (DfEE), and is representative of major institutional change in line with New Labour's overall approach to welfare reform. For Carmel and Papadopoulos, the removal of the words 'social security' from the title of the new department, combined with extensive organisational change, is 'neither merely administrative nor procedural' but rather 'they symbolically marked key shifts in the objectives, logic and organisation of social security policy making' (2003: 32). A crucial feature of this shift involved the creation of a new Executive Agency, 'Jobcentre Plus' which replaced the Employment Service (ES) and the Benefits Agency (BA), providing a focus for a strategic approach to job search support and benefit payments. Integrating services for people of working age in a 'One Stop Shop' is indicative of New Labour's aim to:

> ...transform the primarily "passive" support offered by the post-war welfare state into a more "active" combination of services and benefits thought relevant to the employment and social conditions of the new century.
>
> (Finn, 2003: 112)

The transfer of responsibilities between government departments and the name changes are thus underpinned by the desire to move away from a welfare dependency culture and to create a new operational structure more suited to a 'work first' vision for the future of social security policy. In a practical sense, although organisational, these significant changes represent a continuum of reform measures intended to 'increase the responsibilities of unemployed and inactive out-of-work benefit claimants, and introduce a consistent work-focus to all benefits' (Brewer *et al.*, 2002a: 36). Thus, the actual delivery mechanisms associated with social security policy in Britain, at least with reference to the working age population, serve to further institutionalise and, indeed, provide a centre stage for the perceived positive relationship between paid work and welfare.

With specific reference to the design of benefits, recent reforms have been driven by a 'policy mind-set that divided individuals into two broad groups according to whether they work or receive welfare' (Hewitt, 2002: 190). Thus, in recent years the social security system has been redefined to represent the overall message that citizens will be *supported* through the system wherever possible to work and save. Those individuals perceived to be unable to do so will be provided with *security* in the form of safety net type provision. This apparent redefinition is crucial in terms of identifying the actual function of social security policy in Britain and the resulting mechanisms employed in delivery. As Hewitt points out:

> Traditionally, social security was an area of public policy in which cash in the form of tax and NI contributions was transferred from one sector of the population to another as benefit. Now the stress on the individual's duty to work and save means that social security is

extending its base and moving onto the new territory of markets for waged labour and personal finance. Nonetheless, the government still wishes to preserve the traditional role for social security of guaranteeing minimum income security for those who cannot work. However, the definition of who cannot work has narrowed significantly, and the elements of provision have shifted from universal benefits based on NI contributions and taxation to means-tested and more targeted provision.

(Hewitt, 2001: 190–191)

Delivering on an overall 'Welfare to Work' strategy has thus involved a range of reforms encompassing a broader base than the more traditional system of direct cash transfers. A series of labour market activation initiatives designed to help people into sustained employment have combined with the introduction of a national minimum wage and various work-related benefits with the intention of 'making work pay'. In recognition of barriers to accessing paid work, other than those associated directly with pecuniary gain, the government launched the National Childcare Strategy in 1998. This initiative was primarily concerned with the provision of good quality and affordable childcare for all children aged 0 to 14, with a related and 'particular objective of stimulating labour force participation by welfare dependent households' (Dean and Shah, 2002: 65).

Additionally, a number of measures have been introduced to promote a 'savings culture' with a long term aim of shifting the balance from welfare dependency to self provisioning. Encouraging direct individual responsibility for retirement provision has been a focus of government reforms with respect to pensions from at least the late 1980s (Regan, 2003: 283; McKay, 2003: 194). Furthermore, the introduction of various 'savings vehicles' in the 1990s, such as Personal Equity Plans and Tax Exempt Special Savings Accounts, were representative of government attempts to promote individual savings (Hewitt, 2002: 204). New Labour's pension reform agenda has been driven by a similar desire to promote the private sector over public provision. However, within this context, there has been a significant shift in emphasis from simply creating incentives to a more active role in actually *supporting* individuals in planning their long term financial security. Measures have included the introduction of more tax exempt schemes such as the Individual Savings Account in 1999 and Stakeholder Pensions in 2001 – a low cost personal pension available to individuals with moderate earnings and not in a position to join an occupational pension scheme. In recognition of the need to restore consumer confidence in private financial markets, the government have created a single regulatory body, the Financial Services Authority, to oversee pensions, insurance and savings markets. The new authority has also been given an 'extensive consumer education remit' (Brunsdon and May, 2002:74), which includes a specific 'obligation to promote greater public understanding of the financial system and wider financial literacy' (Hewitt, 2002: 205). More recent developments include proposals to match savings for those on low incomes, and granting 'baby bonds'. The promotion of personal responsibility for economic security is thus central to New Labour's overall approach to welfare reform and the policy instruments employed in delivering on such an objective reach far beyond those traditionally associated with direct income maintenance measures.

With respect to explicit cash transfers, an expansion of the use of means testing has been a key component of contemporary reforms, culminating in an undermining of the contributory principle within the British system. The 1990s witnessed significant changes to the principal insurance-based benefits that involved a tightening of eligibility conditions and the imposition of time limits. Concern regarding costs can be arguably identified as the main driving force behind such changes. However, by effectively restricting access, reforms clearly indicate that a more punitive system of social security was being favoured over the 'rights'-based element of contributory benefits. Despite being against any further moves towards increased means testing whilst in opposition, developments following the election victory in 1997 serve to illustrate that 'expanded means testing became one of the hallmarks of new Labour's social security policy' (Brewer *et al.*, 2002b: 514). In providing an overview of spending on social security in Britain since 1978, Deacon points out that:

> By 2001/02, only 45 per cent of expenditure was on contributory benefits, and nearly all of this was accounted for by pensions and incapacity benefits. Outside these two, contributory benefits have all but disappeared.
>
> (2003: 133)

Although the expansion of means testing within the British system can be identified with an overall desire to target benefits more effectively, thereby containing costs, equally important is its direct relationship with New Labour's ambitious goals of tackling child and pensioner poverty and the 'making work pay' agenda. Thus, recent reforms can be associated with both redistributive and efficiency objectives. Generous increases in existing non-means-tested benefits – relative, that is, to increases in contributory benefits – have been primarily targeted at families with children and pensioners. In addition, some new means-tested benefits have been introduced, such as the winter fuel allowance for pensioners and free TV licences for those over the age of 75. Support for children in 'workless' households has involved substantial increases to the child premium element of IS, the main means-tested benefit for those out of work, and the new Education Maintenance Allowance will provide means-tested support for children aged 16–18 in full time education. With respect to the redistributive element of these changes, it is evident that policy is being directed at the poorest members of society which reflects the 'view that it is only the bottom of the income distribution that the Government should be concerned about' (Brewer *et al.*, 2002a: 11). Thus, policy is driven by political commitments to reduce the poverty experienced by particular demographic groups, and as such the focus on redistribution is concerned with the 'distance between the bottom of the income distribution and the middle, but not between the middle and the top' (ibid.: 7).

As previously argued, tax credits have assumed a more significant role in the British social security system and are a crucial feature of New Labour's reforms to means-tested provision. The primary function of the main new credits is to 'make work pay' by effectively supplementing in-work incomes to ensure the move from Welfare to Work is financially viable and indeed sustainable. The British social security system has a long tradition of supporting the incomes of working families. Various means-tested benefits such as Housing Benefit (HB) and Council Tax Benefit (CTB) provide support for particular costs, whilst Family Credit (FC) introduced in 1988, replacing Family Income Supplement, served to provide families with wages below a certain level a weekly top-up income. In 1999, FC was replaced by Working Families Tax Credit (WFTC) and from April 2003 the adult component of WFTC was replaced by the new Working Tax Credit (WTC) which extended help to a wider range of individuals and couples on low wages. Support for children is now delivered through the new child tax credit (CTC) also introduced in April 2003, which will incorporate all means-tested benefits and tax reliefs for children and will be paid to the main carer. As noted in an earlier chapter, the shift from benefits to tax credits is in accordance with the government's desire to promote a 'work-focused' system of welfare support as opposed to a 'benefit-focused' system of dependency. However, the increased reliance on this in terms of income maintenance policy marks a further move away from universally- or categorical-based provision to an even greater reliance on means testing, albeit delivered via the wage packet or the tax authorities.

Thus it would appear, from the above summary of the main changes in design and delivery, that social security policy in Britain is evolving in line with a vision of state welfare provision which views work as the best route out of poverty. The social security system, then, is primarily considered in terms of *support* rather than direct provision. Of course this is not the case for all individuals, but rather:

> ...the population is divided into children (below working age), working-age people and pensioners. The distribution of rights, responsibilities and risk in social security varies according to this age/labour market status categorisation.
>
> (Carmel and Papadopoulus, 2003: 39)

Benefits will thus be targeted at those groups identified as being most in need whilst, wherever possible, individuals will be categorised as 'able-bodied working-age' and supported through the system to find and sustain suitable employment.

Given the time period involved it is not possible to engage in any meaningful evaluation of the impact of New Labour's wide-ranging reforms in the area of social security provision. However, where research has been carried out with specific reference to the barriers faced by whole sets of individuals in making the transition from welfare to employment or education, the evidence indicates that financial issues remain a significant feature (see for example Gillespie and Scott, 2004). Furthermore, in considering issues relating to gender equality:

> ...the use of joint income assessment in the expanded means-tested programmes for families with children means that some second earners now face considerably reduced incentives to work. This consequence of policy would not be inconsistent with a desire to encourage paid work if the aim is to reduce the number of workless households rather than to simply increase employment rates.
>
> (Brewer et al., 2002b: 513)

The lack of sensitivity to gender differences indicated by the continued emphasis on 'joint income assessments' and a focus on households or couples rather than individuals in establishing benefit entitlement was referred to earlier in Chapter 2. What is worth noting at this point is that financial disincentives to work remain, in part, due to the design and delivery of the tax and benefit systems. Thus, the increased use of means testing coupled with specific delivery mechanisms may not have the desired affect for particular groups of individuals. This is most notable when considering the experience of many women who find their relatively disadvantaged position within the labour market combines with the operation of the tax and benefit system to militate against accessing sustainable employment.

From a micro-analytical perspective then, social security policy has been framed within the context of *active* citizen and *supportive* state. That is, the emphasis has been on promoting individual behavioural responses, with respect to saving and earning activity, through strategic reform to the tax and benefit system, coupled with a series of initiatives intended to restore faith in private financial markets and an extensive range of work activation programmes. However, what appears to be absent from such thinking are issues relevant to the wider socio-economic environment. Private financial markets are notoriously volatile and leave individuals vulnerable with respect to future financial security. Thus, in the longer term, at best savings to the public purse may be negligible and at worst unacceptable levels of poverty amongst the elderly population will become an endemic feature of British society. Furthermore, in assessing New Labour's apparent achievements in increasing overall rates of economic activity, 'the role of sustained economic stability since 1997 cannot be ignored' (Hewitt, 2002: 207). As Deacon points out:

> New Labour's approach is something of a gamble in two important aspects. First, it is assuming that the labour market can absorb all the people that it hopes to move from welfare to work. This leaves it vulnerable to a downturn in the economy and consequent rise in unemployment. Second, New Labour is placing greater and greater reliance on means-tested benefits, which it prefers to call income-related benefits. The government believes that only by targeting benefits in this way can it tackle poverty and yet still release resources for education and health.
>
> (2003: 141)

With an overarching goal of cost containment and a subsequent favouring of private markets over state welfare provision, developments in British social security policy in recent years have been increasingly characterised by an erosion of the contributory principle and an increased role for means testing. However, the shift in focus has not been entirely due to discretionary government policy. Modern labour market structures, which serve to marginalise increasing numbers of individuals within the workforce, rising incidences of lone parenthood and an ageing population are all contributing factors to increases in dependency on social security benefits. The contributory principle does not serve these individuals well due to its explicit link with the formal labour market and its compensation function. Therefore, the increased dependency on means testing is also the result of changing socio-economic structures which demonstrates the point that efforts to cut costs must take account of the fact that spending on social security is demand driven. From a macro-perspective then what is required is a fundamental reassessment of the whole system and how it interacts with other areas of social and economic policy. This would necessitate a clear statement of intent with regard to social security protection as well as an understanding of the current causes and consequences of individual poverty.

Income maintenance: the reform agenda

Although cost considerations have informed social security policy throughout its history in Britain, what characterises policy developments in recent decades is the explicit departure from a commitment to the Beveridge design to a system based predominantly on selective targeting. However, the weaknesses inherent in both the insurance model and the safety-net type approach to income maintenance have been well documented. It is debatable, then, as to whether either of these approaches prove adequate in meeting the needs of modern society. In considering possible reform strategies, the case has to be made, initially, for a departure from the traditional focus on insurance vs. assistance. Only then will room be made for serious consideration of alternative and more radical approaches to social security policy. Thus the reform process necessitates a full-scale review of existing measures, and experiences from the past should be drawn upon. Any future reform package must: take into consideration all of the relevant variables; make clear the objectives of policy from the outset; and take account of the interaction with related policy areas in order to ensure that past mistakes are not repeated. It follows then, that the starting point for designing a reform package should be an identification with the patterns of need emerging in Britain, both on a national level and in relation to our European partners. However, as indicated in the introductory section, any reference made to either policy developments, or changing socio-economic circumstances, occurring in other developed economies is for illustrative purposes only. Although reference is made to a number of comparative studies, a theoretical focus is retained in favour of comparative analysis in demonstrating the convergence of policy and the constraining nature of current debates.

The British experience of escalating costs is not unique. The combined effects of competing demands on public expenditure, low rates of economic activity, and the imposition of political and economic restraints on deficit financing have restricted the capacity of modern welfare states to meet the needs of contemporary society. With regard to social security policy, a number of factors have led to an increasing interest in comparative research. On a national level, countries wishing to embark upon a reform programme may wish to look to alternative schemes operating elsewhere. Additionally, with a given climate of resource restraint, national governments may benefit from gathering information on their relative position in terms of expenditure as a proportion of total output. However, analysing comparative statistics on social security expenditure is problematic. Definitions of what constitutes social security vary across countries; national estimates of social security expenditure are not always readily available nor accurate and absolute comparisons can be misleading given the relative values of different currencies (Eardley et al., 1996: 3; DSS, 1993b: 33). At best comparative statistics perform a descriptive function and by their very nature are normally out of date by the time they reach the public domain. However, comparative research focusing on welfare provision in general, rather than social security expenditure in particular, has proved useful, at least in a British context, in providing evidence to counter the political attack waged on state welfare:

These types of comparison have been influential in demonstrating that the UK does not have a particularly high proportion of GDP devoted to public expenditure, that social expenditure as a proportion of public expenditure is comparatively low, that expenditure on transfers as opposed to expenditure on goods and services is very low, that a larger proportion of transfers are means-tested rather than contributory, that a larger proportion of benefit expenditure is funded from direct and particularly indirect tax as opposed to contributions and that the UK faces a relatively more manageable demographic outlook over the next 40 or 50 years than many other countries.

(Bradshaw, 1993: 53)

Furthermore, available data relating to social security expenditure as a percentage of GDP indicates that the 'UK spends less than the Western European average and more closely approximates the so-called 'Latin Rim' countries in this respect' (Yeates, 2003: 59). Given this evidence it would seem that the zealous campaign to cut costs in Britain has been informed more by political considerations than economic ones.

Research aimed at comparing patterns in policy direction in recent decades has demonstrated common trends. A study commissioned in 1993 by the then DSS in Britain and the OECD compared the structure and operating features of state-provided minimum income guarantees in the following OECD countries: Australia, Austria, Belgium, Canada, Denmark, Finland, France, Germany, Greece, Iceland, Ireland, Italy, Japan, Luxembourg, the Netherlands, New Zealand, Norway, Portugal, Spain, Sweden, Switzerland, Turkey, the UK and the USA. The authors concluded that the increased use of means-tested social assistance was evident in most of the countries studied and a common salient feature of reform debates was the issue of work incentives (Eardley et al., 1996). In an analysis of the 1994 Australian social security reforms, Saunders argues that the proposals were formulated broadly in response to the problem of growing unemployment and as such one of the main intentions was to design a system which would actively promote work incentives. He concludes that the move towards a tax-financed, targeted social security system was considered necessary in the process of designing a flexible approach to income maintenance which would 'respond to, and facilitate, economic and labour market changes' (Saunders, 1995b: 67). Morris and Llewellyn, in their descriptive account of social security provision for the unemployed in the US, Sweden, the Netherlands, West Germany and the UK, found that a built-in feature of all the systems was a concern for the maintenance of work incentives (1991: 121). They further argued that a growth in dependence on means testing was common to all systems, except for Sweden. Furthermore, in all of the countries studied, reforms had been driven by a desire to restrict public expenditure, which had subsequently led to a general limiting of coverage, either through absolute cuts in benefits or the imposition of tighter eligibility criteria, and an erosion in the real value of rates of payment (ibid.: 121). With specific reference to more recent reforms focused on shifting the balance in favour of the tax system 'there has been much policy sharing and policy transfer across countries in respect of tax credits provisions, with the U.S. experience, and values, an important element in this' (Millar, 2003b: 129).

Thus, a focus on work incentives combined with the issue of escalating costs and its effect on future economic growth have become the primary factors influencing the reform debate. This has been accompanied by an overall general favouring of means testing as an approach to income maintenance policy. The selective targeting of benefits to those identified as being most in need is generally believed to be an appropriate response to funding difficulties. The question remains as to whether or not it is an appropriate response to identified modern needs.

Identifying modern demands

Commenting on the 'success' of social security provision involves an awareness of the stated aims of policy. As indicated in Chapter 2, social security has a multiplicity of goals and thus the process of policy evaluation must at the outset determine which goals have been given priority. If it is accepted that the primary purpose of social security provision in Britain has been to protect individuals from poverty, it follows that debates focusing on the future direction of policy should involve an assessment of its redistributive function. This involves commenting on not only the extent to which poverty exists, but also the causes and consequences of poverty. Furthermore, as previously argued, the international reform agenda has been predominantly influenced by questions of work incentives, and concerns regarding the interplay between social security policy and the operation of traditional labour market structures. Assessing the effectiveness of such an approach entails exploring how social security measures impact on individual patterns of behaviour, with particular reference to the world of paid work. It is argued that part of the reason for emphasising the labour market stems from a desire to combat the problem of 'social exclusion'. One of the consequences of living in poverty is that individuals find themselves excluded from participating in mainstream economic and social interactions. In the 1990s, particularly across continental Europe, recognition of this negative aspect of being poor has resulted in the development of measures for 'activating' or 'inserting' those individuals excluded from the social and economic systems which represent the basis for social inclusion in modern welfare states: the labour market and the family (Jordan, 1996: 3). A combination of targeting the 'natural' condition of poverty and tackling the problem of social exclusion through active employment policies has therefore emerged, in recent years, as the dominant approach in the reform of social security. Examining the outcomes of policy in these two specific areas allows for critical comment on the actual 'success' of policy and serves to illuminate the nature of the changing environment in which social security measures currently operate.

Understanding poverty

Social security provision in Britain has indeed, at least since the time of Beveridge, prevented some of the worst evils of poverty in that a minimum income has been secured in times of need for the majority of citizens. Influenced by Rowntree's poverty studies, Beveridge assumed that his social insurance scheme would address the social problem of poverty in that it protected against the main identified causes – the interruption, either temporary or permanent, of earnings. However, in terms of 'eliminating want', the system has to date not proved successful. Vast numbers of individuals in Britain live in poverty. The absence of any official definition or universally accepted notion of what constitutes poverty renders the immediately preceding statement as no more than political sloganising. What is poverty? How many people live in poverty? What are the experiences of those living in poverty? What role does social security play in resolving the poverty issue? In attempting to provide answers to these questions some form of positive methodological analysis must be adopted in order to avoid the problems associated with the use of value judgements.

The practice of defining and measuring poverty has long been debated and throughout this century various methods have evolved in the quest for reliable indicators as to the numbers of individuals living in either absolute or relative poverty (see for example Roll, 1992). No matter what method is employed, the consensus appears to be that numbers are on the increase and not just in Britain, but the experience is similar throughout the capitalist world. The economic growth witnessed in the 1980s was characterised by the production of distinct sets of 'winners' and 'losers'. This was largely due to structural change in the labour market. At the same time as manufacturing jobs were giving way to the service industries, government policy actively favoured 'deregulation' over highly regulated labour markets and the promotion of 'flexible' working practices and patterns. The winners were represented by those groups able to 'monopolise' well-paid non-manual jobs whilst the losers were either denied access to employment, or were forced to accept low-paid, often part-time, insecure jobs and were thus constrained in their individual ability to meet their respective needs. (Massey and Allen, 1995: 124; Green, 1996: 265; Cross, 1993). While unskilled workers have witnessed a deterioration in their labour market position, there has been a simultaneous rise in the relative earnings of highly educated workers. Thus, in recent decades, a common trend of rising earnings dispersions has been in evidence throughout the industrialised world (Hills, 1995). The widening employment gap between skilled and unskilled workers has been accompanied by a general trend towards rising income inequalities (see for example Hills, 1996) Increasing income inequalities can arguably be directly associated with the operation of income maintenance policies. In identifying differences in rates of growth in inequality between countries, Hills distinguishes between the:

> ...automatic reaction of tax and benefits systems to changes in the inequality of market incomes and the effect of discretionary policy changes which may reinforce or counteract these automatic effects.
>
> (1995: 71)

He concluded that in some countries the combination of automatic and discretionary changes served to slow down or even cancel out the effects of growing market income inequality, whereas in others, most notably Britain, Sweden, the Netherlands and the USA, income transfer mechanisms actually contributed to the rise in inequality of disposable incomes (ibid.: 72). In his attempt to develop a comprehensive economic analysis of patterns of income distribution in Britain since 1979, Atkinson argues that for the period studied:

> ...the major recorded redistribution in the UK budget is that associated with cash transfers.... The fact that the redistributive impact of transfers and direct taxes appears to have fallen since the mid-1980s is circumstantial evidence that discretionary policy changes have contributed to the rise in income inequality.
>
> (1996: 42–43)

Atkinson supports his conclusion by referring to specific policy examples. The most notable being those which served to erode the real value of social security payments, and the numerous reforms enacted with regard to unemployment insurance up to 1988, 'the majority of which reduced the level or coverage of benefit' (ibid.: 43). In their assessment of social security policy in Britain under the governance of New Labour, Brewer *et al.* conclude that 'despite large amounts of redistribution to low-income families, and especially to those that have children or are pensioners, reductions in relative poverty and inequality have proved difficult to achieve' (2002b: 528).

Unexpected, or even anticipated, interruptions in earnings represent only one of the many factors contributing to the growing disparities in disposable incomes. This gives rise to questions regarding the quality of existing social security schemes. Is it that levels of benefit are inadequate; or that the system is too complex resulting in low rates of take-up; or that the reliance on labour market participation is outdated and therefore current systems fail to take account of social and economic change? The claim to be made is that these are all valid criticisms of current state-supported income maintenance mechanisms and indeed the situation exists whereby receipt of state benefits can actually contribute to and reinforce individual poverty rather than eliminate it. Any attempt at reversing this situation necessitates an understanding of new forms of poverty.

The overall tradition in terms of preventing poverty within advanced capitalist states has been a reliance on the goal of full employment coupled with state measures at ensuring a national minimum living standard (Mishra, 1990: 27). Such measures have included the provision of universal services intended to meet basic needs in the areas of housing, education and health care. Further policies have been directed at maintaining the incomes of the low paid and the unemployed at minimum subsistence levels. However as Roche points out, the use of the term 'poverty' itself is a highly contentious matter and leads to much debate surrounding the actual definition of poverty, the evolution of various explanations accounting for the existence of poverty, and controversy surrounding the possible cures (1992: 55). If the purpose is to examine the adequacy of state policies aimed at preventing poverty what is required is a workable definition of what constitutes being poor along with an inquiry into the various contributing factors.

The issue of poverty has been a subject worthy of study within a variety of academic disciplines and not just in recent years. However it has not always been a subject considered worthy of similar attention on the political agenda. Within the EC the onset of recession and the persistence of high unemployment in recent years has resulted in more attention being directed at the development of anti-poverty policies (Brown, 1984a). Social policy had previously taken a back seat to economic policy and the emphasis within social programmes had tended to focus on labour market issues with the ultimate goal being to promote the freedom of movement of workers between member states (Brown, 1984a; Schulte, 1993). The recognition of the need for a constructive set of policy prescriptions led to the development of various experimental programmes (Community's Action Programme on Poverty) aimed at tackling poverty within the EC. The definition set out during the course of these programmes was that poverty was experienced by those:

> ...persons whose resources (material, cultural and social) are so limited as to exclude them from the minimum acceptable way of life in the Member State in which they live.
>
> (Schulte, 1993: 40–41)

This rather vague definition was subsequently translated into a tangible yardstick, used by the European Commission in measuring poverty, in that households are to be considered poor if their income falls below 50 per cent of the average income prevailing within the member state in which they live (Atkinson, 1992: 4). The use of this criterion directly led to the:

...widely quoted estimate that there were some 50 million people living in poverty in Europe in the 1980s, a statistic which played a powerful role in mobilising public and political opinion in favour of extending the social responsibilities of the European Community.

(1992: 4)

Accepting the figures derived by the Commission provides policy makers with information on the numbers of households living on low incomes but does little in the way of accounting for the experiences of those households, nor does it furnish any explanation as to the possible causes.

Income levels within a household provide very little information on the actual living standards of that household and measurements of this sort assume a particular concept of poverty. Income may indeed not be equally shared within the household, perhaps going primarily to the wage earner and therefore poverty within such a household remains invisible. Conversely income levels may be no indication as to the resources available to a household and therefore the numbers living in poverty are overestimated. Perhaps a more reliable indicator would be a combination of income and expenditure levels occurring within households. Atkinson distinguishes between the two, arguing that the emphasis on income relates to a particular notion of poverty, that is the notion of 'minimum rights to resources', and concentration on expenditure patterns presents an indication of 'standards of living' (Atkinson, 1989a: 207).

The problem hence becomes one of defining poverty and distinguishing between absolute and relative concepts. Predetermining some absolute minimum level of income, either by using current benefit levels or average earnings figures, is a highly objective approach. Furthermore it provides nothing more than information on the number of households participating in the formal economy, either via the labour market or the official social security system, who are barely able to meet their most basic needs. The idea of relative poverty allows for more illustrative analysis as the concept encapsulates the idea that individuals in society should not only have a right to a minimum income but should also be economically able to participate in that society. Recognition of this fact has led to the development and use of 'consensual' measures of poverty. A practical example of this type of approach is the use of budget standard methodology. Drawing upon research precedents set in North America, Australia, The Netherlands and Scandinavia, the Family Budget Unit, established in Britain in 1987, has engaged in extensive research into the economic needs and living costs of various family compositions (Parker, 1998). The budget approach to measuring poverty brings together a range of 'expert' normative judgements on recognised standards for nutrition, housing, warmth and exercise, and empirical data relating to consumer spending patterns (Parker, 1998: 14). A budget standard is then set which serves as a benchmark representing the costs associated with maintaining a predefined living standard. This type of approach encompasses the point made by Atkinson, referred to earlier, regarding the distinction between income and expenditure in that both resource constraints and consumption patterns are taken into account to provide a more demonstrative analysis of the extent and nature of poverty.

Whatever the standards used, the evidence suggests that the numbers of people living in relative poverty are rising. Within Europe it is estimated that 57 million people live on incomes deemed below the poverty level (European Commission, 1999). However, knowledge of the magnitude of poverty among societies is not sufficient information with which to formulate policy responses. If, for a large proportion of the populace, available resources are inadequate to achieve socially acceptable living standards the solution may be to increase incomes. However such a policy fails to address the reasons why sufficient resources are not being accessed by a significant number of individuals, nor does it explain why for some the actual incomes once secured are indeed inadequate. What is required is an understanding of the individual and social conditions that create poverty. For Cross this understanding has failed to materialise, at least within a European context, because the term 'poverty' is considered:

> ...an organic concept, similar to "ill health", because it implies a "natural" equilibrium state from which this "unnatural" condition departs. Therefore the focus tends to be on identifying the problem and a possible cure, rather than identifying the cause of the problem.
>
> (1993: 6)

Consequently this myopic view of a social problem results in policy proposals being targeted inefficiently.

One of the most obvious causes of poverty occurs when individuals suffer a loss in earning power either through unemployment, sickness, old age or childbirth. Exclusion from the labour market, whether temporary or on a permanent basis, can often be accompanied by an associated increase in living expenses. For example: the costs of job search or retraining; medical expenses; additional household expenses incurred when the pattern of going to work is replaced with spending more time at home; and the extra funds required to provide for a new baby. Such causes of poverty are well documented and were the main motivating factors leading to the design of modern welfare provision. The post-war social security system in Britain has indeed been successful in alleviating the worst aspects of poverty arising out of temporary exclusion from the labour market. A combination of social insurance; a comprehensive National Health Service; a system of family allowances; and a scheme of social assistance proved to be an effective policy package for the purposes of alleviating poverty in the post-war era. Social security acted as a tool for supplementing individual incomes whilst on the macro-level the commit-

ment to maintaining full employment instituted the right to work and witnessed the departure by post-war administrations from laissez-faire type
government to one of intervention. The development of social security
provision in Britain throughout the 1950s and 1960s took place at a time
of broad political consensus. Policies aimed at promoting a mixed
economy and expanding the scope of state public welfare provision
received little criticism. However, this was only to last as long as there was
the guarantee of economic expansion (ILO, 1984: 3).

Although there was a marked development in social security provision
in the immediate post-war years, poverty remained an inherent feature of
British society. Nearing the end of the 1950s, 'evidence began to emerge
about the inadequacies of the Welfare State, and specifically about the
unsatisfactory character of parts of the social security system' (Hill, 1990:
37). The 1960s marked the 'rediscovery' of poverty, at least in the USA
and Britain, with the publication of various academic studies indicating
the current extent of the problem which sparked renewed interest in the
'paradox of poverty amidst plenty' theme (Jordan, 1996: 93–94, Roll,
1992: 26–27). Claims were made that existing provision was inadequate in
terms of levels of benefit but, more importantly, studies pointed to the
poverty experienced by those not covered by the system, either because
they were ineligible for benefit or were in work and earnings were actually
below the state benefit levels. This resulted in various enactments serving
to provide assistance to the working poor and patching up the Beveridge
design for social insurance to account for housing costs and vulnerable
groups, such as those with children and the elderly. Such measures were
piecemeal and failed to address adequately the causes of poverty.

A further development in the study of poverty occurred with the realisation, largely a result of the EC-run experimental poverty programmes, of
the 'new poverty' evident throughout Europe. For Cross, acceptance of
this term does not imply that the 'old' form of poverty has been eliminated, that is poverty amongst the elderly, the unemployed and disabled
people, but rather permits analysis of the problem to go beyond these
parameters and 'focus on the poverty experienced by the able-bodied of
working age who are themselves in the labour market' (1993: 6). Cross
goes on to make a very useful distinction between 'exclusion' and 'marginality' which allows the conceptualisation of poverty to take account of
changes in the structure of the labour market:

> Exclusion is a process of separation from employment which exists
> over sufficient time to force groups, communities and individuals into
> poverty and welfare dependence. Marginalisation is a process of low-
> level and insecure labour-market inclusion into employment, typically
> affecting identifiable groups, with few chances for advancement or
> wealth accumulation.
>
> (ibid.: 7)

In making this distinction Cross implies that:

> ...individuals or households may enter the ranks of the new poor either because they are excluded from employment or because they are employed at levels of income insufficient to sustain their families above the poverty line.
>
> (Op. cit.)

The marginalisation that Cross identifies directly results from new forms of employment. A concentration of job availability in the service sector is characterised by a demand for casual, low skilled labour which is subsequently low paid (Standing, 1992). Subsequently, the type of job creation most evident in today's advanced economies often leaves individuals vulnerable to poverty in that they are unable to secure, for sufficient periods of time, an income capable of meeting their own and the needs of their family. Current reforms to social security policy, which are primarily informed by a 'work-first' agenda, as is the case in Britain, will do little in addressing the poverty experienced by many individuals:

> Encouraging active participation, it is said, is the best weapon against poverty and the best guarantee for a fair income distribution.... Obviously, for many individuals access to the labour market is crucial to escape from poverty. Yet, a cross-country comparison shows that promoting labour market participation is no substitute for income redistribution and the fight against poverty: more work does not necessarily mean less poverty. In the United Kingdom and the United States, for example, more people are at work, and for longer hours. But there is more poverty – in the active age bracket – than, for example, in Belgium.
>
> (quoted from Foreword by Frank Vanderbourke in Esping-Andersen, 2002: xi)

Recent research drawing on information in the UK government's Households Below Average Income Series suggests that low paid work is indeed a growing cause of poverty: households with someone in work account for an average 41 per cent of those living on relatively low incomes during 1999–2002 compared with a third during 1994–97 (Palmer *et al.*, 2003: 23, 34).

Women and poverty

The feminisation of poverty is a well documented phenomenon (see for example Millar and Glendinning, 1989; Glendinning and Millar 1992; Daly, 1992). However, official statistics estimating incidences of poverty tend to be 'gender blind' in that they fail to account for either women's greater vulnerability to poverty or the 'invisible' poverty experienced by women within the household (Lister, 1992: 12). Pahl argues that the feminisation of poverty idea is not a new one, but rather simply the product of better documentation relating to women's poverty and 'their responsibility for managing scarce resources' (1989: 178). It follows that the process of designing policies specifically targeted at relieving poverty should incorporate a gender dimension. In considering the gendered dimension of poverty it is evident that the different experiences of women from those of men arise mainly from their role as wives and mothers. These roles impact on their position in the labour market and the degree of control they are able to exercise over resources within the family unit. In terms of their increased vulnerability to poverty, recent trends in the labour market have served to exacerbate the relatively disadvantaged position of women. Furthermore, whilst the hidden poverty of women is more difficult to quantify, recent developments in social security policy have done little in the way of securing the *actual* economic independence of women, nor have they served to address the negative economic consequences for women arising from the sexual division of labour within the household. These issues will be returned to when discussing the benefits of a CBI in terms of promoting gender equality. At this point, however, a summary of the main factors contributing to women's poverty is provided for the purpose of illustrating their distinctive nature.

Changes in the structure of modern labour markets have resulted in marked differences from the past in terms of the type of labour demanded. The model of full time, permanent employment, viewed as the sole and sustainable source of income, is being replaced by part-time, casual employment to be secured at different points throughout the lifecycle. Consequently such jobs offer little in the way of employment rights, nor do they offer the opportunity to contribute on a long-term basis to some form of occupational pension scheme and the rates of pay reflect this process of deformalisation. The increased participation of women in the labour market throughout the post-war years has been characterised by this growing labour market segmentation, both horizontally and vertically (Ginsburg, 1992: 157; Harkness *et al.*, 1996; Nixon and Williamson, 1993; Lonsdale, 1992: 97). That is, concentration occurs in specific occupations that lend themselves to part-time or casual modes of employment and these jobs are traditionally offered at low rates of pay. At the same time rising unemployment amongst men throughout the European Union resulted in the adoption of a range of strategies intended to encourage women back into the domestic realm (Kofman and Sales, 1996: 37). This structural cause of the gendered nature of poverty is exacerbated by the operation the Keynes/Beveridge design for welfare provision.

Women have long suffered in terms of economic disadvantage arising from their treatment as 'dependants' within the social security system. The combination of social insurance and a macro-economic objective of full 'male' employment presents a socio-economic structure which fails to promote the economic independence of women. Their limited access to benefits, inherent within a social insurance model of welfare provision, places women in an economically disadvantaged position when compared with men, throughout the course of their lifecycle (Lister, 1992; Walker, 1993: 29–30). Women who find themselves unable to secure an independent income are forced to rely on the generosity of men, either directly through the wage packet or indirectly through their contribution records. Subsequently the range of income sources available to women are less secure than those available to men and in terms of benefit structures they tend to be over-represented as recipients of 'inferior non-contributory benefits' or means-tested forms of assistance (Lister, 1992: 28). Furthermore, unpaid work caring for other people remains the primary responsibility of women in the private domestic economy. This serves to threaten their capacity to earn and limits their access to benefits further, due to their perceived 'unavailability' for work in the formal economy (Joshi, 1992; Gardiner, 1997). Thus, women's dependence on either public means of support or the financial contribution of their male partner, their limited access to the labour market and, within a public policy context, the persistent failure to adequately recognise and provide for the traditional caring responsibilities normally assumed by women leaves them extremely vulnerable to poverty.

In addition to these structural factors certain behavioural factors contribute to the gendered nature of poverty. The traditional values and beliefs about the role of women within the family unit and their corresponding responses to financial crises limit even further the opportunity for women to break free of their public or private dependence. It is only when these factors are analysed can the feminisation of poverty hypothesis be fully understood and addressed. Although the unpaid domestic labour of women is traditionally assigned no economic value, and subsequently their contribution is not viewed as part of the household's available resources, they are normally assigned the role of domestic managers, specifically in low income households (Graham, 1992; Parker, 1992; Payne; 1991, Morris, 1990: 110–111, Pahl, 1989). In this sense women are often blamed for 'causing' poverty when managing a household in which another member, usually the male partner, appears to be providing the financial means to support the household, due to their inability to adopt sound budgeting practices (Millar and Glendinning, 1989; Parker, 1992). Men on the other hand are traditionally expected to provide and when this is not possible they can fulfil their social responsibilities by registering at the unemployment exchange as 'actively seeking work'. Blame can be attributed to the functioning of the labour market whereby the failure to 'make ends meet' usually lands wholly at the feet of women with no obvious scapegoat. It is the pressure of such a social obligation that contributes to the situation whereby women often bear the burden of making the necessary individual sacrifices to ensure that the needs of the household are met (Pahl, 1989: 178; Parker, 1992; Payne, 1991). The result is that when poverty is experienced within a household it tends to be felt more severely by the women acting as wives and mothers within that household. Thus, their structural location in work and family life mean that not only are the periods when women are at risk of poverty different from those for men, but also the ways in which men and women encounter poverty and respond to it show a marked contrast (Williams *et al.*, 1999).

The above points have been made in order to illustrate the variety of issues arising out of any attempt to conceptualise and understand the nature of the social problem of poverty. On no account should it be viewed as an exhaustive analysis of the issue of poverty, which is a subject worthy of further research, but rather an introduction to the questions raised regarding the efficiency of current social security measures specifically aimed at tackling poverty. The aim is to draw attention to the fact that the continued existence of poverty, and the failure to come to any universally accepted conclusions as to the causes, is one of the main factors contributing to the criticisms of the modern welfare state, and in particular, the role played by social security.

The consequences of poverty: understanding social exclusion

In debates about Social Europe, the terms poverty and social exclusion have on occasion been used interchangeably. Cynics have suggested that the term "social exclusion" has been adopted by Brussels to appease previous Conservative governments of the United Kingdom, who believed neither that there was poverty in Britain nor that poverty was a concern of the European Commission.

(Atkinson, 1998: 1)

The concept of social exclusion represents wider concerns than the direct economic effects of poverty. That is, the term means more than the lack of income but rather encompasses a range of problems experienced by individuals living in poverty, which serve effectively to exclude them from the social, economic and political institutions of mainstream society. Such problems are normally those associated with concepts of multiple deprivation or social disadvantage, including: inadequate housing; poor health; low educational and/or skills level; family breakdown; and living in communities with high unemployment and crime rates which act to limit the range of services on offer. The most obvious include those services related directly to consumption, such as the location of large supermarkets, leisure and recreational facilities or the provision of public transport and public utilities. However, by way of their postal address, individuals normally residing in areas defined as demonstrating 'multiple deprivation' can often find themselves excluded from a range of financial services which renders them more susceptible to poverty. Lack of insurance, or the denied access to mainstream banking facilities, contributes to the hardship experienced by low-income households. In times of financial crisis they are forced to rely upon the more expensive forms of credit which more often than not transfer into unmanageable debt (see for example Ford, 1991; Berthoud and Kempson, 1990; Parker, 1992).

Combating the problem of social exclusion has become a central feature of social policy in the 1990s at an EU level. However, to date, no legally binding rights and obligations have been set in place, rather the principle of subsidiarity continues to dominate, whereby it is up to individual member states to decide upon and implement policy within a supportive EU framework (Hantrais, 1995: ch 8; Blake, 1996). For Hantrais:

> The growing recognition by the Union that poverty is a result of the inadequacy of cultural and social as well as material resources may help to explain why official documents emphasise the subsidiarity principle in formulating measures to combat social exclusion.
>
> (1995: 160)

Furthermore, what has emerged in more recent years has been a shift in direction from understanding and tackling social exclusion to a policy focus on promoting social *inclusion* (Blake, 1996: 7). On the surface the distinction may seem an arbitrary one to make, but in terms of informing the kind of policies adopted it is crucial. In practical terms it demonstrates a narrow and limiting perspective on the problem of social exclusion, which fails adequately to account for its multi-dimensional nature. The continued reference made to the direct relationship between social exclusion and unemployment within the European policy forum indicates a prioritising of job creation strategies, combined with active labour market measures designed to promote work incentives, as the main weapon against social exclusion (Hantrais, 1995: 166; Atkinson, 1998: 8). It would appear then that the problems associated with social exclusion are perceived to be addressed through inclusion into the formal labour market. Although an emphasis on employment-related rights has been a consistent feature of the European social dimension, the current focus is increasingly directed at tackling the rights of the unemployed rather than the rights of the worker citizen.

In Britain, there has been an explicit recognition of the need to find 'new and more integrated ways of tackling the worst problems' associated with poverty and social exclusion (Scottish Office, 1998), represented by the establishment of the Social Exclusion Unit within the Cabinet Office in December 1997. The current Government's view on social exclusion appears to indicate a move towards a broad based approach to tackling the problem in that a range of both social and economic factors have been identified as contributing to exclusion:

... in particular poor housing, low incomes, lack of work experience in the family, low educational attainment, ill health, family stress and the impact of drugs misuse and crime. The path put of exclusion, for individuals, or communities, is not therefore straightforward. Single interventions may be insufficient to break the cycle – although it will be important to identify where and when interventions can be most effective – and stand-alone policies may be insufficient in themselves to end exclusion.

(Scottish Office, 1998: 7)

However, although a number of key policy initiatives have been taken in the area of child care, housing, education and community safety, the emphasis mimics that adopted on a European level in that the focus of policy is to promote, or in some instances even enforce, 'inclusion'. This is best demonstrated by the most recent developments in social security and employment policy, referred to above.

The combined effect of overall 'Welfare to Work' package of reforms is purposefully to promote inclusion through active labour market participation, by making work financially attractive and by implementing measures which assist individuals, or groups of individuals, in becoming 'employable'. As both current joblessness, and the *dynamics* of unemployment and poverty, are believed to be main contributing factors to the problem of social exclusion (Atkinson, 1998: 8), it follows that advocating inclusion through the formal labour market is believed to be an appropriate policy response. However, it is argued that this response can be criticised in terms of both its limited perspective on the causes and consequences of social exclusion and its 'individualistic' focus. That is, policy is framed in line with a traditional economic perspective that views individuals in isolation and assumes the supremacy of free rational *choice* in determining patterns of behaviour:

In Britain the promotion of employment has now been restored as an objective of policy, but it is not included in the remit of the Monetary Policy Committee.... The instruments adopted for the employment objective are not those of macroeconomic policy. Rather they are those which concentrate on the microeconomic circumstances facing individuals.

(Meadows, 1998: 75)

This microeconomic approach to policy fails to account for the informing role played by social and economic institutions; collective identities; and gender differentials in creating social exclusion.

Exclusion may be directly linked to the behaviour of others over which the individual has no control. For example, the conventional practice employed by financial institutions, referred to earlier, of blacklisting specific postal areas serves to exclude individuals who otherwise may meet all the necessary criteria for utilising the services on offer. Another form of consumption exclusion, which is collectively determined, can be identified as the effects of peer group pressure. This is particularly the case where children are concerned, in that not possessing the necessary items, as dictated by the latest fashion or recreational craze, serves to effectively set them apart from the social norm (Atkinson, 1998: 13). Families, and in particular mothers, struggling to meet their children's relative needs may prioritise expenditure in this area which can result in the neglect of necessary expenditures, thus rendering them more vulnerable to further exclusion (see for example McKay and Scott, 1999). With regard to intra-household resource distribution, certain members of a family unit may be more excluded than others due to their lack of access or control over household income. Again the effects of such are more likely to be felt by women due to their dependent status which is either enforced by the operation of the benefit system or is a result of marked inequalities in earning power. Furthermore, the relationship between employment and exclusion is not as straightforward as 'inclusionary' type policy would suggest. Equalising opportunity is not simply a matter of prioritising education and skills attainment. Discrimination in the labour market, based on factors such as age, gender, ethnicity and disability is well documented, therefore exclusion may be as much to do with belonging to a specific group as it has to do with unemployment. Although the New Deal programme makes explicit reference to the individual job search needs of lone parents, the young unemployed, and disabled people, it remains to be seen whether such will impact on the attitudes and actions of employers, particularly in the long term. A related point when examining current labour market structures refers to the nature of the jobs on offer. Creating incentives to work via a restructuring of the benefit system, combined with a concentration on improving the quality of labour supply, is believed to feed through into the demand side of the equation by reducing replacement ratios, thereby making labour more affordable. However:

> Critics of the American approach of labour market flexibility see it as generating jobs which are less privileged in their remuneration or in their security. The newly created jobs are seen as "marginal" rather than "regular" jobs, where the latter have the expectation of continuing employment, offer training and prospects of internal promotion, and are covered by employment protection. "Marginal" jobs lack one or more of these attributes; they may also be low paid. In this respect, the relativity of the concept of exclusion becomes important. If the expansion of employment is obtained at the expense of a widening of the gap between those at the bottom of the earnings scale and the overall average, then it may not end social exclusion.
>
> (Atkinson, 1998: 9)

Although the introduction of the National Minimum Wage may go some way in addressing the remuneration aspect of the 'junk job' scenario, employment policy targeted almost exclusively at altering the behaviour of the unemployed fails to account for the totality of the social and economic environment in which those individuals operate. This criticism is further demonstrated by the emphasis on a microeconomic approach to employment policy. As well as considering the nature of the jobs available, with regard to both their current status and long term sustainability, the impact of policy aimed at getting people off the unemployment register and into work must be viewed in light of overall economic performance. If individual workers feel 'powerless in the face of macro-economic forces' this may result in disincentives to move from welfare into work due to individual assessments of risk and uncertainty (Atkinson, 1998: 9). This possibility is more likely when the structure of the benefit system makes the transition even more costly in that future job loss is accompanied by laborious and timeous claiming procedures and a potential loss of entitlements based on 'long-term' receipt. Recent research has found this to be particularly relevant when considering the barriers faced by disabled people and lone parents in making the transition from Welfare to Work (see for example Gillespie and Scott, 2004).

In conclusion, the concept of social exclusion is widely understood to be representative of a multi-dimensional problem. However, policy to date has increasingly focused on a uni-dimensional perspective on the relationship between the world of work and exclusion. Furthermore, within that perspective, traces of an adherence to neo-classical assumptions regarding human behaviour are to be found. Policy has been targeted at influencing the consumption patterns of individuals with reference to work and leisure. It is argued that such policy has been formed within a framework bound by the constraining features of rational, individually determined, utility-maximising choice. Thus the outcome of social integration, or inclusion, is believed to be a function of individual action, which is primarily informed by a realisation of the monetary benefits of formal employment. Implied within this strategy is the notion that poverty and social exclusion are inextricably linked and the solution to one provides an answer to the other. Income from work relieves poverty, assures inclusion and thus effectively combats social exclusion. However as indicated above, such a strategy only solves part of the problem and therefore is only part of the answer. A more appropriate response would be to identify the multiplicity of factors which impinge upon individual choice and to design policy with those in mind.

Conclusion

This chapter has outlined the main changes made to social security policy in recent years alongside an analysis of the principal social problems current measures have been targeted at addressing. Throughout the chapter the emphasis has been on demonstrating how policy developments have taken place within an environment where the perceived needs of money-driven market-based economies are prioritised. In particular social security policy has taken a back seat to the efforts devoted to supporting the operating structures of formal labour markets. It has been argued that this approach is a direct consequence of an almost exclusive application of neo-classical economic theory to the study of poverty and social exclusion. Furthermore, the reform agenda is effectively constrained by the dominance of this particular mind set. It follows that future reform proposals will only be taken seriously if they too are presented within a similar analytical framework. In order to move the reform debate beyond such limiting forces it is clear that the first step should involve an explicit recognition of the objectives of social security policy, but also that such objectives should account for the actual nature of the whole range of economic and social exchanges evident in modern society. This is not to say that the formal work-and-pay relationship should be dismissed as a crucial foundation in the design and operation of social security measures, but rather that it should not exist as the sole factor, thus dominating the reform agenda.

What is required is a policy that is independent of traditional labour market processes, but which will operate in such a way that does not adversely affect the efficient functioning of the waged economy. Furthermore, the policy should be flexible in adapting to modern social problems and should serve to complement other forms of state welfare provision. In the search for a reform package that would achieve such a goal a CBI presents as a possible remedy to the related, but yet distinct, problems of poverty and social exclusion and one that positively responds to the dynamics of modern living conditions. The following chapter will provide an introduction to the CBI concept, outlining its defining features and evaluating the main arguments posed for and against its introduction. The claim will be made that a CBI can be viewed as a practical policy option emerging within a tradition of alternative positions on the relationship between work and pay. It is this feature of the proposal that makes it of interest in developing a feminist economics perspective to social security reform. That is, arguing for a CBI provides an opportunity for establishing a framework to critically examine commonly held beliefs about the nature of work and sources of income in modern society. Such a framework would allow for the deconstruction of institutionalised notions about the function of formal paid work in the operation of market-based economies, thus rendering the analytical process more transparent. By identifying the value judgements currently dominating debates on the future of social security policy, the research process can move beyond restrictive practices associated with narrow conceptions of economic efficiency and set in place a framework for recognising the full potential benefits of a CBI.

The following chapter will therefore provide a working definition of a CBI, alongside a summary of the main arguments both for and against the proposal. Attention will be focused on how a CBI has been presented as a package for the reform of income maintenance policy. In this sense it has been viewed traditionally as a measure which would respond to modern demands without threatening the goal of economic efficiency. Thus, it is claimed that the CBI debate has been effectively defined by similar confining parameters to those associated with mainstream economic analysis.

5 Why a Citizens' Basic Income?
The story so far

Introduction

Arguments for a CBI have been framed within a diverse range of perspectives, ranging from the philosophical (see for example Van Parijs, 1996) to ecological considerations (see for example Fitzpatrick, 1999). However, for the purpose of this analysis the focus will be on the economic questions raised by the CBI proposal. As previously argued such questions have persistently dominated debates on social security reform. By providing a critical evaluation of traditional economic arguments posed both in favour of, and against a CBI, the stage is set for incorporating a wider and more inclusive economics perspective into current debates. Thus, in retaining the emphasis on economics, the tendency to attract criticism based on the neglect of a crucial aspect of the operating effects of income maintenance policy is abated, whilst at the same time the truly 'radical' nature of a CBI can be appreciated.

In arguing for reform along the lines of a CBI it is generally assumed that the issues being discussed relate exclusively to the reform of social security systems. This is mainly the result of two associated assumptions regarding the nature of a CBI. First, a CBI involves a transfer of monies from the state to individuals and therefore by definition falls within the realms of state income transfer schemes. Second, a CBI represents an income source unrelated to earnings and as such is categorised as a social security benefit, that is cash received outwith the formal labour market. A CBI will therefore be introduced as a possible social security reform package. However, the wider remit of securing individual autonomy and allowing for the development of social and economic relationships, negotiated outwith the confines of traditional market oriented transactions, has resulted in support for a CBI as a strategy for overall reform of state welfare provision (see for example Jordan, 1996; Purdy, 1994). This aspect of the debate will be explored further in the process of developing a feminist economics perspective on a CBI. For the purpose of this chapter a CBI will be examined with specific reference to the direct association made with the reform of income maintenance policy.

The principal arguments in favour of a CBI point to the potential for promoting fairness of treatment between men and women, the degree of freedom it offers to each individual by removing the economic necessity of employment and the related effect of supporting the requirements of a more flexible labour market. Initial observations indicate that a CBI can arguably be presented as an effective anti-poverty strategy which promotes both economic and social justice, whilst simultaneously responding positively to modern labour market processes. However, arguments against involve the claimed prohibitive costs and the adverse effects such a scheme may have on work incentives. The validity of these specific negative viewpoints are presented as indisputable and indeed such are considered the principal influencing factors in determining whether or not a CBI is implemented. The fact that a CBI is not yet a reality implies that questions of finance and labour market behaviour continue to triumph over any perceived benefits the model may realise.

Outlining the main elements contained within the debate thus far will demonstrate that the world of paid work is central to current discussions. Although the workings of the formal labour market is accepted as an extremely relevant factor in the design of any state-supported income maintenance programme, the prioritising of such above all else is indicative of a biased approach. Value judgements are being made with regard to the worth of paid work, the role of the labour market as a provider of economic and social welfare and the overall objectives of contemporary social security policy. As long as this particular approach dominates, the full potential benefits, particularly those relating to women, of a CBI will remain peripheral to the debate. This argument lays the foundation for the analysis contained within the following two chapters which trace the evolution of the CBI concept. It will be argued that, although the proposal appears within a tradition of establishing an alternative notion of work, income and citizenship rights within capitalist economies, consistency in the analytical framework employed is evident. This consistency represents the dominance of a set of socially constructed ideals regarding the nature of social and economic exchange in market economies. Undertaking to identify and, subsequently, deconstruct such ideals provides a basis for thinking about a CBI in terms of gender justice, free from any preconceived notions about how the world *should* operate.

Defining a Citizens' Basic Income

The characteristics which distinguish a CBI from any existing mechanism of state-supported cash transfer are the principles of universal[1] and unconditional entitlement. In brief, a CBI would involve the granting of a regular equal income to each adult member of society. Grants for children would be paid to parents or guardians.[2] Considering the level at which a CBI should be set involves engaging in debates on the derivation of official poverty lines and subsequent discussion on what constitutes a minimum subsistence income. Clearly these are important issues worthy of further analysis. However, the focus of this study is to show how a social security scheme, not intimately linked to the labour market, can serve to support the workings of market-based structures, whilst at the same time act to promote alternative forms of economic and social organisation. A CBI, therefore, by recognising and allowing for a range of economic activity, is in direct contrast to current social security schemes that serve to favour and even enforce a particular activity – formal employment. The value placed on employment in modern capitalist societies is indicative of patriarchal structures and acts in constraining the choices of many individuals, women in particular. If freedom from such structures is to be realised, the right to an independent income must be wholly separated from the labour market. Thus a CBI must be paid at a level deemed sufficient to meet basic needs, so that any additional income earned is an indication of individual preferences as opposed to being borne out of economic necessity. The grant would be paid regardless of factors such as work status, previous employment records, current levels of income or social living arrangements. A CBI would replace all existing income maintenance benefits and the amount paid would not be subject to tax. The scheme would be financed via general taxation and would involve the abolition of all personal reliefs set against income tax liability.

A CBI would involve full scale integration of the tax and benefit systems, which is one of the principal arguments made in favour of the proposal. Current tax and benefit measures are criticised for their complex delivery structures and their failure to reach predefined targeted client groups. A CBI model benefits from simplicity in administration and the advantages with regard to take-up rates are obvious because of the explicit and uncontroversial eligibility criteria. Perhaps a more crucial positive feature of the integration of the tax and benefit systems is the potential such an approach has to remove the worst aspects of the 'poverty trap', where high MTRs render any rise in gross income financially worthless. With a CBI model, administered by a single government department, such anomalies would not arise. The gains to be made from paid employment would always be positive.

Arguments against a CBI primarily focus on the claimed prohibitive costs and the adverse effects such a scheme may have on work incentives. The tax rates required to finance the granting of an 'adequate' level of income to all citizens are assumed to be both politically unacceptable (Alcock, 1989: 123) and damaging to economic effort (Parker, 1989: 135). In fact, Parker, a supporter of unconditional income guarantees, argues that the tax rates required to finance a full basic income would 'institutionalise' the unemployment and poverty traps rather than remove them (1991: 13). Given that a CBI has not yet been tested these claims are based on theoretical assumptions which lack supporting empirical evidence.

However, it is safe to assume that a policy which advocates paying people in exchange for what is perceived to be 'doing nothing' would not attract much electoral support given the value that modern society attaches to work. For this reason, due consideration has been given to analysing the positive effects a CBI would have on labour market participation rates.

The Citizens' Basic Income and paid work

Much of the literature has been devoted to analysing the effects an unconditional income grant would have on existing patterns of work (see, for example, Atkinson, 1995b; Standing, 1986, 1992; Van Parijs, 1992b). Van Parijs summarises the main issues by outlining three processes he identifies as leading to a more flexible labour market:

> ... basic income can be viewed as an employment subsidy given to the potential worker rather than to the employer, with crucially distinctive implications as to the type of low-productivity job that is thereby made viable. Secondly because it is given irrespective of employment status, the introduction of a basic income abolishes or reduces the unemployment trap, not only making more room for a positive income differential between total idleness and some work, but even more by providing the administrative security which will enable many people to take the risk of accepting a job or creating their own. Thirdly, basic income can be viewed as a soft strategy for job-sharing, by providing all with a small unconditional sabbatical pay, and thereby making it more affordable for many either to relinquish their job temporarily in order to get a break, go self-employed, or to work durably on a more part-time basis.
>
> (1996: 65)

A CBI, therefore, should not be viewed as a proposal that threatens the policy goal of encouraging active labour market participation but rather as one that meets the needs of a labour market adapting to technological change and intensifying international competition.

The provision of income security would enhance an individual's opportunity to make real choices with reference to economic and non-economic activities throughout the course of their lifecycle. Targeted income maintenance programmes pre-define specific life situations which render individuals, or groups of individuals, vulnerable to poverty. An alternative anti-poverty strategy such as a CBI, which does not involve the categorising and continual re-categorising of eligible beneficiaries, appears promising given the volatile nature of modern labour markets and uncertainty regarding the future. A CBI scheme would serve to meet the twin objectives of preventing poverty and enhancing labour flexibility. However, although attempts have been made to illustrate both the social and economic gains to be made by severing the link between work and income, the arguments thus far can be criticised for being too narrow in focus. For instance, the focus within the literature on demonstrating how a CBI could serve to enhance labour market flexibility assumes that formal labour market participation is the desired end result. Furthermore, it is indicative of a perspective that is blinkered to the possible advantages to be derived from alternative 'end results'.

In considering a CBI, which she refers to as a basic income guarantee (BIG) proposal, Orloff agrees with those who advocate the scheme on the grounds that it effectively decreases exit costs thereby allowing both men and women engaged in 'nasty wage-work' to leave those jobs (1990: 3). The subsequent reduction in the 'pool of cheap labour' may indeed lead to an improvement in employment conditions with respect to unpleasant and menial jobs. For Van Parijs this is a 'crucial advantage' of a CBI in that it shifts the balance of 'bargaining power so as to enable (as much as is sustainable) the less advantaged to discriminate between attractive or promising, and lousy jobs' (2004: 17). Orloff, however remains sceptical about the effects the scheme would have on the character of women's paid work. Although the scheme has the potential to increase the relative value of 'bad jobs' it does not offer the same potential in increasing the relative value of women's unpaid domestic work:

> Are there technological innovations which will change the character of the **work** of caring for people, including infants in diapers, sick toddlers, the incontinent elderly, and those ailing in hospitals? And if not just who is going to do **this** dirty work? It is possible that the BIG would function to raise the pay for service sector jobs, but then who pays? The families who rely on this care? Or will women be "encouraged" to "specialise" in doing this work – unpaid, but with a BIG to cover their "basic" need? [Orloff's own emphasis]
>
> (ibid.: 3–4)

Although she argues that the BIG may ease the financial situation of those individuals who opt to specialise in nurturing activities, she dismisses it as a stand alone welfare reform proposal because it fails directly to address traditional gender-based divisions of labour within the domestic economy. Her preference is for a package of reforms that serve to challenge such and she considers the encouragement of paid-work to be an essential component of any future welfare reform proposal:

> ...I would argue that jobs offer far more benefits than does unpaid labor in the home (even with a BIG): in addition to material resources, they provide networks of co-workers, self esteem, an arena for demonstrating competence.... The coming labor shortages in the United States offer an unprecedented opportunity for the feminist

movement to challenge the character of workplace practices, since women are needed as workers; it strikes me as myopic to ignore this potential in favor of arguing for a (better-paid) return to the home. Workplace innovations already suggested by various feminists and family policy reformers include sharing work through a shorter work day and longer vacations. This would not only spread the available work to more of those who desire it (thus paralleling the goal of BIG to share the resources of work); it would make it far more possible for people – men as well as women – to combine parenting and wage work, without giving up the benefits of either – and without suffering from the second-class work citizenship of part-time workers in a world run by full-time workers.

(ibid.: 4–5)

For Orloff then the benefits afforded by a BIG in terms of promoting gender equality are negative in that it merely serves to alter the balance between staying at home to undertake unpaid caring activities and engaging in poorly paid work. The nature of women's unpaid work within the household is not explicitly recognised and it is unlikely that a BIG alone would increase the value society places on such work. Whilst rates of remuneration and conditions of service may improve in other sectors of the economy, due to the introduction of a minimum income guarantee, the same would not be true of caring work. This leaves Orloff concerned about who will remain responsible for this type of work. If the state is not willing to 'absorb the costs of positive alternatives to private caregiving on top of the cost of BIG', Orloff concludes that the BIG may serve to institutionalise womens' position within the home rather than emancipate them (Op. cit.). She believes that the goal of gender justice is best served through the introduction of 'family friendly' policies which make it easier for those who wish to combine paid work with their respective domestic responsibilities.

Although Orloff raises valid concerns regarding the nature and value of caring work and how a minimum income guarantee would impact on such, her tendency to view the BIG as *compensation* for non-access to the formal labour market is limiting. By basing her concerns on the economic and social benefits to be derived from paid work, Orloff appears to be considering a BIG solely in terms of how it will replace current systems of social security provision. The introduction of a guaranteed subsistence income is to be applauded in the sense that it addresses the basic financial needs of the impoverished. However, on its own it has no, or very little impact, on those individuals marginalised or excluded from the labour market and as such find themselves segregated from the mainstream. In fact rather than easing social and economic deprivation 'a grant may be but a more generous pay-off to get the residents of the ghettos to stay where they are' (Orloff, 1990: 5). This line of reasoning can be criticised for failing to recognise the potential a CBI may have in shifting the sands of the world of work. It follows from an irrefutable faith placed in the labour market as the primary source of both economic and social well-being. Given the contemporary character of poverty and social exclusion, identified in the previous chapter, the question remaining is whether or not the labour market can perform such a fundamental role, but more importantly whether it is desirable to expect it to do so?

Responding to this question allows for discussion around the wider benefits to be derived from a CBI. In contrast to existing social security measures, a CBI does not explicitly link income provision with work. In this sense it can be regarded as an emancipatory measure in that it serves to free individuals from the *necessity of toil.* Individual preferences are better served by a policy that allows for freedom of choice as opposed to one that limits choice in favour of labour market participation. A family policy agenda may indeed resolve the difficulties experienced by some in entering, or sustaining, employment but does little for those individuals not constrained by family responsibilities. What a CBI offers is real freedom for all individuals to choose between work and non-work. Rather than being representative of a policy that responds to some pre-determined individual situations, the CBI should be viewed as a measure that adapts to a whole range of individually-defined life choices. Some individuals may indeed derive great pleasure from work, but any policy which has at its core an assumed notion that work is a 'good' thing does not allow for freedom of expression for all in terms of individual preferences. However, it is worth noting that adopting such a line of reasoning does not imply intrinsically an opposition to work but rather takes into account the fact that, for many individuals, the experience of work is not necessarily liberating. For instance, some people may view the work that they are required to perform as unpleasant, or:

> ...see it as something which restricts opportunities for developing themselves in ways they would most like to grow. People have different needs and desires vis-a-vis trade offs between income, work and leisure. Presently, economic reality and public policies do not allow people who define personal happiness and freedom more in terms of greater free time than in terms of work and a high income sufficient avenues to fulfil their desires.
>
> (Needham, 1994: 11)

Justifying a CBI along these lines is a challenging task given the relative worth attributed to work in modern society, and considering the institutionalised nature of both the economic and social structures associated with the world of employment. However, it is argued that any further attempt at moving the debate forward must progress from a focus on the work/non-work dichotomy and instead focus on how a CBI presents as a policy with potential benefits that go beyond the realms of the labour market. In order to strengthen the case made for a CBI, it is considered essential that an investigation is initiated into how the proposal would promote the form of freedom Needham refers to. That is, how would the CBI allow for a greater degree of autonomy in the pursuit of individual preferences and, indeed, is this a desirable public policy goal? Given that the promotion of gender equality is often cited as one of the main benefits of a CBI, and that the issue of caring work remains a controversial topic within the debate, the following section will outline the advantages of the proposal for women.

Women and a Citizens' Basic Income

The existing literature focusing on a CBI as a possible welfare reform strategy is lacking in rigorous feminist analysis, which is disappointing considering the potential such a proposal has for promoting gender justice. Indeed for Pateman, the confining nature of existing debates on a CBI, attributable to the dominance of 'neo-classical economic concepts and theories', is 'exacerbated by the striking absence of arguments and insights provided by feminist scholars' (2004: 92). Although attempts have been made to incorporate the situation of women into the various competing arguments, it is unclear how the resulting analysis can do anything other than 'add women and stir'. That is, within the context of a given set of objectives relating to the operation of formal labour market processes alone the current debate is characteristic of an approach which simply adds 'women as subjects without changing the tools of analysis' (Ferber and Nelson, 1993: 6).

Formal social security arrangements traditionally have served men more favourably than women. This is in part due to the direct relationship between insurance-based benefits and the labour market, but is also an indirect consequence of policies which fail to recognise the diverse roles of women as wives, mothers, workers and carers. Women's historically limited access to the labour market and their lower earnings relative to their male counterparts are well documented. Consequently, women are disadvantaged in terms of rights to benefits within a system based on contributions made whilst in paid employment. Legislation promoting the removal of discriminatory policies has served to enhance women's formal position as claimants and to establish their rights to benefits. However, various social and demographic factors further contribute to gender bias in the operation of social security systems, including: the increase in single parent households (predominately female headed); women's longer life expectancy; and the unpaid work undertaken primarily by women in providing welfare within the household. Ignoring such factors when designing systems inevitably results in unequal outcomes.

References made to women within the CBI literature have focused primarily on the advantages an unconditional income guarantee offers through promoting equal treatment between the sexes; recognising the value of unpaid work; providing income security outwith the traditional labour market thereby strengthening family life; improving work incentives and incentives to invest in human capital; securing financial independence within families; and providing the basis for a more equal sharing of domestic responsibilities between men and women (see for example Jordan, 1988: 118–119, 1992: 171–172; Parker, 1993; Walter, 1989: 116–127). All of these perceived outcomes can be applied equally in an analysis of the benefits a CBI would have for men. Establishing a right to a basic income independent of work would have major consequences for women in determining their life choices and would provide the foundations for a rethinking of the relationships between men and women in families. However the formal establishment of equal rights does not necessarily lead to equal outcomes. Although income security is a powerful tool by which to influence any individual's choices it is not a unique factor in determining those choices. Therefore, although the advantages a CBI would have for women, listed above, may indeed be realised, they follow from generalised assumptions about patterns of men's behaviour.

It would seem then that there is a major gap in the conventional case made for a CBI that results from an androcentric preoccupation with paid work and the labour market at the expense of provisioning/caregiving work performed outside the labour market. More convincing arguments could be made for a CBI on the grounds of gender justice by providing insights into the range of structures constraining women's choices. However, the continued practice of adhering to a neo-classical economic analytical framework 'precludes attention to institutional structures and their interrelationships' (Pateman, 2004: 99). Thus a necessary first step in the process of developing a feminist case for a CBI is to further investigate the assertion made regarding evidence of a bias within the current debate.

Providing evidence of an androcentric bias

The preceding sections indicated that contemporary debates focusing on the CBI proposal have been strongly influenced by an adherence to a traditional economics framework. In critically assessing the focus on *employment* inherent within the CBI literature, Pateman draws attention to the influence of the assumptions associated with neo-classical economics:

> The debates about basic income also center on the figure of a man in – or avoiding – paid employment. This is very clear in one of the major criticisms of, and apprehensions about, the idea of a basic income; that is, that it would encourage free-riding and idleness …

But who is being seen as so prone to idleness and fun? The assumption guiding the discussion of basic income is that the problem is about men and employment.

(ibid.: 98)

In this sense the bias is obvious in that arguments pointing to the negative impact a CBI may have on work incentives are informed primarily by assumptions regarding the behaviour of *rational economic man*. Thus the arguments made so far, both for and against a CBI, remain constrained by narrow and limiting assumptions about the purpose and actual impact of state-supported income guarantees. Tracing the origins of the idea that the state should act to provide some form of universal and unconditional income guarantee provides evidence of the historical nature of the prevalence of such assumptions. However, the process of doing so also serves to verify the existence of alternative and more radical approaches to social security policy. It is argued that such approaches present the opportunity to visualise a wider range of policy options when considering the future of social security arrangements in modern capitalist societies.

The bias, indicated in the literature, towards conceptualising social security policy as a tool for remedying particular market failures, and thus promoting economic efficiency, inevitably results in reform debates being constrained by a set of intractable obstacles. These obstacles effectively serve to limit the consideration given to policy options which focus on objectives other than those specifically related to supporting a traditional work-and-pay relationship. Policy proposals not primarily directed at promoting the efficient operation of the formal labour market remain at the margins of the reform debate. It is for this reason that such proposals are viewed as 'radical'. That is, they represent a departure from the 'norm' by requiring a rethinking of the terms of reference which have come to dominate the reform agenda.

As previously argued, a multiplicity of objectives can be associated with social security policy and ranking the relative importance of such has obvious implications for the resulting policy design. Evidence of the prioritising of objectives can be found in the CBI literature and thus the design of the proposal has been presented in differing guises. However, what emerges from the literature, both historical and contemporary, is a common thematic emphasis on assigning superiority to a particular model of capitalism. That is, it is generally assumed that social security policy should be designed in accordance with the needs of a competitive, growth orientated, monetised market economy.

The following two chapters will explore the development of the CBI proposal, specifically in terms of its relationship to traditional debates on economic efficiency. The argument will be made that the main body of literature provides evidence of a continuing emphasis on preserving a traditional productivist work-and-pay relationship within the debate. This focus is criticised, in general terms, for locating the CBI proposal within a predefined reform programme and, in particular, for illustrating a gender bias in that the life experiences of women are largely ignored. Furthermore, providing an outline of the evolution of the CBI concept will aid in clarifying what is actually understood by the proposal and illustrate that concentration on social security reform as the main agenda is misleading. However, for the purpose of identifying a bias this outline must be developed within an appropriate analytical framework.

Developing an analytical framework

Identifying bias in the method of approach

> It is in the method of attack on its problems, that modern inductive science offers such a striking lesson to politics and legislation; in recognising the existence of certain forces in the universe which have real validity, and that in consequence its triumphs must be achieved by ascertaining the nature of these forces and, taking them as they are, employing and combining them to achieve the desired result. But the whole of our modern civilisation is hedged in, distorted, and confused by a number of limitations which have no validity other than that which we choose to give them.
>
> (Douglas, 1924: 45)

The concept of a basic income for all has attracted attention, on an academic level, from a wide range of disciplines within the social sciences. Support for the proposal has also been heralded by practitioners in the political arena, from both left and right wing perspectives, and from those actively involved in campaigning for state action to improve the living conditions of impoverished members of society. The wide and varied base of support indicates that arguments in favour of a CBI originate from a diverse range of viewpoints regarding the nature and purpose of state activity in the field of income maintenance. However, it is possible to categorise these viewpoints in terms of two general concerns regarding the outcomes associated with the free operation of market economies. The process of economic exchange in an unregulated market generates income inequalities and, in many cases, renders inefficient results due to the inherent nature of identified market failures. Promoting the objectives of economic efficiency and/or social justice is normally cited as the justifying principle for state intervention within a predominately capitalist framework. It is not contentious to assert, then, that the accepted starting point in arguing for social security policy involves a consideration of the dual objectives of efficiency and equity.

With regard to economic efficiency, the theoretical framework and policy prescriptions are made quite explicit within the neo-classical model of economic analysis. By accepting the validity of certain behavioural assumptions, the consequences of a particular action, or even inaction, can be predicted. Commenting and acting upon the objective of equity is not so straightforward, at least in a technical sense. The concept of equity is essentially normative in nature in that it involves making judgements as to the relative 'fairness' of differing patterns of income distribution. Thus, arguing for policy on the grounds of promoting equity implies that some notion of social justice has been decreed and, subsequently, employed in the analysis. Policy recommendations, in this instance, will be informed primarily by moral value judgements as to what constitutes a socially just allocation and distribution of resources. Any useful analysis of social security policy must therefore account for influences that are 'political' in nature:

> Social Security measures are generally perceived as required because market related economic processes generate inequalities, with consequences in terms of individual deprivation which are deemed to be politically unacceptable, either because of the threat they pose for social order or because of political movements and ideologies which demand remedial measures.
>
> (Hill, 1990: 3)

It would appear, then, that debates on social security reform could be broken down into two distinct processes. Questions of economic efficiency are considered within a framework of deductive reasoning, based on 'factual' propositions about human behaviour. The practice of doing so gives rise to claims of positive scientific analysis in that theories can be tested by appealing to the relevant empirical evidence. The focus on equity, however, follows a more normative route in that discussions are largely informed by the opinions of policy analysts. Particular values and subsequent policy prescriptions will be ranked in accordance with perceived notions as to what constitutes a just society. Ascribed values are therefore given as the justifying principles for state intervention, which inevitably leads to a great deal of controversy regarding policy direction.

Making the distinction between positive and normative constructs in the analysis of social security policy mimics the process adopted within traditional economic theory. By emphasising the preserve of scientific methods, the traditional economics approach is dominated by techniques believed to be wholly objective. The inherent preference for 'positive economics', displayed in neo-classical paradigms, is transferred to the social security reform agenda. The process of categorising analytical frameworks is arguably a mechanism for establishing a hierarchical structure in considering the objectives of policy. Those which can be analysed within a model which employs logical methods of scientific reasoning will be favoured in the research process over those which are subject to scrutiny in terms of identifying and prioritising a particular set of subjective values. Thus, in the ranking of objectives, superiority is assigned to achieving economic efficiency. This is mainly because, as a concept, it is technically easier to quantify. Furthermore, by appealing to theories based on assumptions derived from observed patterns of individual behaviour, the process of justifying policy prescriptions can claim to be value free. This effectively reduces the potential for controversy by presenting policy as an essential remedy to previously identified, and agreed upon, real world phenomena.

However, claims of objectivity should be treated with caution. The basis of any positive statement is in itself normative. To illustrate this point Culyer considers the essentially positive statement, widely used in the economic analysis of social policy, that the introduction of a subsidy to the price of a service will result in increased levels of consumption of that service (1983: 3). Although the statement itself can be categorised as positive, in that it can be tested by examining the consumption patterns of individuals before and after the subsidy is introduced, the fact that it is considered a proposition worthy of study at all stems from a value judgement relating to desired consumption levels. That is, explicit interest in the analysis of behavioural responses to subsidies suggests an implicit interest in the outcomes of such a policy. Concern regarding outcomes is inextricably linked with subjective notions of what is considered to be an acceptable level of consumption, both at an individual and at a social level. This acceptable level may be determined by appealing to a range of arguments such as those relating to economic efficiency, equity or political expediency. Whatever the justifying principles employed, the process of prioritising objectives and expressing an interest in a desired outcome provides evidence of the existence of value judgements in any positive analytical process.

However, as Culyer argues, this does not mean that the practice of distinguishing between the positive and the normative in the analytical framework is meaningless. What is crucial is that the practice of making *judgements* is identified and understood in the use of the normative and positive dichotomy:

> Note that both involve *judgement*: one can never be perfectly *sure* either that a behavioural prediction will actually be borne out (our theories are too imperfect for that) or that others will interpret the evidence in the same way as oneself (the evidence is rarely unambiguous enough for that), nor can one be perfectly *sure* either that one's values are shared by others or that one's own values are perfectly consistent with one another. There is however, an important difference of principle between the two kinds of judgement, for in the case of positive judgements concerning "what will happen if..." it is possible to reduce arguments, where people differ in their judgements, to questions concerning the relevant and valid use of logic and the relevant

and valid interpretation of the facts. In the case of value judgements, argument ultimately boils down also to questions of logic and fact but also – and herein lies a major difference – to differences in views about equity, social justice, political values, and so on: in short to differences in what may turn out to be fundamental views on what constitute the good society.

(ibid.: 4)

Culyer, although a subscriber to the traditional economics framework of favouring positive scientific analysis in the study of social policy, recognises that value judgements are an inherent feature of such an approach. For Culyer, the principles of 'logical validity and empirical validity' prove to be valuable tools provided they are not employed in a limiting sense, that is with regard to a single set of values, but are drawn upon to 'explore a variety of *different* values' (ibid.: 5).

Therefore, although most economists would accept that claims of objectivity in the application of economic analysis to social policy are flawed, the practice of adhering to the positive approach serves to counter this criticism. That is, by emphasising their technical expertise in explaining the implications of policy, both existing and proposed, economists assume the role of specialists in informing value judgements as to what 'constitutes the good society'. However, it can be argued that the focus on achieving the goal of social efficiency, both in the allocation and distribution of resources, demonstrates a particular bias and thus policy will be directed in this area. Although the methods employed in the traditional economics approach approximate a scientific impartial methodological framework, it is assumed implicitly that the principal goal of policy is to maximise the fulfilment of individual preferences, which in turn will promote the ultimate aim of achieving efficiency. Thus the normative content of the neo-classical framework involves more than 'questions concerning the relevant and valid use of logic and the relevant and valid interpretation of the facts'. The generalised thesis of the economics model is that scarcity implies choices. The maximisation of social welfare and so efficiency, will be the end result if resources are allocated in accordance with individual preferences, which are in turn indicated by their individual choices. Thus:

> The efficiency criterion can rank alternative situations by reference to their ability to satisfy the preferences of consumers, *given* their money incomes, but produces no agreed method for deciding what relative incomes should be.
>
> (Wiseman, 1991: 60)

Intrinsic to this thesis is the assumption that individuals will always act to maximise their own personal satisfaction and, in doing so, their choices are both freely made and expressed. Constraints on choice, other than those associated with money incomes, are effectively ignored. Issues concerning the distribution of resources, therefore, remain outwith the scope of the model. Commenting on equity is thus considered a matter determined by the personal value judgements of the commentator, rather than a practice that can be supported by appealing to a process of logical deductive reasoning. For Wiseman, this illustrates the limitations of the welfare economics component of the neo-classical framework:

> The explanation of this situation lies in the fact that, although it purports to be a generalised logic of choice, this welfare thesis is essentially concerned with choice-through-markets.
>
> (ibid.: 62)

Herein lies the most crucial value judgement contained within the traditional economics approach to policy analysis, which tends to go unrecognised (at least in a formal sense) – the accepted dominance of markets in determining social arrangements. As Wiseman goes on to argue:

> ...the market operates in the context of a set of institutions and constraints which are themselves in one way or another also the outcome of the choices of citizens. The relationships between such institutions (constitutions, governments, legal systems) and markets is intimate and complex, and there is no obvious reason to evaluate the efficiency of social arrangements by reference to the operation of only one of them.
>
> (Op. cit.)

The overarching emphasis on efficiency over equity; the unremitting attachment to 'scientific' methods of analysis, and the exclusive focus on the market constitute the basic elements of the neo-classical construct. It is argued that these elements themselves originate from statements of subjective value and thus the analytical framework is essentially normative in nature. The traditional economics approach to policy analysis can in itself be described as comprising a set of generalised beliefs as to what constitutes a 'good society'. However, this is not always immediately apparent and as Wiseman argues; 'the neoclassical construct facilitates the introduction of personal value judgements which then assume an unmerited 'scientific' status' (ibid.: 64). It follows then that the practice of making scientific conclusions based on empirical evidence, which forms the basis of the neo-classical framework, is fundamentally premised on a set of personal value statements regarding the 'right' way of doing things. To claim therefore that this approach to policy analysis represents an unbiased methodological framework for the purposes of explaining policy outcomes, and thus informing policy direction, is erroneous. Furthermore, a continued exclusive adherence to this approach represents a particular bias, albeit disguised, with regard to the nature of social and economic arrangements.

Any useful analysis of social security policy must account for this bias and attempts should be made where possible to distinguish vested interests from fact. In examining the CBI literature, evidence emerges of a continual emphasis on preserving a traditional work-and-pay relationship. It is argued that this emphasis represents a similar bias to that found in the welfare thesis of neo-classical economic theory. That is, policy is considered in terms of its intrinsic relationship to the workings of a market economy. Certain assumptions are held regarding the behaviour of individuals, particularly with reference to motivational issues; the role of government and the functioning of market-determined transactions. Following on from these assumptions, a process of logical deductive reasoning produces policy prescriptions that conform to the ideals associated with an efficient market economy.

As indicated in the introductory chapter, the purpose of social security policy can be directly associated with both economic efficiency and equity goals. That is, systems are designed with specific reference to the goal of supporting the workings of the market economy, but state administered income maintenance measures can also be considered in terms of the role they play in promoting social citizenship rights. This dual, and often conflicting, function of social security policy informs the analytical process in that systems are assessed according to their impact on both efficiency and equity. More specifically, the tendency in the practice of analysing state-supported income maintenance schemes has been to concentrate on three distinct but interrelated principles: 1, the advancement of the right to a minimum income; 2, the body of work devoted to analysis of the traditional wage mechanism in an attempt to separate work from pay; and 3, the concern for the furtherance of the principles of individual freedom and personal autonomy. Reference to these principles, with varying degrees of emphasis, is to be found in the literature pertaining to the CBI concept. However, it is argued that common to the various arguments is an underlying focus on the question of economic efficiency. Although reference is made to the objective of equity and the promotion of citizenship rights, such issues have been considered within the confines of market-based economies. In accounting for the evolution of the CBI concept it can be demonstrated that the continued application of neo-classical methods and theories have resulted in 'interests' being subsumed in what has been presented as fact. Thus the constraining features of a socially constructed academic discipline spill over into applied areas with equally limiting consequences.

In order for the debate to progress beyond such a confining framework it is crucial that these 'interests' are identified. It is in this sense that the analytical approach adopted is similar in content to the methods employed in a feminist economics analysis. That is, the intention is not to disregard or even exclude questions of economic efficiency from the debate. The purpose is rather to engage in discussion which formally recognises the inherent bias displayed in both historical and contemporary debates regarding the CBI proposal, thus enabling the development of a broader discussion, incorporating a wider range of 'interests'.

The purpose of inquiring into the origins and development of the CBI concept is, therefore, to demonstrate the limiting effects of adhering to a particular set of assumptions regarding the nature of social and economic arrangements. However, in doing so it is equally important to note the relevance of external influencing factors. An intellectual history of the CBI idea which reads like a 'list of who said what' would merely provide a chronology of ideas. The evolution of theories concerning minimum income guarantees must be examined with regard to the prevailing political structure and socio-economic organisation of the period. The task then becomes one of identifying the various social, economic and/or political pressures and assessing their relative importance in the forming of policy. The primary focus remains that of tracing a common and dominant practice of prioritising the goal of economic efficiency, defined in accordance with a traditional neo-classical model of the market economy. However, the analysis will also serve to identify and dissect various attempts to wed philosophical ideals concerning social justice with the practical solutions advocated, giving due consideration to the influence of the existing political and economic climate as well as to that of opposing doctrines. In this sense the approach adopted can be described as a 'political economy' approach. That is, the analysis combines questions of economic efficiency with the goal of promoting moral and social justice and situates such within a framework that accounts for the numerous factors that influence the policy process.

Identifying bias in the subject matter: incomes in a market economy

Individual incomes in modern market economies are primarily determined by the degree of control or ownership an individual commands over the factors of production: land, labour and capital. Subsequently, alterations in patterns of income distribution will result from market transactions that effectively serve to alter patterns of resource allocation. Within the neo-classical framework it is assumed that individuals, motivated by a desire to maximise their own personal utility, will act independently and autonomously when engaging in their respective market transactions. Thus, sources of income are derived directly from individual action in the market place and the level of such can be attributed to an individual's ability to accumulate resources. For Heilbroner, it was this 'idea of gain as a normal guide for daily life' that marked the end of societies organised around the principles of tradition and custom and the birth of the modern capitalist economy (1980: 24). Accepting the market as the guiding principle of economic organisation gives rise to new forms of social and economic relationships which, as Heilbroner argues, are primarily informed by the actions of 'economic man':

> The problem of survival was henceforth to be solved neither by custom nor by command, but by the free action of profit-seeking men bound together only by the market itself. The system was to be called capitalism. And the idea of gain which underlay it was to become so firmly rooted that men would soon vigorously affirm that it was an eternal and omnipresent part of human nature.
>
> (ibid.: 35–36)

Setting aside inherited property and capital ownership, paid work is the main source of income, or rather the main means of accumulating resources, for the majority of individuals in market-based economies. Paid work, therefore, is an essential feature of the market economy:

> ...present-day market-oriented economics was conceived by Adam Smith at the same time that markets for hiring labor were becoming more widespread, suggesting an intrinsic link between the wage system and the market economy. Not surprisingly, anyone who would dare to question the wage system is automatically seen as either anti-capitalist or utopian, and certainly as a most questionable economist.
>
> (Lutz and Lux, 1988: 154)

Furthermore, as Lutz and Lux argue, viewing paid work, or rather the operation of the traditional wage system, as a necessary ingredient in the functioning of the modern economy is an uncontroversial hypothesis across the political spectrum. They point out that contemporary orthodox Marxists have a problem with paid work only when it results in the generation of private profit:

> Eliminate these "fruits of exploitation" and there is not much that is wrong with the paying of wages. There is, then, a strange common ground shared by the two rival ideologies of today: they both are committed to the institution of wage labor.
>
> (ibid.: 155)

It can be argued then that, although the promotion of and adherence to the capitalist mode of production and distribution resulted in a growing awareness of the 'evils' of such a system in terms of wealth distribution, the traditional wage system has been accepted as an unquestionable and immutable element of capitalist economies.

It follows that attempts to resolve questions of equity, economic efficiency and citizenship rights within a capitalist market-based framework have tended to focus on the workings of the wage mechanism. The subject of work and pay has attracted the attention of those with an interest in preserving existing capitalist institutions in their bids to ensure greater efficiency. Similarly, attempts at promoting greater equity or advancing the rights of citizenship, within the confines of a market economy, have generally targeted issues such as low pay, employment rights, the role of the state as compensator for loss of employment and actively securing adequate levels of work. Finally any proposal which posits alternative forms of political and economic organisation must contain some reference to issues pertaining to work and pay given the current prominent role such plays in the functioning of modern socio-economic relationships. Thus the desire to re-evaluate, or even restructure, the traditional relationship between work and pay, emerges as a common doctrine amongst economists, social reformers and political analysts alike.

The CBI debate has not escaped this primary focus. Evident throughout the literature is an overarching theme of questioning the existing wage system. As previously argued, the emphasis may differ in terms of the motivating force in arguing for a CBI. Concern regarding the income security of individuals operating in a market economy has attracted many to the CBI concept with a view to instituting and preserving a notion of citizenship rights within an economic system governed by market principles. Furthermore, questions of wealth distribution and its impact on the efficient workings of the market economy have resulted in attention being drawn to the threat that widespread poverty poses for the functioning of capitalist structures. A CBI becomes relevant to such questions in that it presents the opportunity to promote efficiency in the labour market. Finally, a CBI has been viewed in terms of its potential for promoting individual freedom. The free market holds no guarantees in terms of gender or racial equality, personal autonomy and independence, as well as income security. A CBI can be conceived of as a mechanism for promoting such goals without radically altering the relationship between the state and the market, thus preserving the fundamental principles of capitalist societies.

All of the above arguments have been employed in the literature supporting a CBI. Accepting, and indeed actively promoting, the principal role of formal market-oriented work in determining individual incomes, leads to the subsequent assumption that any alternative source of income is either secondary, temporary or compensatory. The implication for the CBI proposal is that it is placed within a dualistic hierarchical structure with obvious negative consequences in terms of implementation prospects. Policies aimed at promoting and preserving the traditional work-and-pay relationship will be favoured over those that can be construed as radically opposed, or even independent to that relationship.

Thus, the task for those who support a CBI has been to make the glove fit. Arguing for a CBI on the grounds that it is a policy proposal that conforms to the model of modern capitalist development proves to be the favoured approach. In doing so the demands imposed by accepting the supremacy of the market economy, along with the implicit assumptions relating to the behaviour of 'economic man', are met.

Conclusion

At first sight a CBI presents as a promising proposal for the reform of income maintenance policy. On a macro-level it has the potential to promote both overall economic efficiency and social justice, while on a micro level, a CBI can arguably be viewed as a measure that corresponds with, and indeed assists in, the functioning of flexible labour markets. Conversely a CBI can be construed as damaging to economic performance in that it threatens the incentive to engage in paid work. Assessing the validity of such claims, both for and against a CBI, although considered a necessary feature of the reform debate, was not the prime intention of this chapter. The purpose was rather to show how thinking about a CBI in these terms is indicative of a narrow and limiting approach. It follows from a failure to fully appreciate the purpose and nature of social security policy and a subsequent limited understanding of the CBI proposal which, in turn, results from a continued and exclusive adherence to neo-classical economic theory in the analytical process.

A CBI has the potential to promote real freedom for all, but this aspect of the proposal will never be fully recognised as long as it continues to be regarded within a framework defined by the governing principles of mainstream economic thought. The implicit faith bestowed upon a particular model of economic and social organisation, inherent within neo-classical theory, occupies the policy agenda. Thus, reform proposals are considered with this agenda in mind. With reference to income maintenance policy in particular, this results in a privileging of the traditional work-and-pay relationship. That is, policy is considered, first and foremost, with respect to the impact such will have on formal labour market processes and any other possible outcomes are subsequently neglected in the analytical process. Arguing for a CBI within this perspective indicates that the whole range of potential benefits to be derived from the implementation of such a proposal, particularly those relating to gender justice, are overlooked. Rather, paid work is emphasised as the main source of economic and social welfare, therefore the efficient functioning of modern labour market structures is assigned priority.

However, the idea of an unconditional minimum income guarantee is not unique to contemporary debates on state welfare reform. Tracing the origins of the CBI concept provides evidence that it appears in various guises as a fundamental component of attempts to establish alternative notions of work, income, and citizenship rights within capitalist economies. Such attempts have produced convincing theoretical positions in support of a CBI and, in the process of doing so, have produced valuable insights in the search for an alternative economics. However, a critical assessment of this literature indicates that, while the limitations of conventional economic theory may be recognised, the focus remains firmly grounded within a view of the world that implicitly assumes the dominance of capitalist-based principles of social and economic organisation. Arguing for a CBI, therefore, displays a long established tradition of adherence to a socially constructed analytical framework which favours a particular vision of how the economy should operate. This continued practice serves to negate our understanding of the range of possible outcomes associated with the CBI proposal.

6 Arguing for a universal income guarantee

The reformist case

Introduction

As previously argued, the problem of poverty amidst plenty has been the prime motivating force behind the development of state-supported income maintenance schemes. Although differences in design can be attributed largely to the influence of disparate ideological beliefs, the rationale for state involvement in the relief of poverty can be presented in positive economic terms. A fundamental feature of traditional economic theory is the formal recognition of particular market failures, not least of which is the inability of the free market to ensure sufficient incomes for all. However, this does not imply that an alternative system of economic organisation is preferred. Rather, the case is made that the operation of the free market remains the single most effective method of ensuring individual freedom, and that the process of both resource allocation, and distribution, should take place within a market-determined framework wherever possible. State intervention is deemed necessary only in those instances when the market fails.

The purpose of this chapter is to trace the evolution of the minimum income guarantee concept and to identify the arguments employed in justifying such a scheme. The rationale for providing such an historical account is to demonstrate the relevance of mainstream economic theory in arguing for a universal minimum income proposal. This is not to say that all justifications have been framed within the market failure approach. The idea of a minimum income guarantee appears within alternative views regarding the actual structures of economic organisation. However, the claim is made that common to all arguments is an accepted belief that the economy is governed exclusively by the principles of free market capitalism. In this sense the universal minimum income proposal is presented as a practical policy response to a particular set of problems associated with capitalist development. State action is required to ensure a minimum income for all citizens; however; the nature of such action should be designed in accordance with the needs of a market economy.

A number of schemes supporting an unconditional and universal minimum income guarantee have been proposed under different names, such as social dividend; social credit; social wage and demogrant. Such schemes, although varying in detail, share a common aim – the formalisation of the right to an income predicated by citizenship. Furthermore, all such proposals have at their core an implicit assumption regarding the responsibility of the state as a provider of welfare. That is, the state in capitalist society has a duty to promote the freedom of all citizens and to act in ensuring that the process of wealth accumulation benefits all members of society. With this in mind, proposals for a minimum income guarantee can be grouped within two main categories: those which emphasise the rights of citizenship, and those which appear within attempts at developing an alternative view of the relationship between work, income and property in capitalist economies. It is worth noting that these two categories are not mutually exclusive and that justification for a minimum income guarantee is often sought by appealing to both considerations. However, making the distinction serves to illustrate the relevance of differing influences on the actual form policy should take.

This chapter will therefore begin by outlining the various proposals for a universal minimum income which originate within a predominantly rights-based theoretical framework. A further section will introduce similar proposals which have emerged as a fundamental feature of debates focused on rethinking the formal relationship between work and pay, as it exists within capitalist society. A final section will examine proposals for a universal minimum income guarantee that were presented as an alternative to the social insurance model of provision. Such proposals are treated distinctly, not because of any detraction from the past in terms of justifying principles, but rather because they appear at a time of consensus regarding the role of the state in the economy. That is, the notion of the 'mixed economy' bestowed upon the state a broader set of responsibilities, particularly in the area of welfare provision. Thus, less attention is devoted to justifying state intervention per se, but rather the focus is on the actual mechanisms to be employed. The conclusion will be drawn that the evidence indicates an established and heterogeneous tradition of attempts at justifying some form of CBI. Although such attempts provide useful insights into the potential economic and social benefits to be gained from a CBI, it is argued that they remain constrained by an implied acceptance of an entrenched set of governing principles that dominate all spheres of economic and social life. In this sense, proposals for a minimum income guarantee present as practical policy solutions, responding to the needs of a dynamic capitalist economy. It is not until the onset of the perceived 'crisis in welfare' theory that the CBI proposal emerges as a radical alternative to existing provision. The extent to which it is presented and understood as such will be explored in Chapter 7.

Tracing the origins: the rights-based justification for a Citizens' Basic Income

The idea of the right of every individual in society to a minimum of existence dates back to the end of the eighteenth century when Thomas Paine, in his attempt to explain the widespread poverty evident in advanced civilised nations, became one of the earliest advocates of a social security system sponsored and regulated by the state. Van Parijs refers to Paine as one of the 'most outspoken forerunners of basic income' and the author of 'what can plausibly be viewed as the first elaborate proposal of a genuine basic income' (1992b: 9, 11). Paine was born in England in 1737 and raised within a Quaker community. The Quaker tradition of egalitarianism, hostility to authority, and the emphasis on simplistic lifestyles are values found throughout Paine's life and work.

Paine began his career as a writer espousing political causes with the publication in 1792 of *The Case of the Officers of the Excise*, which drew attention to the low wages and mundane duties of the excisemen. Paine pointed out that such conditions resulted in the existence of strong temptations for dishonesty on the part of excisemen that had obvious negative consequences for government revenue. Although motivated by a concern for the poor conditions suffered by his fellow workers, Paine took care to attempt to appeal to the authorities. Rather than justify his claims for improvement on humanitarian grounds, he raised the issue of efficiency by pointing out the consequential indirect effects on government revenue by implementing policies that would serve to weaken the financial motives for participating in the informal economy. Higher wages would not only ensure a better standard of living for the excisemen but would also alleviate the temptation to engage in smuggling. This would further improve overall efficiency as providing sufficient reward, in terms of adequate wages, may result in workers being more diligent in their duties. It would appear then that Paine shows great insight in his attempts to promote the cause of the low paid. Rather than relying solely on an appeal for improving social justice he relates his demands to the objectives of both macro- and micro-efficiency in the sense that his claims of higher productivity and the curtailment of illegal activities will result in increased national wealth.[1]

Paine's life history illustrates that he was a committed champion of political and economic reform which served to promote the rights of the citizen and the preservation of individual liberty (see for example Oser and Blanchfield, 1975: 340 and Claeys, 1989: chs 2,3). He travelled to America and France in support of the revolutionary cause and wrote extensively on the subject of republican government in the name of freedom and justice for all citizens. An examination of Paine's thesis on income distribution, to be found in a text primarily concerned with the reform of agricultural society in the latter half of the eighteenth century, demonstrates that the rationale for his concept of the right to a

guaranteed income was primarily motivated by a concern for the rights of
citizenship and democratic government.

In *Agrarian Justice* (1796) Paine started from the premise that:

> It is a position not to be controverted that the earth, in its natural,
> uncultivated state was, and ever would have continued to be, the
> common property of the human race.
>
> (Paine, 1796: 611)

Paine is concerned with the fact that as society moves from a natural state
to a civilised state by means of essential and beneficial agricultural
improvements, advances in manufacturing technology and progress within
the arts and science domain, poverty, which does not exist in the 'natural
and primitive state of man' becomes apparent (ibid.: 610). He concludes
that while the process of 'civilisation' leads to affluence for some, it also
exacerbates the deprivation suffered by others. Paine witnesses this poverty
to be 'the condition of millions, in every country in Europe' and that such
individuals would have been better off in the state of nature (Op. cit.). The
remainder of Paine's essay attempts to show how poverty occurs as a consequence of civilisation and indeed how governments should intervene to
ensure that each member of society is not robbed of their natural rights,
that is, the right to 'natural property, or that which comes to us from the
Creator of the universe – such as the earth, air, water' (ibid.: 606).

In doing so, Paine distinguishes between natural property and what he
refers to as 'artificial or acquired property' (ibid.: 606). He explains that,
as land is cultivated only the value of the cultivation should become
private property:

> ...as it is impossible to separate the improvement made by cultivation
> from the earth itself, upon which that improvement is made, the idea
> of landed property arose from that inseparable connection; but it is
> nevertheless true, that it is the value of the improvement, only, and
> not the earth itself, that is individual property. Every proprietor,
> therefore, of cultivated lands, owes to the community a ground-rent
> (for I know of no better term to express the idea) for the land which
> he holds; and it is from this ground rent that the fund proposed in
> this plan is to issue.
>
> (ibid.: 611)

This then was how Paine envisaged the financing of his system of social
security and in the name of justice, not charity, the funds so raised should
be distributed as such:

> ...there shall be paid to every person, when arrived at the age of
> twenty one years, the sum of fifteen pounds sterling, as a compensa-

tion in part for the loss of his or her natural inheritance, by the introduction of the system of landed property. And also, the sum of ten
pounds per anum, during life, to every person now living, of the age
of fifty years, and to all others as they should arrive at that age.

(ibid.: 612–613)

Paine goes on to emphasise the role of society in his plan for social security and thus justifies taxation as a means of finance in the name of moral
justice:

> I have made the calculations stated in this plan, upon what is
> called personal as well as upon landed property. The reason for
> making it upon land is already explained; the reason for taking per-
> sonal property into the calculation is equally well founded though on
> a different principle.... Personal property is the effect of society;
> and it is impossible for an individual to acquire personal property
> without the aid of society as it is for him to make land originally....
> All accumulation, therefore, of personal property, beyond what a
> man's own hands produce, is derived to him by living in society; and
> he owes on every principle of justice, of gratitude, and of civilisation, a
> part of that accumulation back again to society from whence the
> whole came.

(ibid.: 614)

Although simplistic it would appear that Paine writing in the eighteenth
century provides us with a proposal for a genuine CBI, financed from a
form of progressive taxation, and further provides a powerful rights-based
justification for such a proposal. Paine does not distinguish between rich
and poor when calculating his payment plan but places emphasis on the
right to compensation for loss of natural inheritances. A system which
does not involve the direct transfer of funds from those in work to those
out of work but rather depends upon taxation, justified in terms of an
individual's debt to society, avoids the social evil of stigmatising the poor.
For these reasons, that is the development of the notions of compensation
due and debt owed which were not explicitly linked to the formal labour
market, the Paine doctrine for social security is to be viewed as radical. It
can be argued that such radicalism would not be welcomed in eighteenth
century Britain as it involved a substantial transfer of funds from the pros-
pering property owning classes, who were emerging as an increasingly
dominant force both politically and economically.

However transfer by taxation and the state provision of a minimum subsistence level of income did in fact emerge in practical policy terms. The
Speenhamland system of poor relief administered in Britain in the late
eighteenth century reflects these aspects of the Paine philosophy. The
system developed as a direct result of the following event:

> The justices of Berkshire, meeting at the Pelikan Inn, in Speen-hamland, near Newbury, on May 6, 1795, in a time of great distress, decided that subsidies in aid of wages should be granted in accordance with a scale dependent on the price of bread, so that a minimum income should be assured to the poor irrespective of their earnings.
>
> (Polanyi, 1968: 78)

This system of relief, originally intended as an emergency measure was copied widely throughout England in subsequent years, and although never became law 'received the stamp of common acceptance' (Gregg, 1965: 34). However as Polanyi points out:

> ... it introduced no less a social and economic innovation as the "right to live", and until abolished in 1834, it effectively prevented the estab-lishment of a competitive labour market.
>
> (1968: 78)

The problem of the free-rider emerged in that relief was now provided regardless of whether an individual was in work or not. Relief payments were criticised specifically for promoting idleness; encouraging the breed-ing of illegitimate children for the purposes of maximising allowances; and for preventing individuals from assuming responsibility for their own economic misfortunes (Gregg, 1965: 180–181). Furthermore, the system created disincentives in terms of labour productivity:

> Hence, no labourer had any material interest in satisfying his employer, his income being the same whatever wages he earned ... however little he (the employer) paid, the subsidy from the rates brought the workers' income up to scale.
>
> (Polanyi, 1968: 79)

As a direct consequence labour productivity began to decline and this in turn provided employers with an added justification for reducing wages even further. However, the system proved to be universally popular, at least in the short term, in that:

> ... employers could reduce wages at will and labourers were safe from hunger whether they were busy or slack; humanitarians applauded the measure as an act of mercy even though not of justice and the selfish gladly consoled themselves with the thought that though it was merci-ful at least it was not liberal; and even ratepayers were slow to realize what would happen to the rates under a system which proclaimed the "right to live" whether a man earned a living or not.
>
> (ibid.: 79–80)

It was clear, that in the longer term, the Speenhamland system of poor relief was doomed to failure. Costs escalated beyond control system and the system actually resulted in the irony that individuals were compelled to offer their labour in order to earn a living whilst at the same time that labour was being deprived of its market value. Abolishing Speenhamland to make way for the more stringent system implied by the Poor Law of 1834, can be arguably viewed as a measure conducive to the needs of a competitive labour market. The principles of the 'Workhouse Test' and 'Less Eligibility' ensured that poor relief was targeted at the truly needy and receipt of such was conditional upon individuals subjecting them-selves to harsh conditions of deprivation. The underlying philosophy of the 1834 Act followed a Malthusian line in that it was believed that the condition of poverty itself would serve as a natural check on population growth, thus curbing any further increase in overall poverty levels. Although primarily based on religious doctrine and political philosophy regarding the natural order of society, such beliefs were in accordance with the economic theories espoused by Adam Smith. The new system of poor relief conformed to the ideas of individualism and the assumed inherent efficiency of the operation of the free market. Poverty was believed to be a condition which an individual could control by their own independent action and state support should only be provided in the most extreme circumstances in order to avoid any damaging effects on the structure and functioning of the market:

> Far better was private charity, which of its goodness relieved necessi-tous cases and had the discrimination to pass over the idle and dis-solute. The labouring population would thus be kept down to the level at which there was work for all, and a sequence of work, wages and contentment would be set in train, with the unavoidably needy relieved by the charitable rich. . . . Each man had to work, not in the position to which God and birth had called him, but in the place into which his own exertions had brought him. Supervising his efforts and ensuring that the sum total of all such activity in the community would result in the greatest possible good was an "Invisible Hand". So, in place of God and birth, the economists substituted the invisible hand and competition, which, in the long run, came to the same thing.
>
> (Gregg, 1965: 184–185)

The Poor Law Act of 1834 therefore effectively removed any notion of rights to income maintenance that had developed under the auspices of Speenhamland and served to stigmatise the poor. The selective granting of relief was strongly favoured over the previous universal system as experience had proved that such was detrimental to the efficient workings of the market economy. This leads Green to conclude:

> The failure of this first experiment with a guaranteed minimum income left as a legacy to the future grave doubts about the workability of any plan that provides a minimum income to all citizens.
>
> (1967: 51)

By driving wages down to levels below their natural market clearing rates the Speenhamland experiment created disincentives to work, which took effect on a large-scale basis, thus rendering the scheme prohibitively costly (Brittan, 1988: 203). National productivity suffered and the widespread dependency on public assistance led to an increase in rates of poverty. Although supportive of a CBI, Brittan argues that in order to avoid the pitfalls associated with the Speenhamland experiment, there should be a 'fairly large gap between national income per head and the basic income' (ibid.: 299). Thus basic income guarantees should be set at a level 'well below the average or median wage if they were not to be ruled out on "incentive" grounds' but the level should also be sufficient to ensure at least a standard of living which is above subsistence levels (ibid.: 202). For Brittan this scenario is possible in 'affluent' modern market economies and represents a practical solution to the problems associated with work-induced poverty:

> Classical economists who rightly argue for market rewards to factors of production usually fail to face the problems of those whose work has a low market value. The challenge for economic and social policy is to find a way of obtaining as much as we can of the benefits of an American-style labour market, without incurring the cost of American-style poverty.
>
> (ibid.: 301)

Although advocating a rights-based minimum income guarantee, Brittan's arguments are primarily founded on economic efficiency grounds and the scheme he envisages is to be designed in accordance with the requirements of modern capital and labour markets. That is, the system should operate in such a way as to ensure sufficient profits are to be realised from individual effort, thereby promoting continued economic growth, which in turn would safeguard the nation's ability to pay. The demise of the Speenhamland system can be arguably attributed to its failure in meeting such conditions.

Thus, while Paine provides us with the theoretical justification for a state-supported minimum income guarantee, the economics of such a scheme had not yet been well thought out. Practical experience in the UK in the late eighteenth century demonstrated that any proposal for the implementation of a system of state-provided income maintenance, which does not entail a work test, financed via general taxation would not be politically expedient given the historical context in which it was proposed.

During this period, the advancement of a capitalist system based on laissez-faire principles of socio-economic organisation took precedence and the relief of poverty was mainly viewed as a private concern. It is perhaps for these reasons that the concept of a CBI does not appear again in the literature until the beginning of the twentieth century.

However utilising Paine's terms of reference provides a powerful basis on which to build in that a CBI can be supported within a theory of natural human rights. In seeking further justification, the purpose is not to dismiss such a theory but to elaborate on it, as will be demonstrated by an examination of the notion of 'Cultural Heritage' which emerges in various forms in the subsequent literature. As capitalism develops in the industrialised world the growing numbers of individuals experiencing the poverty that Paine witnessed occurs simultaneously with a general increase in national wealth due to economic growth. This pattern of events leads to concern among academics, politicians and social reformers alike within the area of income distribution.

Accepting that great disparities in patterns of wealth distribution pose a threat to the functioning of the liberal market economy gives rise to questions concerning the appropriate mechanisms to be employed in addressing distributional imbalances. Whether the emphasis is placed on achieving social justice or promoting a more efficient (in strictly economic terms) allocation and distribution of resources, the poverty issue provides justification for state intervention. Given the political and economic structures associated with capitalist forms of organisation, the policy instrument most suited to achieving such goals is the use of transfer payments. However the question remains as to: which method of transfer is indeed the most effective in securing continued economic growth and addressing deficient demand; how are such transfers to be implemented within the prevailing socio-economic structure; and how do transfer payments relate to the dominant political philosophy? That is, the overall desire to preserve freedom whilst maintaining limited state intervention in the workings of the economy. The concept of a CBI has featured prominently in debates focused on resolving such issues. However it has also been presented, although at times somewhat modified, as part of a range of measures intended to alter existing structures of resource allocation implied by adhering to a strictly capitalist model of economic organisation. In this sense a CBI is viewed as an alternative to the more traditional approach to income redistribution involving straightforward transfer by taxation. The differences in emphasis result in differences in design but the ultimate goal remains the same. That is, promoting a socially efficient allocation and distribution of resources, whilst at the same time preserving individual freedom in an economy which is largely governed by the operational principles of the market place. If it is assumed that paid work, as previously argued, remains a primary source of income, then, it follows that debates focused on the relevance of a CBI to issues of income distribution originate from concerns relating to perceived inadequacies of the functioning of the labour market. Attempts to resolve such issues, taking into account the lessons learned from past experiences with transfer payments, have resulted in a great deal of attention being paid to the formal relationship between work and income in a modern market economy.

Work and pay

Transfer payments represent a shift in income from higher income groups to lower, from taxpayers to non taxpayers, from younger to older workers, from active, productive members of the economy to those no longer contributing to output. Whatever the arguments about justice, and aside from the effects on the direction and level of output, transfer payments indicate a vital, growing area where "work" and "pay" are not closely related.

(Lovenstein, 1966: 113)

Writing in the 1960s Lovenstein, an economist, draws attention to the fact that transfer payments are a logical solution to the problem of an unequal distribution of income. Furthermore, as a policy measure, it conforms to the capitalist structure of reliance on the market recognising the responsibility of the state to promote stability and economic growth. For Lovenstein, the granting of a 'guaranteed income' is such a transfer payment and serves not only to fulfil the government's objective of ensuring sufficient purchasing power within the economy to sustain growth, but also contributes to the process of separating work and pay.

The separation of income and work has been the subject of many a political tract and economic theory. However it is not the purpose of this chapter to examine such literature but merely to demonstrate the strong link with the CBI proposal and the belief that the employment of one's labour is not the sole source to the means of subsistence. A dual concern for the level of national output and the rights of the individual attracted many contributors to the CBI debate. Within such contributions, however, there is no concrete policy proposal for an unconditional minimum income to be paid as of a right and on an individual basis. It is not until the emergence of the contemporary literature, responding to the flaws and inadequacies of existing transfer payment systems, that a CBI is more explicitly defined. However many of the proposals advocated during this precursor phase contain some of the more radical elements of the CBI philosophy and hence require attention in that they promote an understanding of the underlying theoretical concepts.

Guild socialism and the social dividend

Guild Socialism, primarily a British movement, reached its height around the time of the First World War. The Guild Socialists were a moderate group advocating a type of socialism that relied on gradualism and reform. Its leading exponents were a group of middle class intellectuals dissatisfied with the performance of the Labour Party. The Guild Socialists claimed to represent everybody's interests with an emphasis on the needs and interests of workers. The economic basis of the Guild Socialist movement centred around an attack on the traditional wage system. That is, utilising the Marxian analysis of 'surplus value' the movement criticised the appropriation of value from the efforts of workers in the form of the capitalist's profits. The traditional system of wages would hence be replaced by a system that would more adequately reflect the value of labour and the contribution made by that labour to the end product. The political question to be resolved was the lack of control afforded the individual in a system relying upon the electoral process as the only means of voicing discontent. Economic freedom and political freedom would be advanced in a new form of organisation. Each industry or craft guild would be responsible not only for the management and control of production and distribution within their own particular sphere of economic activity, but would also be responsible for the care of those outwith the traditional labour market. This would include the old, disabled people and the unemployed within the relevant guild. The establishment of the Joint Council would serve to promote the collective wishes of all guilds and hence a more democratic form of government would ensue. The movement attracted widespread support due to its twin pronged attack on the wage system and undemocratic government, in the sense that it attracted those committed to the Marxist ideology regarding the role of labour and those committed to devolved power. However events in Russia led to a focus of attention on the Bolshevik revolution. The Guild Socialists found it increasingly difficult to retain supporters influenced by the communists' success. Indeed, the move towards the idea of revolutionary change, an attempt to prevent mass exodus of the more extreme socialists, served to alienate the more moderate supporters, whilst the extremists left to join the newly formed Communist Party in Britain (Finlay, 1972: 83). Despite the political demise of the Guild Socialists the analysis contained within the philosophy regarding the relationships between income and work provides a concrete link to the CBI proposal.

The Guild Socialists sought to:

> ...combine Syndicalism with the Ruskin-Morris belief that work should be a creative, life enhancing experience, fearing that both Fabians and Marxists gave too much power to the state.
>
> (Burkitt, 1984: 121)

Bertrand Russell, essentially a Fabian but attracted to the anarchist philosophy, wrote in 1918 that:

> Marxian Socialism would give too much power to the State, while Syndicalism, which aims at abolishing the State, would, I believe, find itself forced to reconstruct a central authority in order to put an end to the rivalries of different groups of producers. The best practible system, to my mind, is that of Guild Socialism.
>
> (1918: 13)

Russell is, therefore, attracted by the movement and in common with the Guild Socialists he develops a theory which contains elements of a CBI. However, Russell's argument for a form of minimum guaranteed income finds justification in the earlier work of Paine as well as going further to examine the relationship between work and pay. In a chapter entitled 'Work and Pay' Russell begins by stating that it is economic fact that 'Nature only yields commodities as the result of labour' (ibid.: 99). For Russell, then, labour is an essential ingredient for economic survival. However, he remains concerned about the traditional means of rewarding productive activities which 'yield commodities', that is the wage mechanism. He hence looks to alternative systems of political and economic organisation for inspiration. He begins by drawing similarities with the Socialists and Anarchists who propose the abolition of the wage system in the name of a more equitable distribution of the nation's resources:

> Defenders of the existing system maintain that efficient work would be impossible without the economic stimulus, and that if the wage system were abolished men would cease to do enough work to keep the community in tolerable comfort. Through the alleged necessity of the economic motive, the problems of production and distribution become intertwined. The desire for a more just distribution of the world's goods is the main inspiration of most Socialism and Anarchism.
>
> (ibid.: 105)

The primary concern of the Socialists is to retain the willingness to work, according to Russell, as a condition of receipt of the minimum right to subsistence. Whilst the Anarchists wish to provide everyone with as much as they can consume of necessities with no corresponding conditions of entitlement. The 'rarer commodities' would be rationed and subsequently divided equally amongst the population. For Russell, then, both systems of redistribution are compatible with the common ownership of land and capital but the difference is that socialists would impose an obligation to work whilst anarchists would not. Two very distinct forms of economic organisation would hence evolve. The problem for Russell is how to deal with the problem posed by work no longer requiring the economic stimulus of income. If equal incomes are to be granted to all those workers willing to work, under the more 'thoroughgoing Socialist' system, and an equal share of all commodities is to be the result under Anarchism then how would society ensure that enough of the necessary unattractive work would be done in a society where the 'idler received just as much of the produce of work' (ibid.: 107). This is the problem that Russell sets out to resolve. He points out that the main criticism of the Anarchist system is that as long as work remained unpleasant no individual would engage in such employment for the mere fact that they were no longer forced to for reasons of economic survival. Russell counters this criticism by pointing out that:

> A certain amount of effort, and something in the nature of a continuous career, are necessary to vigorous men if they are to preserve their mental health and their zest for life.
>
> (ibid.: 112)

Income is therefore not the only stimulus. There are other rewards and for Russell these factors will outweigh the pay factor for the vast majority of citizens. There will always be work which is disagreeable however and therefore 'special privileges must be accorded to those who undertake it if the anarchist system is ever to be made workable' (Op. cit.). Such privileges are not within the Anarchists terms of reference and hence Russell concludes that inflexibility on the part of the Anarchists leads to their plan being unfeasible.

Russell remains concerned about the removal of the obligation to work. With this in mind he turns to the Socialists and states, 'Anarchism has the advantages as regards liberty, Socialism as regards the inducements to work' (ibid.: 118). In attempting to outline the problem inherent within the Anarchists' plan regarding the work requirement, Russell's attraction to Guild Socialism can be traced:

> Anarchists always assume that if their schemes were put into operation practically everyone would work; but although there is very much more to be said for this view than most people would concede at first sight, yet it is questionable whether there is enough to be said to make it true for practical purposes. Perhaps, in a community where industry had become habitual through economic pressure, public opinion might be sufficiently powerful to compel most men to work; but it is always doubtful how far such a state of things would be permanent. If public opinion is to be really effective, it will be necessary to have some method of dividing the community into small groups, and to allow each group to consume only the equivalent of what it produces.

This will make the economic motive of each operative upon the group, which, since we are supposing it small, will feel that its collective share is appreciably diminished by each idle individual.

(ibid.: 116)

Such a scheme is again not consistent with the Anarchist system. However it appears that the organisation proposed by Russell is indeed compatible with the plan advocated by the Guild Socialists.

In trying to combine the advantages of both the Socialist and the Anarchist systems of distribution of society's resources Russell advocates the following plan:

> ... that a certain small income, sufficient for necessaries, should be secured to all, whether they work or not, and that a larger income – as much larger as might be warranted by the total amount of commodities produced – should be given to those who are willing to engage in some work which the community regards as useful.

(ibid.: 119)

Continuing concern for the problem of choice in occupation, and the resulting effects on levels of production, leads Russell to further propose some sort of system which would enhance the incomes of those who engaged in disagreeable trades over those who are employed in more pleasant or skilled jobs. It would seem then that Russell is advocating a CBI scheme which for him:

> ... combines freedom with justice, and avoids those dangers to the community which we have found to lurk both in the proposals of the Anarchists and in those of orthodox Socialists.

(ibid.: 120)

Russell's plan fits the definition of a CBI and although primarily motivated by the separation of income from work debate, he does find justification in the equal right to freedom, therefore developing the rights based approach:

> When education is finished, no one should be *compelled* to work and those who choose not to work should receive a bare livelihood, and be left completely free; but probably it would be desirable that there should be a strong public opinion in favour of work, so that only comparatively few should choose idleness.

(ibid.: 193)

In *Roads to Freedom* Russell also presents a powerful argument to counter those who criticise universal minimum income guarantees on the grounds that the free-rider problem would render such schemes economically inefficient:

> There would, of course, be a certain proportion of the population who would prefer idleness. Provided the proportion were small, this need not matter. And among those who would be classed as idlers might be included artists, writers of books, men devoted to abstract intellectual pursuits – in short, all of those whom society despises while they are alive and honours when they are dead. To such men, the possibility of pursuing their own work regardless of any public recognition of its utility would be invaluable.... Freedom for such men, few as they are, must be set against the waste of the mere idlers.
>
> (ibid.: 115)

Although Russell uses this argument to defend the criticisms of the Anarchist system, which requires no work obligation, his observations prove relevant in arguing for a CBI. Russell raises the issue of 'productive leisure activities' which constitutes an important element in contemporary debates. However, at this stage the points Russell makes are worthy of comment, due in part to their relevance in negating claims of the economic inefficiency arising from the granting of a universal minimum income.

It would appear that by making the distinction between those engaged in 'intellectual pursuits' and 'mere idlers', Russell envisages a privileged CBI. That is a minimum income would be secured to those individuals who spend all of their time furthering the arts and sciences for no immediate financial gain, however the same minimum income should not be paid to those who merely refuse to work. Such a system is not in accordance with the CBI proposal in that it distinguishes between classes of individuals in much the same way as means test would. However it is not entirely clear that this is what Russell is proposing. For instance, he does draw attention to the fact that the gains to be made from granting a minimum income to the 'intellectuals' is to be set against the waste incurred by the loss in productivity from allowing some individuals the opportunity to become free-riders. By referring to this 'waste' he seems to be advocating that the minimum income is due to all and that in doing so the gains in terms of personal freedom will offset any efficiency loss. The Russell doctrine therefore presents a case whereby the question of economic efficiency is combined with the political concern of promoting individual liberty.

Although it has been illustrated that Russell was attracted to the Guild Socialist plan for reform, his basic income philosophy was distinct, though similar in aspects, to the policy proposed by the movement itself. One of the major academic contributors to the Guild Socialist doctrine was G.D.H. Cole, a professor of economics at Oxford University. Cole although an adherent of the socialist cause, remained committed to the idea of *active* as opposed to *passive* democracy and the avoidance of central control by impersonal state bureaucracies, which become unresponsive to the needs of the citizens it is elected to represent.[2] This is primarily what attracted him to the movement. His thoughts on Guild Socialism appeared on a regular basis during the 1920s in the *New Age*, a publication edited by R.A. Orage, a fellow Guild Socialist. Cole's association with this publication is illustrative for the purposes of this analysis due to the journal's strong link with the Douglas Social Credit movement, to be discussed below. Given the academic environment in which Cole was operating and his contact with fellow distinguished theorists advocating social reform, his role in the evolution of the political economy of income redistribution is an influential one.

Cole draws an analogy with the political and economic system of capitalism and religious doctrine. He identifies those in control as the money makers and the economists, whom he refers to as the 'high priests' and 'lesser priests' respectively, with the economists being the servants of the high priests. In doing so Cole draws attention to the supremacy of the role of money in the economy and to the dominant nature of those in control of managing the money supply. His reference to religion also reveals the fact that a great deal of mystification surrounds the present system but any criticism may be viewed as heresy. This scenario results in a strong solidarity amongst those in control, but the problem remains as to how to address the growing unrest from the 'flock'. For Cole, capitalism is 'the religion of economic inequality' and in order to survive must find a means of solving the issue of growing inequality (Cole, 1935: 13).

Writing in 1935, Cole attempts to develop a practical analysis of the principles and methods of economic planning within a society, exercising a parliamentary system of control, which would be institutionalised without revolutionary change but rather through a process of constitutional reform of the existing economic and political structure. *Principles of Economic Planning* is therefore an account of how planning could be introduced taking into consideration that capitalism, despite suffering recent setbacks in the form of being unable adequately to address the social problems of increasing levels of unemployment and poverty, remains an omnipotent and positive force throughout the Western world. Cole takes care to point out that he is not adverse to revolutionary change, nor does he rule it out as a future option. However, given the existing dominant economic and political order he is merely recognising that change is necessary, and operating within this structure, he presents:

> ...an outline of the problem as it meets us here and now – compelled as we are under the existing conditions to make a choice between working for the revival of private enterprise on the old lines and attempting to substitute a different economic system designed to

unloose the chained up forces of production and to give to the entire people a wider and more abundant life.

(Cole, 1935: ix)

The stimulus for Cole and consequently the reason we need to 'unloose the chained up forces of production' is his concern for underconsumption and the resulting effect of widespread unemployment. He further distinguishes between unemployment and leisure, maintaining that the present system ensures that unemployment is degrading and shameful to those suffering it directly when in fact the recent advances in productive capacity should allow us to experience more leisure time without being financially worse off. He criticises the classical doctrine of laissez-faire, with its emphasis on the supremacy of free markets in allocating resources efficiently and scolds the economists who attribute unemployment to high wages. However, he recognises that there is a growing number of economists in favour of a new order, involving increased management in terms of preventing downturns in the trade-cycle by encouraging investment as opposed to savings. Furthermore, there is a growing awareness amongst those controlling business that unemployment affects them directly as the resulting lack of purchasing power within the economy leaves their machines idle and their warehouses full. However, those exercising control over the means of production are a powerful group and therefore the instinct is to opt for 'planning' and not socialism, as this would mean relinquishing political and economic power. Cole's purpose then, is to develop a planning mechanism 'without a good deal of socialism' (ibid.: 16).

If, as illustrated above, Cole was motivated by a concern for underconsumption and the realisation of the economic importance of leisure time, his analysis of economic planning would obviously have something to say about the distribution of incomes. It is in this area that he introduces the social dividend. Cole begins, in a chapter entitled *Planned Distribution of Incomes and Production,* by acknowledging that the price standard is insufficient as a measure of value. Prices reflect a willingness to pay, and therefore indicate the relative scarcity of a particular good or service. Such prices can only be attached to purely economic goods and if the question at issue is how best to use the productive resources available then some measure must be devised which takes into account 'considerations of justice and well being' as well as the economists' criterion of 'preparedness to pay' (ibid.: 220). Cole then goes on to determine what criteria of social justice and social well being should be applied in a planned economy.

In his analysis, Cole categorically states that need should take precedence over demand:

> ...the need for a generally diffused supply of all things which can be regarded as necessaries of civilised living will constitute the first

overriding claim upon the available resources of production. A satisfactory minimum of food, fuel, clothing, housing, education and other common services will come before anything else, as a social claim that a planned economy must meet.

(ibid.: 224)

In the resource allocation process, the provision of necessaries for all citizens therefore assumes the highest priority. Cole then outlines his notion of what constitutes a necessity by taking into consideration individual tastes and developing a definition of relative as opposed to absolute standards of living. Goods that are not believed to be absolute necessaries in any civilised society, such as leisure goods or a greater quantity than is essential for survival of basic goods,[3] may be considered a necessity by some in order to achieve an acceptable and tolerable standard of living. The individual must be afforded the opportunity to consume such goods and hence the provision of a minimum income, with which the individual is free to devote to the purchase of these 'second class' goods and services, becomes the subsequent claim on available resources. This leads Cole to his logical assumption that the planned economy must intervene in the area of income distribution:

In the field of primary necessaries there will be no doubt about what the planned economy is to set out to produce, though there will be doubt about the level at which the necessary universal minimum is to be set, and therefore about the total size of the primary claim. But in the secondary field of what we may call "substitutable necessaries", there will be doubt. It will be desirable for the most part to leave the individual citizen the widest range of choice in deciding which of these secondary goods and services he prefers, and is therefore prepared to pay for out of his limited income. But as soon as this freedom of choice is assumed, it is at once apparent that the structure of demand for substitutable necessaries to which the planned economy will have to respond will depend on the distribution of incomes, and that no plan for their production can be made except with a definite distribution of incomes in view.

(ibid.: 225)

Cole maintains that the planning of production on the basis of 'social justice or expediency' will be extremely inefficient, at least at the micro level, unless it is preceded by planned income redistribution. Utilising the economists tools of merit goods and externalities he outlines how reliance on the operation of the price mechanism as a way of influencing demand will fail in its ultimate purpose of correlating consumption patterns with planned output. The planned economy, like the free market economy, must match up what various producers are willing and able to sell with what consumers are willing and able to purchase. It is assumed that in the free market economy this equilibrium will occur through the automatic and unfettered operation of the price mechanism. The planned economy has to find an alternative method of responding to signals and allocating scarce resources.

Given the criteria of 'social justice' and 'expediency' the planning authorities can readily determine the level of output required to provide everyone with the predefined primary necessaries, and select an efficient method of distribution, such as free provision, without requiring any prior knowledge of income distribution, or indeed assuming responsibility of any future control of income distribution. However, this is not the case when considering the production and distribution of 'substitutable' necessaries given the objectives of social justice and well-being. After having provided 'the minimum requirements of decent and healthy living' for all citizens it is assumed that individuals are free to choose how to spend their incomes and society has no interest in determining or indeed influencing these choices. However such an assumption fails to take account of situations where there may be sound social and or economic reasons for wishing to influence consumption patterns. The planning authorities can attempt to affect consumption by the direct use of pricing policies. Goods that are considered meritorious can be priced low to encourage consumption and likewise goods and services considered harmful to society can be attributed high prices to discourage consumption. However, as Cole points out, the actual effect of pricing policies will depend largely on the distribution of incomes at any given time, and hence without prior knowledge of such distribution the results may be inefficient.

Cole then goes on to explain how the planned economy may run into problems when trying to account for changes in demand without first considering the distribution of income. By anticipating how much of a particular good or service will be demanded at the proposed price the planners will set output levels correspondingly. Mistakes in the estimated amounts will be evident in the form of either surplus or gluts on the market. The planned economy in attempting to rectify for such errors can attempt to mimic the free market by fixing prices in the short run and altering production levels in the long run. Fixing prices will serve to deplete existing stock-piles or to curtail demand until such times as supply can be increased and the altering of output levels will reflect the change in market conditions in the next time period. However, as the overall level of demand in any economy is subject to regular fluctuations, any authority assuming the responsibility of planning the level of production in all productive sectors must remain extremely flexible in order to emulate the market process. Such a degree of flexibility at the micro level is administratively difficult and very costly to achieve. Planners, therefore, can resort to influencing demand in such a way that their decisions regarding output appear to be in line with consumer tastes. In other words, individual choice is manipulated to suit the planned output. Cole maintains that this monopoly power, accruing in the hands of a large state bureaucracy, is indeed the principal danger of a planned economy in that it serves, just as a large monopolistic industry in a free market, to severely curtail individual choice (ibid.: 230–231). This leads Cole to his conclusion that the success of the planned economy in responding to the frequent changes in demand conditions requires the adoption of policies directed at income distribution:

> If, however, consumers' incomes can be so raised as to give everyone a surplus to be spent on substitutable necessaries and cheap luxuries, the consequent enlargement of freedom of choice is likely very much to outbalance any tendency of the planning authority to persuade consumers into buying what they do not want.
>
> (ibid.: 231)

Cole does not rely on this justification alone but goes on to examine macro-economic issues which affect the level of demand. The planning authority requires information regarding the total level of purchasing power in the economy and a general concept of the division of the national income between geographical areas as well as between groups of individuals. Equipped with this information, the planned economy will be more successful in estimating the level of demand for particular goods and services and the pattern of allocation of that demand. Providing the analytical reasons why knowledge and control of the distribution of income is important, Cole then goes on to say how the planned economy should operate in this area.

Cole starts by stating that incomes perform two roles in the economy. They provide the means of financing the purchase of consumer goods by all individuals and they contribute towards the accumulation of capital goods through the process of savings and investment. The savings and investment function is not only represented by the actions of 'businesses and other corporate bodies' but also by individuals who choose not to spend all of their incomes in the immediate time period or by individuals who are forced, out of necessity, to 'put away resources to provide for a "rainy day", for their old age, or for giving their children a start in life' (ibid.: 232). He argues that:

> The sum accruing as incomes to the members of the community is therefore meant to be large enough to buy not only the current supply of consumers' goods and services, but a proportion of the investment goods as well.
>
> (ibid.: 232–233)

In a planned economy this scenario will be replaced by a system that distributes incomes sufficient for the consumption of all consumable goods and holds back an amount deemed necessary for the supply and accumulation of capital goods. It will therefore no longer be the responsibility of specific individuals to provide for the purchase of investment goods. This is not to say that individuals should not save a part of their incomes if they wish to do so but as this activity 'will be of no economic service' the savings will not accrue any interest. The balance between consumption and the accumulation of capital will be determined by the state in accordance with the national plan. Preference for saving on the part of individuals will be met by a reduction in the amount held back by the authorities and an equivalent increase in the amount available for distributing as incomes. Likewise, any shortfall in the savings level, as determined by the state, will be rectified by decreasing the sum available for distribution and translating this amount into collective savings. The planned economy will therefore operate in such a way as to ensure that in any given time period the total level of income circulating within the economy will be sufficient to purchase the total amount of goods and services supplied. What remains to be explained is how the national income will be distributed.

Reliance on a system that provides incomes either in the form of earnings or payments from the public purse (which Cole refers to as 'doles' and includes payments of interest on public debts, pensions, insurance and means-tested benefits) leads invariably to long term deficiencies in disposable income. Any down turn in the economy will be equalled by a reduction in available incomes, as 'doles' are currently financed by taxation. An increased demand for 'dole' payments results in further reductions in purchasing power and therefore unemployment becomes:

> ...self-perpetuating, because incomes cannot be increased until production has been increased, but production will not be increased until incomes are available to purchase the extra products.
>
> (ibid.: 234)

For Cole, then, the under-utilisation of productive resources could become a long-term phenomenon in the unplanned economy and the market will not automatically return to equilibrium. The issue becomes one of discovering some alternative means of distributing incomes from that which depends upon payment for services to production and state handouts financed via general taxation. Cole attempts to build a model that will ensure continued full employment in that:

> A planned economy will seek to begin at the other end, by distributing enough income to buy at the planned prices all the consumers' goods and services which can be produced with the available productive resources, so as to leave adequate provision for the making

of the requisite supply of capital goods. There will be a planned total of incomes as well as of products, and the aim of the plan will be to balance these two at the highest practicable level.

(ibid.: 234)

It is at this point that Cole presents the 'social dividend'. He wishes to replace 'doles' with a social dividend whereby income will no longer be derived from tax-financed state handouts or from payments of interest. Direct services to production will be rewarded in the form of wages and further income will be due to each citizen directly from the state as a 'recognition of each citizen's claim as a consumer to share in the common heritage of productive power' (ibid.: 235). The dividend will be due as a 'civic right', paid universally on an equal basis for each adult with appropriate allowances for children, and from the very onset should be '...at least large enough to cover the bare necessities of every family in the community' (ibid.: 235). Earnings from work would no longer be the means of economic survival but rather a means of securing an income over and above the minimum. Cole answers the criticism that work incentives would thus be destroyed within such a system by stating that the desire to obtain a degree of luxuries and a greater supply of what he previously referred to as 'substitutable necessaries' is in fact 'the keenest of all human demands' (ibid.: 236).

Cole is aware of the *possible* threat to work incentives within a scheme abolishing the traditional wage system altogether and replacing it with equal incomes for all and therefore is keen to ensure that an element of reward remains for participating in the labour market. However, the price mechanism will no longer be the main method of income distribution but will be complementary to a scheme of primarily distributing incomes on the basis of need. Hence, the main slice of national income will now be accounted for by the priorities of the amount set aside to provide for the accumulation of capital and the distribution of the social dividend. Any amount remaining will be available for payment to individuals engaging in work. Cole actually emphasises the growing importance of the social dividend when he refers to the primacy that the payment of the dividend will have over the wage mechanism:

> I believe the tendency will be for a planned economy steadily to reduce the proportion of total income distributed in the first of these ways, (rewards for work) and steadily to enlarge the amount of the social dividend.

(ibid.: 235)

In adopting these policy measures in the field of income distribution, the planned economy will be better equipped in forecasting the level of demand and in accounting for fluctuations – the problem Cole set out to resolve. All that is now required is an estimate of the overall level of basic needs. This will now be an easier task, as the demand for basic necessities remains more stable than the demand for 'substitutable necessaries' and luxury goods. Individual demands will indeed vary over time quite considerably, but knowledge of the average level of demand for the bare essentials of life can be much more readily acquired than the information required to establish the market conditions in each industry. Uncertainty of demand will not be completely abolished but the move towards equality will diminish the extent of this uncertainty, at least in the short run. The expenditure of incomes derived from sources other than the social dividend will be much more difficult to anticipate. However, in drawing up a plan of national consumption, the authorities will be aware of the supplies and output required to fulfil basic needs and, by retaining flexibility in the 'finishing trades' in terms of capital structure, it will be easier to switch resources from one area to another in response to fluctuating demand. Within this chapter of Cole's thesis on economic planning, the recurring theme of citizens' rights is coupled with an analytical illustration of the inadequacies of the current means of distributing wealth (with its accent on the price mechanism leading to rewards and ownership) to develop a justification for a guaranteed minimum income scheme. Cole is therefore essentially utilising the economist's tools of analysis to develop a more efficient means of wealth distribution. However, his contribution to the CBI debate contains a theoretical aspect that complements his practical analysis.

In an appendix Cole goes on to provide a more theoretical justification for his social dividend:

> The power to produce wealth is a social power which arises out of the entire development of the society in which it exists. This power can be increased by individual skill or effort; but the skill and effort of individuals are exercised upon a situation which embodies the entire social heritage of the community to which they belong. When economists speak of a man's "productivity", they really mean that part of the productivity of society which is realised more or less effectively with his aid. It follows that no man really "produces" the full value which is attributed to him in economic theory, and that no other factor of production really possesses a "productivity" corresponding to that which it is credited. Most of the product achieved by the employment of the factors of production is attributable to society: the individual is responsible only for relatively small variations in its value, according as he uses well or ill the available resources of production.
>
> (ibid.: 251)

In 1936 Cole published a pamphlet titled *Fifty Propositions about Money and Production*[4] in which he states:

14 The productive power of the community is a social power: it depends on the accumulated capital resources and knowledge at the disposal of the community as well as upon the current efforts of individuals. Wealth creation is a social, as well as an individual, process.

15 Accordingly, the entire body of citizens has a social right to share in the current product of industry, not only as a reward for current service rendered, but as a right of citizenship.

(1947: 360)

Witness the recurring theme of citizenship coupled with the separation of work and income. Cole goes on to say:

20 It is implied in the above proposition that the social dividend should be equal for all citizens. Every citizen has an equal right to share in the social heritage.

Note – This does not exclude decisions by the community to make additional grants to certain citizens on grounds of special need, e.g. to the sick or infirm, or decisions to vary the dividend in the case of children who are receiving free services such as education, or of other persons receiving special free services at the public expense.

(ibid.: 360)

Clearly, then, the social dividend envisaged by Cole in the 1930s was one which should be paid unconditionally to all citizens. There was to be no work test and the amount paid would have no link to individual effort, and therefore not be viewed as a reward for work. However, Cole does appear to develop a concept of debt to society in that he assumes a preparedness to work on behalf of all citizens making a claim on the nation's cultural heritage. He is unclear how the system is to be policed in light of individuals' failing to 'pull their weight', but he is resolute that some form of provision should be made for at least meeting the basic needs of those who 'forfeit their claims' (1935: 264). In making this claim, Cole reinforces the important issues his thesis raises with regard to the responsibility of modern civil society in providing for the *needs* of its citizens as opposed to their individual *wants*. Cole further recognises the relationship between social security and other forms of state welfare provision when discussing the criteria for determining the amount of dividend payable. The Cole doctrine, then, represents a significant contribution to the CBI debate.

However, the arguments presented by Cole display limiting characteristics due to his acceptance of the dominant and monopolising force of capitalism in determining the socio-economic base of society. He takes care to point out that his model does not imply the demise of capitalist-based structures. Rather, he presents it as means of securing a more efficient use of a nation's resources by exercising a degree of carefully managed and democratically-based control over the process of market allocation. Inherent within his plan is a mechanism that ensures that the basic needs of economic survival are met from a source alternative to the processes associated with the traditional buying and selling of labour. By defining his 'social dividend' as a claim on the nation's common heritage, he further separates his plan for income redistribution from the formal labour market. Furthermore, this aspect of his model emphasises the notion of collective responsibility, which is distinctively opposed to a focus on the individual, a fundamental feature of capitalist organisation. However, Cole's thesis is first and foremost an analysis of the economic planning of income distribution in a capitalist economy. As such, his 'social dividend' is to be regarded as an income maintenance measure that complements the traditional work-and-pay relationship. The focus on an equitable distribution of wealth being a necessary condition for achieving efficiency in the utilisation of productive resources implies that the direction of social policy is being driven by economic considerations. Although explicit links to the labour market are effectively removed, the concept of the 'social dividend' remains implicitly a function of production and consumption in a market-oriented economy. However, Cole's plan does represent a crucial turning point in the CBI debate in that for the first time the relationship between the economic planning of income distribution and the formation of social policy is defined and analysed. Cole apparently historically coined the term 'social dividend' in his thesis on economic planning in a capitalist economy (Van Trier, 1989). However, the concept of a guaranteed minimum income appears throughout the literature on how a socialist economy could reach the equilibrium afforded by the market. An examination of this literature provides further justification for a CBI.

The neo-classical view

In 1938 Oscar Lange, an economist, attempted to deal with the objection from the capitalist economists Von Mises and Hayek that a socialist economy was impracticable in that it would fail to solve the problem of rational allocation of scarce resources. Lange, utilising neo-classical analysis, spoke of the social dividend:

> ... there must be some connection between the income of a consumer and the services of labour performed by him. It seems therefore convenient to regard the income of consumers as composed of two parts: one being the receipts for the labour services performed and the other being part of a social dividend constituting the individual's share in the income derived from the capital and the natural resources owned by society.
>
> (1964: 74)

Lange therefore envisages a system in which dividends are due to citizens from the state in a planned economy in the same way that privately owned industries distribute dividends to shareholders in a capitalist state. That is, by virtue of their ownership of the means of production as a natural right. Again, the rights-based justification for state-supported schemes of income support is raised. However, Lange is not primarily concerned with justifying a CBI on the basis of citizenship rights but is rather working out a theory of distribution within state socialism that will resolve questions of allocative efficiency. Work is no longer the sole source of income but the relationship between labour provided and financial reward, in the form of pay, remains unaltered. Pay rates act as signals to providers and purchasers, indicating degrees of relative scarcity, and ration resources accordingly. Therefore, when discussing the distribution of this social dividend Lange points out that it must be entirely independent of the choice of occupation so as not to distort the price mechanism operating in the distribution of labour, hence ensuring that 'a substitution of planning for the functions of the market is quite possible and workable' (ibid.: 83). Lange addresses the distribution of the social dividend in practical terms using neo-classical tools of marginalism:

> Freedom of choice of occupation assumed, the distribution of the social dividend may affect the amount of services of labour offered to different industries. If certain occupations received a larger social dividend than others, labour would be diverted into the occupations receiving a larger dividend. Therefore, the distribution of the social dividend must be such as not to interfere with the optimum distribution of labour services between the different industries and occupations. The optimum distribution is that which makes the differences of the value of the marginal product of the services of labour in different industries and occupations equal to the differences in the marginal disutility of working in those industries or occupations. *Therefore, the social dividend must be distributed so as to have no influence whatever on the choice of occupation.* [Lange's own emphasis] The social dividend paid to an individual must be entirely independent of his choice of occupation. For instance, it can be divided equally per head of population, or distributed according to age or size of family or any other principle which does not affect the choice of occupation.
>
> (ibid.: 83–84)

Lange therefore is not proposing an unconditional guaranteed income payable to all, in the CBI sense, as he points out that his scheme does not necessarily entail equal distribution of the social dividend per head of population. His contribution to the debate though can be viewed in the separation of income from work analysis in that he views two sources of income in a planned economy, that is wages for work done and the social dividend. Lange's social dividend is hence merely a policy instrument to be adopted by the planners of a socialist economy to ensure a more efficient distribution of income. The price mechanism would remain as the primary economic force within labour markets.

Lerner, writing in 1944, utilises the same tools of analysis (later to become known as the Lange–Lerner model of the price mechanism of a socialist society) to illustrate how in a socialist economy governments can avoid the evils of inflation whilst attempting to maintain full employment:

> In the collectivist economy this can be done in two ways. The first is through adjustments in the rate of interest. This affects both the rate of investment and the rate of consumption. Second, and more important, is the direct effect of government action on income and through income on consumption.
>
> The consumers receive part of their income from their work in payment for their labour by the managers of production, who hire labour in accordance with the Rule. The rest of the income of consumers comes to them from the government. This can be considered as the citizens share of the earnings of the factors of production other than labour, but however it is considered, the government must distribute just enough to induce consumers to spend the right amount which, together with the investment demand for factors, will provide full employment.
>
> (Lerner, 1970: 267)

Governments therefore have to be aware of the right amount of dividend due in accordance with production plans and it would appear that flexibility is a part of the Lerner model in that the dividend should be adjusted accordingly as production plans are altered. Although, in using marginal analysis Lerner was essentially a Keynesian and to describe him as a 'neoclassical' economist is 'a bit misleading' (Van Trier, 1989: 43). Van Trier draws attention to the fact that:

> Although studying and teaching at the LSE, being the "protégé" of Lionel Robbins, very much influenced by Hayek and von Mises, and intellectually committed to the elegant logic of marginalism, Lerner's socialist values led him to accept Keynes's scheme. For Lerner the (allegedly small) losses in efficiency from a Keynesian type of intervention did certainly not outweigh the social costs of mass unemployment.
>
> (ibid.: 43)

For Lerner then, the social dividend plays a very different role in guiding the allocation of resources compared with its role for Lange. Justified in the same way, that is, as a means of reimbursing citizens with their share of the social product, Lerner views the social dividend as more than a policy instrument to redistribute income. It is also viewed as a mechanism government could, and indeed should, utilise to guarantee an effective level of demand to ensure full employment:

> The only proviso that must be made in the interest of the optimum use of resources is that the amount paid out to any individual should not in any way be affected by the amount of work he does. This is because of the desirability of having the wage equal to the vmp *(value of marginal product)* of labour (which is what the manager will be paying the worker quite apart from any "social dividend") so as to induce neither too much or too little labour. In the name of the optimum division of income it can be argued that the distribution of the social dividend should not be very unequal. My personal inclination is for an equal share to be given to each member of society as his right as a citizen, with no questions asked and no exceptions. There could be no better safeguard of the freedom and independence of the individual.
>
> (Lerner, 1970: 267)

Van Trier summarises the differences between the Lange and Lerner social dividend schemes:

> ...for Lerner the social dividend is clearly a steering device, keeping the economy on the right but narrow track between inflation and depression. Lange's view, on the contrary, put the social dividend in a more strictly distributional framework. Secondly, whereas for Lange social dividends should not correlate with the choice of occupation, Lerner stresses the necessity of its being independent from the amount of work done. Thirdly, for Lange the rate of equality of the distribution was optional; Lerner, on the other hand, states his preference for an equal distribution, based on a dual argument: citizenship rights on the one hand and a more utilitarian argument in terms of the optimal income distribution on the other hand.
>
> (1989: 48)

The Lange–Lerner model therefore contributes to the CBI debate in an influential way. Both develop a state scheme of income maintenance based on citizenship rights and fiscal policy measures to ensure full employment. The right to work is linked with the right to an adequate income whilst at the same time developing a model which successfully separates work from income. The use of neo-classical marginal analysis, combined with Keynesian demand-management type measures, illustrates the flexibility of the concept of a minimum guaranteed income for all individuals across the political and economic divide.

Poverty as a natural consequence of progress

Continuing with the theme of financial reward for work, strands of the CBI proposal can be found in theories of poverty as a natural consequence of progress:

> Where the conditions to which material progress everywhere tends are most fully realised – that is to say, where population is densest, wealth greatest, and the machinery of production and exchange most highly developed – we find the deepest poverty, the sharpest struggle for existence, and the most of enforced idleness.
>
> (George, 1913: 9)

Concern for the effect on the labour market of increased mechanisation has attracted many individuals to a CBI. Parker (1989) points out that two former soldiers, Major C.H. Douglas and Jaques Duboin, at the time of the First World War, were motivated by such concerns:

> In France, Verdun veteran Jacques Duboin, who watched the newly manufactured tanks succeed where echelon after echelon of men had died, argued passionately for institutional change that would completely uncouple income from work. In order to prevent mass unemployment and to take advantage of the material abundance made possible by new technologies, he proposed that each country's national income should be shared out equally between its citizens, with a tax of 100 per cent on all their other income.[5]
>
> (ibid.: 126)

When developing a historical sketch for his book *Basic Income Freedom from Poverty: Freedom to Work* (1989) Tony Walter takes a similar starting point; that is the proposals associated with the aforementioned Major Clifford Douglas. Douglas, an engineer by profession, was spurred by a concern for the effect of expanding industry during the war and how was this to be consumed. The possible failure of society to fully appreciate and benefit from ongoing advances in modern technology led Douglas to turn his attention to the study of economics. He began to work out and subsequently advocate a plan that would address the decline of traditional liberal orthodoxy within the economics discipline (Finlay, 1972: 1). Although the Douglas proposal can be criticised with regard to providing a workable solution to deficient demand:

> ...the body of work published between 1918 and 1924 in collaboration with Orage forms a coherent critique of the capitalist financial mechanisms which regulate production and distribution in a technologically advanced society.
>
> (Burkitt, 1994: 19)

The central issue for Douglas was how to address the scenario of overproduction and unemployment and his remedy was the Social Credit. Douglas based his theory on the idea that:

> What backs the value of currency is not the banks but the productive capacity of the people and therefore credit ultimately derives from and is due to the people.
>
> (Walter, 1989: 23)

Douglas therefore became associated with the founding of the theory of Social Credit and his work was expounded in *The New Age* throughout the 1920s. The link with *The New Age* is worthwhile noting for two reasons. Douglas was not an economist by profession and as such was not afforded the academic credibility essential for ensuring his doctrine was brought into the public domain. Douglas hence required a public stage that would be sympathetic to his cause. *The New Age* turned out to be that stage:

> At length, at the end of 1918, a New Age editorial drew attention to "an ingenious and convincing article" by Major Douglas appearing in the "English Review" of December that year. The article itself was reprinted in *The New Age's* first issue of the new year, and Orage and his paper were launched upon a championing of Social Credit to which both were to remain loyal to the death – that of Orage dramatically on the night after his BBC talk on Social Credit, that of *The New Age* in 1938, when it faded out unable to pay its way.
>
> (Finlay, 1972: 62)

The journal itself served to promote both the political and economic aspects of socialist beliefs and under the editorship of Alfred Richard Orage it commanded a certain degree of literary and academic prestige. An association of this kind allowed the opportunity for the Douglas doctrine, essentially a treatise on monetary reform, to become connected with and to incorporate, with the aid of Orage's editorial skills, the social and political values of a progressive liberal movement. The second, related point to note regarding the link with *The New Age* regards the audience Douglas's Social Credit theory received. As mentioned earlier, G.D.H. Cole was a regular contributor and therefore it can safely be assumed that Cole was more than familiar with the Douglas proposal. As an economist, it follows that he would be interested in the function of money in the economy and therefore may have been influenced by Douglas.

The main thrust of the Douglas proposal was that in order to rectify any deficiency in purchasing power within the economy, governments should distribute additional money to consumers and grant subsidies to employers in order to divorce the production process from the price mechanism. It remains to be explained how this was to be done and whether the Social

Credit envisaged by Douglas bears any relation to a CBI, which would serve to separate work from income. Charles Sanderson, in a booklet published in 1936, attempted to outline the pros and cons of the Douglas plan, pointing out that Douglas was initially concerned with the problem of under-consumption. Consequently, his proposal set out to ensure sufficient purchasing power existed within the economy to buy what was being produced. That is, the central tenet of the scheme was demand management. According to Sanderson:

> ...Social Credit offers a scheme which it believes will cure under-consumption without interfering in any way whatsoever with the present economic organisation. It leaves ownership untouched, it leaves management untouched, it leaves profits untouched, it leaves interest untouched; it leaves the present economic organisation just as it is. It applies itself directly and entirely to the financial side.
>
> (1936: 5)

The scheme therefore offers a mechanism by which governments can control the amount of financial credit available within the economy to ensure that total national consumption would be equal to total national production. This mechanism was two pronged, involving the National Discount affecting product prices and the National Dividend affecting incomes. It would appear at first glance, then, that Douglas is an early Keynesian. However, further interpretation of the Douglas proposal is necessary to illustrate that this is not the case and that Social Credit did entail much more than, as Sanderson advocates, reform of the financial sector. Douglas's critique of the workings of capitalist economies does provide useful insights into the relationship between social and economic policy, previously viewed as separate. Furthermore, the Douglas doctrine contains strong elements of the notion of rights of citizenship and the abolition of the work requirement, albeit for a temporary five year period, as a condition of state-supported income maintenance schemes.

Douglas wrote in the preface to the revised edition of his original text, published in 1924, that his book *Social Credit* was issued:

> ...in order to correlate the financial theories, which have since become widely known under the same title, with the social, industrial, and philosophic ideals to which they are appropriate.
>
> (1935: v)

Douglas thus recognises that his ideas on financial reform are to be viewed as a new social order if his scheme is to be at all successful. Douglas is not prepared to accept that the adoption of his Social Credit scheme should involve revolutionary change, nor should it be a natural evolutionary process, but rather a combination of the two. The scheme proposed is to address the growing awareness that present financial and social arrangements throughout the industrialised world are unstable and that change is inevitable. In fact he writes:

> Nothing will stop it; "Back to 1914" is sheer dreaming; the continuation of taxation on the present scale, together with an unsolved employment problem, is fantastic; the only point at issue in this respect is the length of time which the break-up will take, and the tribulations we have to undergo while the break-up is in progress. But while recognising this, it is also necessary not to fall into the error which has its rise in Darwinism; that change is evolution, and evolution is ascent. It may be; but equally it may not be. That is where the necessity for the revolutionary element arises; using of course, the word revolutionary in a constructive sense.
>
> (ibid.: 197)

This provides some indication as to Douglas's political motivations. He goes on to state that:

> There is, at the moment, no party, group, or individual possessing at once the power, the knowledge and the will, which would transform the growing social unrest and resentment (now chiefly marshalled under the crudities of Socialism and Communism) into a constructive effort for the regeneration of Society.
>
> (ibid.: 197)

The simple solution to the negative balance between potential supply and effective demand, that is demand backed by a willingness and ability to pay was, for Douglas, money (Douglas, 1924: 27). In developing his scheme for financial reform Douglas adopts the attitude that the individuals comprising a community rightfully own the productive capacity of that community. His justification for this is based on his belief that accrediting all wealth formation to the collective values of the three traditional factors of production; land, labour and capital, is an erroneous assumption as it fails to recognise the contribution made by individual enterprise (ibid.: 56–57). This process of deduction provides Douglas with a theoretical justification for income redistribution based on the premise that individuals are naturally entitled to a share of the nation's wealth by way of their inherited ownership as citizens. The rights-based approach to an income guarantee is very much a part of the Douglas doctrine. However, Douglas does not rely solely on this justification, and the concept of a 'Cultural Heritage', that he refers to is strengthened by his analysis of the role of credit. Douglas tackles his analysis of deficient purchasing power by attempting to distinguish between financial credit and real credit. He begins by stating his concerns regarding the role of money in the economy, which subsequently leads him to his plan for financial reform. The emphasis on money as a measure of the value of a particular service or commodity is fiercely criticised by Douglas and he himself views this criticism as fundamental to his theory:

> *The proper function of a money system is to control and direct the production and distribution of goods and services.* [Douglas's own emphasis]. It is, or should be, an "order" system, not a "reward" system. It is essentially a mechanism of administration, subservient to policy, and it is because it is superior to all other mechanisms of administration, that the money control of the world is so immensely important.
>
> (ibid.: 72)

The financial organisation of an economy leads to the scenario of deficient effective demand in light of increasing supply. Individuals within such an economy are unable to purchase the goods they require or those goods and services which producers are willing and indeed 'anxious' to supply, due to the lack of money necessary to make such purchases. The Socialist retort to this theory would be that the problem stems from an unequal distribution of wealth but for Douglas this is a misconception:

> The point we have to make is not merely that financial purchasing power is unsatisfactorily distributed, it is that, *in its visible forms*, [Douglas's own emphasis], it is collectively insufficient.
>
> (ibid.: 95)

Douglas therefore builds his analysis around the theme of the role of money in the economy. The fact that money is viewed as a tool for measuring value results in a possible disequilibrium between supply and demand. If, as Douglas argues, the reason for underconsumption is due to individuals not having enough money in their pockets to buy goods produced, and as money represents the value of these goods, then he must turn to an examination of the price system. Prices represent money values and if money is deficient in the hands of the consumer then this leads Douglas to the assumption that prices are prohibitively high. If prices are determined by the need to cover costs of production then what does this say of the behaviour of producers. The problem arises when some of the costs being covered do not represent costs of final goods or services offered for sale but rather contribute towards the financing of capital goods. Not all money in the economy is spent on consumable goods but is saved in order to pay for capital goods, which become the property of those doing the saving, that is the capitalists. If the ultimate motivation is profit maximisation then the accumulation of capital goods is viewed as a future investment which will ensure the production of new goods, which in turn will be sold at a price sufficient to cover total costs, that is both 'old' and 'new' costs. If this process continues, then, it is 'self-evident' to Douglas that even if there were sufficient money to purchase all goods produced at any one point in time, the filtering of money into the production of 'new' goods results in a disparity between total costs and current prices in the successive period:

> The condition then is, that there are more goods in the world at each successive interval of time, because of the financial saving, and its application to fresh production, while the interest, depreciation, and obsolesence, on this financial saving has to be carried forward into the prices of production during a succeeding period. Each pound saved would be a pound withdrawn from consumption and put into production. Since costs must be less than prices, it only requires a very simple examination of this condition to see that the cycle becomes unworkable in a very short period of time, since no one would be able to buy anything.
>
> (ibid.: 98–99)

The process of depreciation, then, is diminishing the purchasing power available in the economy and requires intervention from the financial sector to prevent economic collapse. Assuming that money, in the form of legal tender, is the only form of purchasing power, then following Douglas's argument there will never be enough circulating to meet increases in production. This deficiency of purchasing power can be met by the creation of 'bank money' (ibid.: 101). The granting of financial credit ensures the survival of the production process, which as a consequence becomes debt driven. For Douglas then, it is the banking system that controls and determines production and the distribution of incomes. The creation of credit in the form of loans creates bank deposits which individuals can draw upon in the form of money used to purchase goods and services. However, the repayment of these loans serves to reduce bank deposits and thereby reduce effective demand. Due to what Douglas refers to as the existence of a system of punishment and reward, the cost of providing producers with financial credit must be recouped in monetary form. It is therefore passed on to consumers in the form of higher prices and thus the cycle continues as these higher prices stifle the additional demand that the original creation of credit was intended to address. The financial system not only controls the production process but also determines the distribution of incomes by affecting prices:

> ...a policy of increasing issues of money or credit, in such a manner that it can only reach the general public through the medium of costs, and must, therefore be reflected in prices, has one thing and one thing only to be said for it at this time; that it is absolutely and mathematically certain to reduce any financial and economic system to ruins.
>
> (ibid.: 118)

Douglas is scathing of the financial system in that it has developed into a powerful monopolistic organisation operating in such a way as to continually cream off purchasing power from the individual. This is represented by higher prices, justified due to increased costs of production arising from the repayment of debt, to reap the financial rewards of providing the service of issuing money in the first place. Thus:

> The capitalist financial system facilitates production and distribution of goods only incidentally, as an adjunct to its primary *raison d'être*, to secure a title of the share of those goods and services (the "real credit" of the community) through the agency of interest payments.... The recurring cycles of debt creation and repayment with interest require a constant growth in the overall economy if it is to function effectively.
>
> (Hutchinson, 1995: 44)

Any attempt, given the current financial system, to reduce prices would subsequently lead to a reduction in profit margins and if this was to fall below the amount needed to cover costs, production would come to a halt and unemployment would occur. The current system of financial organisation means that policies of deflation will be at the expense of the producer. Bankruptcies will increase which will directly affect the consumer in terms of unemployment and policies of inflation will negatively affect purchasing power, therefore affecting the producer in the long run. This leads Douglas to his conclusion:

> ...the consumer cannot possibly obtain the advantage of improved process in the form of correspondingly lower prices, nor can he expect stable prices under stationary processes of production, nor can he obtain any control over the programme of production, unless he is provided with a supply of purchasing-power which is not included in the price of the goods produced. If the producer or distributor sells at a loss, this loss forms such a supply of purchasing-power to the consumer; but if the producer and distributor are not to sell at a loss, this supply of purchasing-power must be derived from some other source. There is only one source from which it can be derived, and that is the same source which enables a bank to lend more money than it originally received. That is to say, the general credit.
>
> (ibid.: 114)

Douglas therefore seeks a new method of income distribution. The 'savings' that Douglas referred to allowed the owners of factors of production to re-invest in capital goods and to accumulate profits. These profits were realised in the form of dividends payable on shares. However, these savings were not the result of forgone consumption but were created by the banks in the form of paper transactions; therefore such individuals were claiming a share of the national wealth to which they had not directly contributed in the form of a personal sacrifice. That is, rewards were accruing to those who had no claim in terms of individual effort other than their ability to secure the financial credit from the banks. It would appear from this argument that Douglas is accepting the Marxist principle of surplus value (Finlay, 1972: 112). For Douglas, then, there would never be enough purchasing power in the economy to buy back the total products of industry. Under-consumption would persist, posing a threat to the process of economic growth:

> Economic growth requires a constant expansion not only of production but more particularly of consumption, where "consumption" is defined as "purchase on the market with the use of money".
>
> (Hutchinson, 1995: 44)

What was required was some regulatory mechanism that served to increase the level of purchasing power within the economy, so ensuring that total national consumption was equal to total national production. The Douglas social credit scheme proposed that government should increase demand by paying everyone a National Dividend and that this dividend should be financed from increasing the money supply. Douglas justified this dividend by referring to his concept of the 'Cultural Heritage' and in an earlier book *Credit, Power and Democracy* he referred to the dividend as 'the natural successor to the wage' (1920: 43). It is in this sense that the Douglas proposal is relevant to the separation of income from work debate.

The National Dividend was to be granted as a right of every citizen and thus 'established the principle of payment of an unearned income from the state, unrelated to work record or to any other tangible contribution to the formal economy' (Hutchinson, 1995: 45). In his attempt to illustrate the specific benefits of his income distribution scheme with regard to the labour market, Douglas contrasts his proposed National Dividend with existing unemployment allowances, which he refers to as the 'Dole'. He regards the dole as the 'Cinderella of Dividends' and criticises it for: stigmatising recipients; creating unnecessary and damaging divisions within society between contributors and beneficiaries; imposing harsh regulations which stifle work incentives; and for being set at levels determined by concepts of absolute as opposed to relative poverty (Douglas, 1924: 126–128). Furthermore, he suggests existing mechanisms of income maintenance are designed, not only in accordance with the needs of a policy goal of full employment, but also there is a hidden agenda:

> . . . it must be evident that the soundness of this stress on the prime necessity for continuous and general employment, using that term in the narrow sense of commercial employment for wages, rests on quite

other grounds than the use of employment as a means for distributing wages, – can, in fact only rest on the premises of the Modernist, or Classical idea.

(ibid.: 130)

He goes on to argue that actively promoting full employment, defined in terms of 'every individual capable of employment ... employed and paid according to the existing canons of the financial system' would prove disastrous, on both a political and economic level, for any government. The result would be 'fantastic' inflationary pressures or 'the military consequences of an enhanced struggle for export markets' (ibid.: 131–132). He claims, therefore, that the focus of attention directed at the formal labour market primarily derives from:

> ...a widespread feeling on the part of executives of all descriptions that the only method by which large masses of human beings can be kept in agreement with dogmatic moral and social ideals, is by arranging that they shall be kept so hard at work that they have not the leisure or even the desire to think for themselves. The matter is rarely stated in so many words. It is more generally suggested that leisure, meaning by that, freedom from employment forced by economic necessity, is in itself detrimental; a statement which is flagrantly contradicted by all the evidence available on the subject.
>
> (ibid.: 132–133)

In arguing existing welfare strategies reinforce the traditional work-and-pay relationship, Douglas views such as barriers to individual enterprise and hence will stifle economic progress. Douglas regards this scenario as an inevitable consequence of a society governed by the principles of 'rewards and punishments' which effectively acts to subordinate the rights and interests of the individual to that of the community as a collective. Determining the social and economic order of a society around such ideals may have been expedient in the past, but for Douglas the whole process of industrial progress has rendered the system 'undesirable and actively and practically vicious' (1924: 80). In developing his line of reasoning, Douglas appears to be making similar observations to those made by the psychologist Abraham Maslow concerning the hierarchy of human needs. That is, once the basic physiological needs of any individual are satisfied, that individual is then free to devote attention and energy to the securing of a further category of needs, which are more social or moral in nature:

> In other words, human needs manifest themselves in a series of stages and, according to Maslow's classic original conception, you have got to get through one stage before you can go on to the next. These

stages can be seen as priorities, so that a more crucial priority must be heeded before another priority can claim attention. This can be seen to define the process of growth. It has been summarized by Maslow in the following phrase: "Man does not live by bread alone – *if* he has enough bread".

(Lutz and Lux, 1988: 11)

In his efforts to demonstrate the outmoded nature of relying upon the sanctions imposed by a system of punishments and rewards, Douglas refers to his own conception of a hierarchy of human needs:

So far from the mere sustenance of life through the production of food, clothing and shelter from the elements being, with reason, the prime objective of human endeavour, it should now be possible to relegate it to the position of a semi-automatic process. Biologists tell us that the earliest known forms of life devoted practically the whole of their attention to the business of breathing. Breathing is not less necessary now than it was then, but only persons suffering from some lamentable disease pay very much attention to the process.

(Douglas, 1924: 83)

For Douglas the new direction of human energy, implied by reaping the benefits of industrial progress, is being hindered by adherence to a system that was designed with the old direction in mind.

The National Dividend scheme proposed by Douglas therefore represents a mechanism capable of re-orientating society, in that an obsolete system of restraint is replaced with one of co-operation and assistance. As a proposal for welfare reform, it effectively severs the traditional link between work and pay by providing an income guarantee for all citizens, explicitly detached from the processes associated with modern labour markets. His form of a CBI would free individuals from the economic necessity of employment and enable them to pursue a range of non-material needs. As a consequence, individuals are afforded the opportunity to ascend to a higher level of personal development, which in turn will benefit further economic progress. This particular aspect of the Douglas doctrine represents an important contribution to contemporary debates focusing on the efficacy of current income maintenance measures given the dynamics of modern socio-economic conditions. Furthermore, his critical analysis of the role of money in the economy, and his assessment of the motivations behind all human endeavour prove relevant in developing a feminist economics perspective in support of a CBI. The preceding discussion of the Social Credit movement, and in particular the proposals advocated by Douglas, has therefore indicated the strength of the arguments, central to both, in promoting a 'new economics'.

The method of income distribution proposed by the Social Credit movement was essentially premised on a critical appraisal of mainstream economic theory regarding the relationship between ownership and control of the factors of production. Theories advocating a 'social dividend' scheme as a fundamental element of a planned economy, either capitalist or socialist determined, accept as a starting point that prices are not a true reflection of value. This phenomenon occurs when ownership is separated from control and the prices accruing to factors of production are not representative of actual economic values, but rather are determined by the degree of power which can be exercised in the market place. Deficient levels of aggregate demand may therefore be a natural, and indeed permanent feature, of the capitalist system due to artificial distortions of market equilibrium prices and output levels. The 'social dividend' represents a scheme for income distribution that effectively serves to redress the unequal balance between ownership and control arising from the economic processes associated with a free market economy.

The Douglas analysis formally recognises the economic consequences of ownership of the factors of production being divorced from the control of those factors. However, rather than placing faith in the ability of a centralised planning authority to direct both production and consumption patterns, Douglas focuses on the structure of the financial system. For Douglas, control over production and distribution lay in the hands of financiers, and thus the level of aggregate demand in the economy was nothing to do with ownership of factors of production but a function of power with regard to access to financial credit. Furthermore, the financial system was a human construct and therefore any claims to legitimacy were political in nature (Burkitt and Hutchinson, 1994). To illustrate this point, Douglas draws upon the British experience in financing the First World War. The government effectively 'created' the money to pay for the war by employing the mechanisms associated with the workings of the existing financial system. By abandoning the gold standard, the government was able, 'through a complicated series of paper transactions', to transfer the National Debt into a National Asset (Hutchinson, 1995: 45; Burkitt and Hutchinson, 1994: 24). The interest accruing to individual owners of Government War Securities did not represent direct payment for a current material contribution to the formal economy but rather was a claim to be drawn against future production. Thus, the government:

> ...established a precedent for the payment of dividends, a share of national wealth, to individuals whose contribution to the creation of that wealth was ephemeral. The National Debt is "clearly a distributing agent".
>
> (Burkitt and Hutchinson, 1994: 24)

For Douglas then 'financial credit' was merely a convenient way of *representing* the 'real wealth' of a community; and wealth should be a communal possession rather than reside in the hands of the bankers (Finlay, 1972: 112). His package of proposals was, he believed, a way of reforming existing capitalist structures in order to restore power to the individual, without at the same time incurring the need for large scale bureaucratic planning authorities, which in essence posed a further threat to individual liberty.

The Douglas proposal is distinct from a CBI as previously defined, as it involves direct transfer of funds from the state to the individual to be financed by increasing the money supply, rather than via the tax mechanism. In addressing critics who pointed to the inflationary pressures implied by such a system, Douglas again emphasised the importance of the production and sound management of social credit. The price system would be self-regulating in that consumption would match production, and vice versa, provided the restraints imposed by the requirements of 'financial credit' were eliminated. Furthermore, by removing the economic necessity to work, Douglas believed his model for the future development of capitalism was better suited in meeting the demands of technological development. Douglas foresaw that continuing advances in technology meant that future work would give way to more leisure time but that current financial structures would not allow the individual this option. Industrial progress, combined with the present system of income distribution, based primarily on the principle of financial punishments and rewards, would serve to further subject the individual to wage slavery. His belief in the intrinsic value of work, and the potential of the capitalist model in stifling individual creativity and innovation, implied that he was radically opposed to conceptions of 'rational, self interested economic man'. As Burkitt and Hutchinson argue:

> This rejection of the inherent disutility of labour, with its denial of the necessary centrality of financial reward, was among the factors that rendered Douglas' writing uncongenial to mainstream economists of the inter-war period.
>
> (1994: 25)

Douglas therefore presented a case for questioning the efficacy of traditional economic theory in explaining economic practice. The laws of supply and demand did not provide a framework for determining the value of commodities, in particular labour. Rather, the concept of scarcity was an artificially generated phenomenon emanating from the practices of capitalist financial structures. Individuals, as consumers, are not free to choose but remain servile to those with power over the whole production process – the financiers. Given his heretical views on such fundamental concepts of orthodox economics it is not surprising that mainstream economists would treat Douglas's proposals with caution.

However, it was not only the economics profession that questioned the validity of the Social Credit movement. The blatant attack on financiers not only disturbed the bankers themselves, but was also viewed as being potentially anti-Semitic (Walter, 1989: 23; Finlay, 1972: 176–179). Furthermore, Douglas's outspoken disapproval of a system dominated by the process of centralised economic planning and state ownership gave rise to criticism from those espousing the socialist cause (Finlay, 1972: 12–113). In fact:

> Throughout the inter-war years Social Credit aroused powerful negative reactions in practically all established centers of male socio-economic power – among mainstream economists, socialists, communists, trade unionists, bankers and politicians of all parties.
>
> (Hutchinson, 1995: 39)

The movement witnessed some success when the Social Credit Party was founded in Alberta, Canada in 1935 and dominated politics within the province until 1971. However, the Party more or less abandoned Douglas's theories early on and went on to advocate policies such as employee participation in profits and shareholding, more a workers co-operative theory. The social credit theory was ultimately a political failure.

Despite this, the economics of Major Douglas and his contemporaries provides some useful insights into the relationship between economic policy and social policy. As a model for welfare reform, social credit established a principle whereby the economic necessity of formal employment would no longer dictate the forming of both policy and institutions aimed at promoting social justice. In this sense the social credit doctrine proves relevant to contemporary debates on the future direction of income maintenance policy. Given the dynamics of modern socio-economic conditions, social credit may provide the mechanisms for minimising the negative consequences of the continual strive for sustainable economic growth. That is, the maximising of economic conflict and the associated problems of social exclusion and marginalisation. Specifically, the collective regulation of financial instruments, along with the payment of a national dividend, could effectively act to promote the socio-economic status of those individuals who devote the majority of their time engaging in 'non-economic' activities. Reform along this route, would have obvious advantages for women, but could also prove conducive to an economic system based on alternative ways of organising and doing work. This particular point is of interest in developing a feminist case for a CBI and thus will be explored further in Chapter 8.

In analysing the Douglas plan, the purpose has been to illustrate the distinctiveness of social credit as a proposal for a state-supported minimum income guarantee. It is argued that the innovative nature of the Douglas scheme rests in its explicit rejection of the principles governing the traditional work-and-pay relationship. In doing so, Douglas effectively presents a logical case for dismantling and restructuring the principal organising features of an economy dominated by a strict adherence to the canons of competitive free market economics. Although this would prove, in practice, to be politically unacceptable, the insights to be gained relate to the contribution of the social credit approach to economic reform in the process of developing a 'new economics'.

However, both in practice and in theory the Douglas scheme was overtaken by Keynesianism. The publication of *The General Theory of Employment Interest and Money* by J.M. Keynes in 1936 brought about the dawning of a new age in economic and political organisation. When criticising the classical economist's assumption that supply creates its own demand, Keynes refers to his analysis as supplying us 'with a explanation of the paradox of poverty in the midst of plenty' (Keynes, 1951: 30). For Keynes, the problem lies with effective demand and he draws attention to the fact that this area has been sadly neglected within the economist's discipline for 'more than a century' (ibid.: 32). Although the existence of deficient or excessive demand was observed and recognised by some, the lack of positive economic analysis explaining why aggregate demand could indeed be deficient, led to the widespread appeal of the classical model with an emphasis on the supply side, free markets and flexible prices. In fact Keynes points out that the inability to scientifically analyse the theory of aggregate demand and its effects on the level of employment and national income meant that:

> The great puzzle of Effective Demand with which Malthus had wrestled vanished from economic literature. You will not find it mentioned even once in the whole works of Marshall, Edgeworth and Professor Pigou, from whose hands the classical theory has received its most mature embodiment. It could only live on furtively, below the surface, in the underworlds of Karl Marx, Silvio Gesell or Major Douglas.
>
> (ibid.: 32)

Keynes, therefore, was aware of the Douglas proposal but viewed the Major as somewhat of a crank:

> Since the war there has been a spate of heretical theories of underconsumption, of those which Major Douglas are the most famous. The strength of Major Douglas's advocacy has, of course, largely depended on orthodoxy having no valid reply to much of his destructive criticism. On the other hand, the detail of his diagnosis, in particular the so-called A + B theorem, includes much mere mystification. If Major Douglas had limited his B-items to the financial provisions made by entrepreneurs to which no current expenditure on replacements and renewals corresponds, he would be nearer the truth. Major Douglas is

entitled to claim, as against some of his orthodox adversaries, that he at least has not been wholly oblivious of the outstanding problem of our economic system.

(ibid.: 370–371)

Keynes sets out to provide a 'valid reply' to Douglas's 'destructive criticism' and, through a process of positive macro-economic analysis, develops a model justifying state intervention in the economy for the purposes of effective demand management.

The National Dividend proposed by Douglas, although unique in terms of its criticism of traditional economic theory, should not be set apart from the arguments in support of a universal minimum income guarantee discussed above. Common to all proposals is a concern for the rights of the individual citizen within the confines of capitalist-based market economies. Questioning the traditional relationship between work and pay is evident throughout the literature. Furthermore, taking into account the historical perspective, the proposals discussed thus far were argued for at a time when there was no established principle for state intervention in the field of income maintenance. Mechanisms for the relief of absolute poverty, argued for on the basis of religious, philosophical or moral grounds, had not managed to secure a concrete foothold in the political or economic base of industrial society. Arguments for state intervention based on economic considerations were equally marginalised in that they remained subordinate to the demands imposed by the operation of competitive free markets. Attempts, therefore, at justifying a form of CBI, prior to the development of the modern welfare state, can be categorised as practical policy solutions responding to the perceived social evils of capitalist development. In other words they were not presented as an alternative to existing provision but rather as proposals for social and/or economic reform which assumed a common starting point – the dominance of laissez-faire market economics in forming the structural base of society.

The development of the modern welfare state can arguably be pinpointed as representing the break-down of this dominance. The explicit political acceptance of Keynesian economics in post-war Britain demonstrated a departure from a sustained and prolonged attachment to orthodox neo-classical economic theory in the design of social policy. Future proposals for a universal minimum income guarantee would therefore have to be framed as an alternative to the new orthodoxy. The following section therefore traces evidence of proposals for a form of CBI, presented as practical policy options conforming to the principles of demand management and a general consensus regarding state responsibility for securing the welfare of those individuals and their families excluded from the labour market.

A practical policy alternative

The Beveridge Report of 1942 provided the British wartime Government with a range of policy options designed to ensure the effective implementation and operation of a state-supported income maintenance programme. The Beveridge plan was to replace the current system of social security with a comprehensive, universal scheme providing freedom from 'Want' from the cradle to the grave. The actual Report not only contained a list of policy proposals but also contained detailed analysis on administrative procedures and the method of finance. Public support for the document itself (Abel-Smith, 1992: 13; Jacobs, 1992: 6; Thane, 1996: 237) coupled with the fact that Beveridge had been thorough, both in his consultation with the Treasury regarding affordability (Abel-Smith, 1992: 12; Thane, 1996: 228), and in laying out the specific details of his plan, resulted in the Government being more or less forced to take it on board.

The central tenet of the Beveridge scheme was social insurance. This in itself was not a new idea as schemes similar were developing elsewhere in the world.[6] What was new was the fact that the plan for social insurance entailed universal coverage; flat rate contributions; flat rate benefits; centralised administration; and a residual safety net designed to meet the needs of those who were denied access to the labour market and who were therefore unable to contribute. Furthermore, Beveridge outlined three related policy areas necessary for the effective operation of his scheme. First, to complement social insurance, a scheme of family allowances was proposed to cover low-income families in work. Second, a comprehensive health service should be established to provide access to adequate health care free at the point of use based on the rationale that industry requires a healthy work force. Third, Beveridge assumed that in order for social insurance to operate, and effectively continue, governments should be committed to ensuring full employment within the economy: employment being the central concept in a contributory-based plan for social security. Thus Beveridge can be credited with institutionalising the concept of the right to work. Furthermore, the emphasis on a commitment to full employment, contained within the Beveridge doctrine, incorporated Keynesian demand management techniques and hence provided a basis for a new economic, political and social order. Government acceptance of the Keynes/Beveridge model was made explicit with the publication of the *Social Insurance* White Paper and the *Employment Policy* White Paper in 1944. For the first time in UK history, social policy was inextricably linked to macro-economic policy.

In the post-war period, social insurance, with its emphasis on employment, became the prevailing doctrine with regard to income maintenance policy, not only in the UK but also throughout Europe. As Parker so cogently puts it, 'social insurance quickly established itself as one of the institutions no self-respecting social democracy could be without' (1989:

12). It would appear, then, that the uncoupling of income from work concept within the realms of social security policy had drawn its last breath with the overwhelming acceptance of variants of a system based on contributions from employer, employee, and the state. However, an alternative to the Beveridge plan was proposed which did in fact contain elements of the CBI concept.

The idea of a CBI, or social dividend, has been proposed as an alternative to the Beveridge plan for social security reform in recognition of the limitations of social insurance (Atkinson, 1995a: 299). The 'Social Contract' advocated by Lady Juliet Rhys Williams, an independent economist, was presented as such an alternative:

> The basic idea of the Social Contract was originally put forward in August 1942, in a privately circulated[7] pamphlet under the title of *Something to Look Forward To*. A shorter booklet, bringing the proposals up to date in light of the Beveridge Report, was published in January, 1943, under the title of *Some Suggestions for a New Social Contract. An Alternative to the Beveridge Report Proposals*. The present book is an elaboration of the suggestions contained in these two publications.
>
> (Rhys Williams, 1943: vii)

Lady Rhys Williams was concerned, like Beveridge, with the problem of ensuring 'freedom from want' for the citizens of the UK in the post-war years. Painfully aware of the existence of poverty in light of progress she saw the greatest problem facing UK society as the distribution of wealth question:

> We have got to discover a means of distributing the wealth of which there is, in peace time, such comparative abundance, to those who need it, and we have got to do this *without destroying the will to work of those engaged in its whole production*. [Rhys Williams's own emphasis].
>
> (ibid.: 10)

The work incentive is important for Rhys Williams. She explains that the existence of poverty is not a direct product of the system of social and economic organisation. Therefore, in the UK, the inability of a great number of individuals to purchase the necessaries of life cannot be blamed on the capitalist system but rather is a function of the 'peculiarity of human nature' (ibid.: 11). Her conception of human nature leads Rhys Williams to the assumption that individuals illustrate an unwillingness to engage in work unless forced to do so, or are adequately rewarded. It would appear then that, unlike Douglas, Rhys Williams favours the framework of punishment and reward, brought about by the operation of existing financial systems. There would be no problem distributing the abundance of goods in the economy to all citizens on an equal basis and thereby eliminating

want if it were not for the fact that such a method of allocation would
result in a drastic decline in the nation's wealth. Rhys Williams comes to
this conclusion by adopting assumptions associated with mainstream economic theory. She asserts the view that if goods are received with no work
requirement then the incentive to free-ride would be so strong that 'the
production of new wealth would come to an end, and the whole community will starve together' (ibid.: 11). No system of social, political or economic organisation would be successful unless the current motives of
reward and punishment for working are replaced with an alternative
motive. Rhys Williams goes on to develop a plan which will solve the
problem of distribution whilst addressing the effects of the removal of
work incentives in the form of fear of poverty and hope of gain:

> The cause of the whole difficulty of distributing wealth and abolishing
> poverty does not lie in the material sphere of economic and political
> systems, of Governments and their policy, or of the laws of supply and
> demand; it lies in the psychological sphere, and depends upon the
> discovery of some motive for labour, other than the fear of want,
> which does not involve resort to even more unsatisfactory and primi-
> tive motive from which we have so recently escaped, and to which a
> Nazi victory would have condemned us to return, namely the fear of
> punishment at the hands of a Gestapo.
>
> (ibid.: 11)

Aware of the apparent failure of the classical model to provide answers
to the problems of increasing unemployment and the humility suffered by
those forced to claim benefits from the state via Public Assistance, Rhys
Williams recognised that the time was ripe for political and economic
reform. However, the preservation of individual freedom is paramount
and any attempt to abolish poverty by instituting a 'new order' should not
be at the expense of such freedom. The dangers of Fascism are to be
remembered and lessons learned:

> In our determination to abolish want and the fear of want, we must
> beware of those panaceas which promise these reliefs only at the cost
> of surrendering the greater part of our hard-won political liberties,
> including the right to withhold our labour and to select our employ-
> ment.
>
> (ibid.: 19)

Rhys Williams therefore seeks a system which will serve to uphold the
supremacy of individual liberty whilst at the same time institutionalising a
programme of social planning which is fully democratic and does not
necessitate coercion by the state in the name of the National Plan. With
the ultimate goal of ensuring freedom from want, that is the complete

abolition of poverty, any future reform must address the problem of distribution in such a way:

> ...that no human being can ever be in such a condition, regardless of his own actions or of external circumstances, since while poverty remains at all, the fear of it can never be removed from the hearts of men.
>
> (ibid.: 22)

The question remains as to how this is to be achieved without destroying the will to work, which, for Rhys Williams, is the means of wealth creation. Given this assumption it follows that her plan for state-supported income maintenance would remain inextricably linked to the labour market. It would appear from her initial statements that she wishes only to propose a more socially just proposal for social security whilst operating within the parameters of traditional economic liberal orthodoxy. That is, she is ultimately concerned with economic efficiency and the creation of wealth although she wishes to remedy the fact that a growing number of individuals are not afforded the opportunity to participate in the labour market and are therefore unable to meet their most basic needs. This scenario is unacceptable in a society committed to the principles of liberty for all and state action is required and justified in these terms. Further examination of her proposals will illustrate that her motivations were grounded in making a capitalist system more economically efficient and therefore her particular proposal can be categorised as displaying the limiting characteristics implied by adopting such an approach. However, her contribution is important given its historical context and her criticisms of the Beveridge plan, which became the accepted policy option. This becomes more crucial when discussing the crisis in welfare literature in that if the Rhys Williams plan had been adopted instead of social insurance the idea of a CBI may appear less radical as a contemporary reform package.

Rhys Williams illustrated great insight in her warning of the pitfalls of the dilemma, which has come to be known as the poverty and unemployment traps. She recognised that if the Beveridge plan was to become law, the social security scheme in Britain will serve to seriously undermine the work incentive by 'subsidising the idle and not the worker' (ibid.: 144). The solution, according to Rhys Williams, is the adoption of a new social contract where the State assumes responsibility for the welfare of all citizens and therefore benefits should be paid on an equal basis to all regardless of employment or health status. She categorically states that:

> *The prevention of want must be regarded as being the duty of the State to all its citizens, and not merely to a favoured few.* [Rhys Williams's own emphasis] The notion that only the unemployed, the sick, the improvident and

the unfortunate should obtain the *largesse* of the State, and never the hard-working, the energetic, the thrifty and the successful should be replaced by a fresh and insistent interpretation of the conception that all men are equal in the eyes of the law.

(ibid.: 145)

This provides Rhys Williams with a theoretical framework in the acceptance of an obligation on the part of the State to provide for all citizens in the form of the 'Social Contract'. In practical terms this contract would involve the payment of an 'average benefit' from the public purse paid on an individual basis to every man, woman and child, with actual benefits due taking into account rent levels 'prevailing in the district concerned and the children's allowances could be graded in accordance with the age of the child' (ibid.: 145). This benefit would replace all existing forms of public assistance and render the means test redundant. Evident in the Rhys Williams proposal is the emergence of the concept of an unconditional income due to all citizens by the State. However, further analysis of the doctrine points in the direction of conditionality as the use of the term contract implies some form of responsibility to be undertaken by both parties. Rhys Williams views this responsibility as availability for work:

The payments would be made available immediately upon the signature of the contract, and every week thereafter, provided that proof was supplied, say, once a month, to the local Labour Exchange, that the signatory was gainfully occupied, or if unable to find employment, then that he was willing to accept suitable employment offered by the Exchange ... at standard rates of pay. In the event of refusal to accept such employment, or to remain in it or in alternative employment, the benefits would cease, as in the case of unemployment assistance today.

(ibid.: 145–146)

Rhys Williams incorporated this conditional aspect as she was ultimately concerned with the effects on the labour market of the receipt of state income maintenance. Further evidence of this concern can be traced to her treatment of women within the social contract. She makes a positive contribution to the feminist cause for a CBI in that she stipulates that women with caring responsibilities 'would receive the benefits of the contract without being required to register for employment' (ibid.: 146). She appears, then, to recognise the economic value of unpaid domestic work. However, she does not fully accept the idea of complete economic independence for women as she wishes to institutionalise the concept of male dominance in the labour market when she states:

Single women and widows under sixty without dependent children, although free to take up full-time work, would not be required to do so, but only to do part-time work, if available, for eighteen hours a week, since the labour market would otherwise be overcrowded.

(ibid.: 147)

Her opinions with regard to the productive capacity of labour operating within traditional commercial labour markets are evident throughout her proposal. She believes that the Social Contract will provide individuals with sufficient incentive to engage in paid work, as such activity will render financial gain and result in higher standards of living. The Social Contract does not destroy this motivation nor does it require any form of coercion to be exercised by the State. The work requirement test exists to prevent abuse of the scheme from the 'work shy' and hence the Social Contract proposal leaves individuals free to choose both where they want to work and whether they want to work part-time or full-time. Although this argument may not have proved critical in the early 1940s, given that the labour market was characterised by a full-time male employment norm, it is frequently employed in the contemporary literature with reference to meeting the requirements of modern 'flexible' labour markets.

An interesting point to note when examining the relevance of the Rhys Williams scheme to the evolution of the CBI concept is that she advocates voluntary exclusion from benefits by way of not signing the contract:

There would be no compulsion to enter into the contract. Those unwilling to hold themselves out for employment on account of private means could simply refrain from signing. They would thereby forfeit the benefits, but would not be exempt from the Social Security tax which would be necessary to finance the Scheme, and which would represent their contribution to the resources of the country in lieu of personal service.

(ibid.: 146)

A scheme based on the weekly distribution of benefits to be paid through the issuance of order books redeemable at the post office and with receipt being conditional upon periodical visits to the local labour exchange, to illustrate willingness to work, is not to be viewed as stigma free. The option of voluntary exclusion within such a scheme would be attractive to those unwilling to accept the necessary intrusion into their work patterns, or those unhappy about weekly trips to the local post office to collect state benefits. Given sufficient private means were available, such individuals may see the costs of claiming and collecting the social dividend as outweighing the financial benefits of receipt. Such a proviso would ultimately lead to the stigmatisation of those individuals currently in receipt which defeats the purpose of a guaranteed minimum income paid as a right.

When discussing the method of financing her scheme, Rhys Williams draws upon the Douglas Social Credit plan. She, like Douglas, recognises the problem of deficient demand and agrees that the state should assume responsibility for ensuring sufficient purchasing power is maintained within the economy. However, she remains concerned about the effects a direct injection of new money of a predetermined amount would have on the general price level. Rhys Williams draws attention to the fact that conditions of production are regularly in flux and therefore a set weekly dividend, which assumes a corresponding set increase in national output, is too rigid. Such a mechanism must be counter balanced with taxation measures designed in such a way as to take account of the amount of money currently in circulation. This would avoid the situation whereby too much money would be chasing too few goods with resulting inflationary pressures (ibid.: 116). She therefore goes on to describe a mechanism that does just this:

> What is required, then, is some machinery for issuing money directly to the individual consumer, which will be closely linked to the other machinery for taking it away again, either up to the precisely similar amount, if no increase in the amount of money in the hands of the public is required; or up to a less amount, if some increase is permissible, owing to the expansion in the quantity of goods available; or in the event of some catastrophe such as war involving the sudden decline in the amount of purchasable goods, then up to a greater amount, in order to produce a deflationary effect. It is clear that if such machinery could be devised it would be of immense assistance to those in whose hands the task of balancing our monetary system with our productive power would lie after the war, since in this way a stable price level could be maintained.
>
> (ibid.: 150)

The Social Contract scheme is such a machine and whilst serving ultimately to abolish 'want' it provides the government with a mechanism by which to ensure and maintain a stable price level. The proposed tax structure is to take the form of a single social security tax. It is in this area that the Rhys Williams doctrine is to be viewed as important for the purposes of examining the evolution of the CBI concept.

Complexity and costly administrative processes would be avoided with the abolition of all personal tax reliefs to be replaced with a single social security tax, payable by each individual. Justification for the abolition of personal allowances for dependants is to be found in the fact that dividends would be paid directly to the individuals concerned and therefore each individual would be secured a subsistence income (ibid.: 151–152). The scheme would be entirely self-financing in that revenues raised from taxation would fund the dividends due under the contract. This system, according to Rhys Williams, would not only be simpler to understand and ensure the maintenance of a stable price level but would also resolve the 'old antagonism' between taxpayers and those in receipt of state benefits, 'inasmuch as every individual would be a beneficiary as well as a taxpayer' (ibid.: 155). Obviously those with larger incomes would contribute more to the scheme but for Rhys Williams the 'justice of this is not in doubt' (ibid.: 155).

The Rhys Williams plan is, hence, essentially a transfer by taxation scheme which carries a work test and could ultimately lead to stigmatisation of the poor due to the voluntary exclusion clause. However, the establishment of the right to a minimum subsistence income, in return for an obligation on the part of the individual to contribute to the creation of wealth within society by striving to engage in the traditional labour market, is important in that it removes the need to resort to a means test. The only intrusion into an individual's life is the monitoring by public officials regarding work patterns. For these reasons it is not a CBI scheme. Nevertheless, the Rhys Williams plan is viewed as constructive in that she does provide useful insights into the benefits of integrating the tax and benefit systems. Considered in an historical context she builds on previous doctrines, namely the Douglas Social Credit plan, and provides a radical alternative to the Beveridge Report. However, she does not develop any powerful justification, other than that the system would result in a more efficient allocation of resources given the existing political and economic structure. The fact that her plan was not politically successful, although widely referred to in the literature, can perhaps be attributed to this neglect on her part. The Beveridge scheme was viewed a more appropriate mechanism for achieving such a goal.

Some trace of the move to separate income from work is to be found in the Social Contract, in that the dividend constitutes income paid whether in work or not and is not removed as income increases. However, as explained, inherent within the Rhys Williams plan is the explicit assumption that paid work remains the most important contributor to not only individual welfare but to the welfare of the community as a whole. Thus, the Rhys Williams model for reform of tax and income maintenance measures conforms with a traditional approach to social security policy. That is, the function of social security is, first and foremost, to support the efficient operation of traditional labour market structures. This subordination of social security policy in the overall workings of the capitalist economy has, as previously argued, negative consequences for the reform process. By acquiescing to a given set of assumptions regarding the nature of work and pay, debates on the future direction of social security will remain bound by the doctrine of punishments and rewards. Reform of the tax and benefit systems along these lines can arguably be viewed as a process of manipulating existing measures to meet newly emerging demands, as and when they arise. A more comprehensive approach would involve examining the justifying principle and basis of income transfers in light of the dynamics of modern socio-economic conditions. In other words, an approach which is more 'radical', rather than 'reformist', in nature.

The Rhys Williams plan for social security reform can arguably be viewed as a radical alternative to the Beveridge scheme. However, as indicated, the underlying foundations of the Social Contract were dictated by the principles of Keynesian economics. Subsequently, in terms of social policy reform it represented a continuance with existing norms regarding the relationship between social security measures and economic policy. Taken in this context any attempt at restructuring the relationship between work and pay is to be considered in a strictly reformist sense. That is, it is implicitly assumed that any restructuring will be either temporary or peripheral. The ultimate result will be the permanence, and indeed predominance, of traditional market-oriented work-and-pay structures. In tracing the development of minimum income guarantee proposals, post the institutionalisation of social insurance, it becomes apparent that this assumption is a common feature. Although contemporary debates focus intensely on the nature of modern labour markets, it is argued that the total separation of income from work has not yet been envisaged. However, this is not to say that the reform agenda has been lacking in originality. The process of justifying a minimum income guarantee has produced a wide range of theoretical positions regarding the nature of citizenship rights in a predominately capitalist market economy. One such position is encountered in the analysis of the role of social security policy within the writings of the New Right.

Tax and benefit integration: a new right agenda?

The classic statement of New Right economic philosophy is to be found in Milton Friedman's *Capitalism and Freedom*, originally published in 1962. The basic premise of the Friedman doctrine was that laissez-faire capitalism was the only mechanism by which individual political and economic freedom could be guaranteed. He therefore attacks the growth of government throughout society and advocates a limited role in similar terms as those expounded by Adam Smith in the eighteenth century. He further argues that since limited government intervention is justified in the name of preserving freedom, in order to prevent the possible abuse of state control, government power should be decentralised and reduced to the local level wherever possible. Subsidiarity would allow for a more democratic and responsive government in that individuals are more able to use their exit option as a means of voicing protest at the local level than at the national level. The central theme therefore of the Friedman school is to promote the:

> ...role of competitive capitalism – the organisation of the bulk of economic activity through private enterprise operating in a free market – as a system of economic freedom and a necessary condition for political freedom.
>
> (Friedman, 1982: 4)

Whilst doing this, Friedman also finds it necessary to devote time to considering the role of government in a society committed to the preservation of individual freedom, and the dominance of free markets, as a means of organising economic activity. His proposals for the role of government in the provision of social welfare are therefore determined by this ideology. What remains to be examined is whether or not Friedman's proposals for social security and tax reform represent a radical departure from an income transfer system premised on employment-based rewards and punishments, and if so how his plan relates to the CBI debate. Although Friedman's Negative Income Tax (NIT) proposal attempts to depart from the model of work status benefits, it does so with the ultimate goal of developing a mechanism in which work and pay would eventually not be uncoupled.

Friedman's philosophical thesis was written at the height of the Keynesian Welfare State consensus and hence was outside the existing mainstream body of thought. Friedman himself is aware of his marginal position when he notes in the preface to the 1982 edition of *Capitalism and Freedom*:

> Those of us who were deeply concerned about the danger to freedom and prosperity from the growth of government, from the triumph of welfare-state and Keynesian ideas, were a small beleaguered minority regarded as eccentrics by the great majority of our fellow intellectuals.
>
> (Friedman, 1982: vi)

However, he draws the reader's attention to the relevance of new radical ideas in times of consensus for the purpose of aiding future policy reform. He is not perturbed by the fact that upon first publication his philosophy was given the 'silent treatment' by the national press as his book exists to:

> ...keep options open until circumstances make change necessary. There is enormous inertia – a tyranny of the status quo – in private and especially governmental arrangements. Only a crisis – actual or perceived – produces real change. When that crisis occurs, the actions that are taken depend on the ideas that are lying around. That, I believe, is our basic function: to develop alternatives to existing policies, to keep them alive and available until the politically impossible becomes politically inevitable.
>
> (ibid., 1982: ix)

He is in no way a radical nor does he represent a philosophical departure from traditional views. He is merely restating classical traditional economic thought in modern terms and he believes his time will come. His ideas on social security reform should therefore perhaps be viewed as stemming from concern over 'crisis' in current welfare provision. Although writing at a time when the concept of the welfare state was enjoying much public acclaim, he pre-empts its failure to address the problems of banishing 'want', whilst at the same time holding the freedom of the individual as sacred, by providing policy makers with a viable alternative which will preserve the capitalist system.

He develops his NIT proposal in a chapter entitled *The Alleviation of Poverty*. The title in itself suggests that Friedman does not want to put an end to the existence of poverty but merely wishes to alleviate its worst aspects. He does however recognise the relative nature of poverty and admits that while the majority of individuals throughout the Western world have escaped from poverty in an absolute sense (which he attributes to the benefits derived from the capitalist model of free enterprise), there are many who are experiencing deprivation defined according to the acceptable standards set by the society in which they live. The most consistent remedy to this condition, given the Friedman philosophy, is reliance on acts of private charity. However, the increase in government intervention in the arena of social welfare policy has resulted directly in a 'corresponding decline in private charitable activities' (ibid.: 191). Even if this turn of events had not taken place the assumption of rational self-interest as the dominating motive for all human behaviour would ultimately render private charity inefficient in alleviating poverty as communities grow in size. This is due to the strong incentive to free-ride. That is, although the existence of poverty causes distress on the part of those experiencing it, it also causes disutility for those witnessing the hardship experienced by others. Such disutility can be overcome by contributing to the relief of poverty either by donating to a charity dedicated to such a worthwhile cause or by personally giving money to the beggar in the street. This type of charitable activity may be sufficient in small, localised communities where individuals are known to one another and public pressure limits the opportunity to rely on the donations of others to solve the problem. No such pressure exists in larger communities, hence the rational self interested actor will realise that benefits can be derived from the charitable activities of others. There is, therefore, no reason to incur personal costs when one can free-ride on the actions of others. If sufficiently numerous individuals adopted this line of reasoning, very few donations would be made to the social goal of alleviating poverty and it is this line of reasoning which allows Friedman to justify government action in the sphere of poor relief.

The primary objective of governments should be to establish and maintain a set standard of living which no one individual in the community should fall below. This is to be achieved through the direct targeting of resources to the poor and any policy aimed at doing so should not interfere with the operation of the free market. That is, no attempt should be made to distort the flexibility of the price mechanism through policies such as minimum wage legislation or price subsidies. The answer for Friedman is the implementation of a 'negative income tax' (ibid.: 192). In summary the NIT proposal is a combined system of tax and benefits which would involve setting a minimum level of income to which every individual would be entitled. Any earnings above the fixed level would be subject to tax – the amount paid depending on the tax rates charged on various levels of income. If income received were below the set minimum, a subsidy would be due from the government, which would represent payment of 'unused tax allowances'. For Friedman, the NIT has 'enormous advantages', but only if it replaces all current income maintenance measures within existing welfare systems and does not simply become 'another rag in the ragbag of welfare programmes' (Friedman and Friedman, 1980: 122). Such a comprehensive reform would not only cut down on direct administration costs but would also lead to reductions in the overall welfare burden. By emphasising that the role of the NIT is to alleviate poverty caused by low incomes, the claim is made that although some individuals or families may need further assistance due to specific circumstances, 'that assistance could and would be provided by private charitable activities' (ibid.: 123). By operating in ways that stifle such activity, existing welfare systems are imposing unacceptable costs upon both current and future taxpayers. Thus the NIT is ultimately a reform proposal which effectively serves to redefine the role of the state, as provider of welfare, by promoting the notion of self-help.

Variations of Friedman's NIT scheme have emerged in the literature on tax and benefit integration (see for example Brittan and Webb, 1990; Clinton *et al.*, 1994; Parker, 1989). Exploring the relatively minor technical differences of such schemes is not considered crucial in this analysis. What is important is the relevance of the results of the Friedman scheme and the role played by the NIT model in the CBI debate. The NIT does allow for integration of the tax and benefit system, which is synonymous with a CBI, but this is where the similarity ends. The continued emphasis on income testing is argued to be more economically efficient in that it does not weaken the incentive to work in the same way that universal non means-tested programmes, such as a basic income grant, would (Garfinkel and Kesselman, 1978; Clark, 1977). In the US, the NIT scheme received a much more positive reception than in Britain[8] following Friedman's publication in 1962, and in fact has 'been the subject of voluminous theoretical analyses, cost estimates, field experiments, and legislative proposals'[9] (Garfinkel and Kesselman, 1978: 180). A possible reason for this difference across the Atlantic in terms of attraction to the idea could be the fact that the concept of universal payments based on social insurance and not income tests were already very much a part of the British welfare system by 1962. These institutionalised benefits would be almost politically impossible to remove and replace with an income-tested scheme.

In conclusion, then, Friedman does provide policy makers with a scheme that grants all individuals a minimum income and hence represents a safety net. However, the emphasis remains strongly on the centrality of the labour market in providing individual welfare. The prime purpose of a Friedman style NIT scheme would be to enforce labour market participation by redressing the balance between incomes in work and incomes out of work. Targeting income transfers at those demonstrating actual need as opposed to potential need is argued to be more efficient and such theorising forms the basis of the main tensions surrounding contemporary social security reform debates. In this respect the NIT model is often directly compared with a CBI (see for example Brittan and Webb, 1990: 9–11; Creedy and Disney, 1985: ch 9; Commission on Social Justice, 1994: 258–265; Parker, 1989). Brittan goes as far as to argue that when considering the redistributional impact of the NIT model, compared with a CBI scheme, the differences relate to the level of the basic payment and/or the rate of withdrawal. He refers to such as 'differences of degree within the same framework' and thus the 'differences are along a continuum rather than between incompatible proposals' (1990: 11). However, arguing along these lines fails to account for a fundamental distinction between the NIT model for reform and a CBI, that is the primary motivational aspect of promoting paid work. In this respect, any scheme which proffered the granting of a minimum income guarantee to all citizens would obviously raise suspicions regarding the possible negative impact on work incentives. In fact it was this issue that was used to undermine the whole idea of the NIT in America. Critics questioned the results of the NIT experiments, claiming that they had 'greatly underestimated the potential reduction in work effort amongst low-income workers' (Parker, 1989: 97). However, as Parker indicates, such criticisms were biased in that the focus was on emphasising the negative impact on incentives as opposed to any possible positive incentive effects. She thus concludes that opposition to the scheme was primarily driven by political considerations and it was the unconditional nature of the Friedman NIT scheme which ultimately led to its political demise (ibid.: 97). The practical experience of the NIT model therefore serves to demonstrate the limiting nature of the welfare reform agenda. By adopting an uncompromising position with regard to the relationship between income transfers and the labour market, policy makers are loath to consider any scheme that may be construed as threatening to that relationship. This position proves hostile to the conditions necessary for any serious consideration of reform along the lines of a CBI.

Friedman himself recognised that, given the political and economic climate of the late 1970s, the political will necessary to implement his plan for welfare reform was not evident:

> Too many vested interests – ideological, political, and financial –
> stand in the way. . . . The political obstacles to an acceptable negative
> income tax are of two related kinds. The more obvious is the vested
> interests in present programs: the recipients of benefits, state and
> local officials who regard themselves as benefiting from the programs,

and above all, the welfare bureaucracy that administers them. The less obvious obstacle is the conflict among the objectives that advocates of welfare reform, including existing vested interests, seek to achieve.

(1980: 120, 124–125)

Friedman thus draws attention to the institutionalised nature of modern welfare state policies and the subsequent difficulties associated with attempts made at replacing them. He further indicates that for reform of any kind to take place there must be a broad base of political consensus. Given the radical nature of his plan and the right-wing label attached to the NIT model, 'enactment of such a programme seems a utopian dream at present' (ibid.: 120). Friedman, however, is prepared to be patient and considers his plan as a guide for a future time period when it is evident that the 'tide of opinion' has turned in favour of limited government and greater economic freedom. The election of governments committed to such a philosophy, on both sides of the Atlantic in 1979 and 1980, is perhaps indicative of the 'tuning tide' Friedman hoped for. Such developments, coupled with the associated perceived 'crisis in welfare' debates gave rise to a whole new way of thinking about social security reform, and in effect meant that arguing for a CBI could take place on a different stage. The extent to which this shifting environment has been embraced by advocates of a CBI proposal, and how it has informed the justifying principles employed in arguing for such a reform package, will be examined in the following chapter.

Conclusion

Support for variations of a CBI can be traced to, at least, the beginnings of modern welfare state development. Advocates have either presented the idea of an unconditional minimum income as a necessary component in the process of capitalist development, or have argued that the proposal presents as a more effective and indeed efficient alternative to existing schemes of social security provision. Either way, during this period, the CBI has been framed as a reform proposal that conforms with, and supports, the needs of ongoing capitalist development. Presenting the proposal as such is arguably a necessary precondition in the reform debate given that the policy process is determined by the acceptance, and strict adherence to, a set of unifying political and economic structures associated with capitalism. Thus the reform agenda is hindered from the outset in that it is bound by the continued dominance of a particular mind-set. The truly radical nature of the CBI proposal is not fully appreciated until the validity and sustainability of those structures and processes are questioned. The following chapter will outline contemporary developments in the CBI debate, with the purpose of demonstrating the extent to which the hurdle of 'reformist' to 'radical' has been overcome.

7 Arguing for a CBI
A radical policy response?

Introduction

As discussed in Chapter 4, the attack on social security policy has been consistent and policy developments have contributed to a withering of employment-related insurance based benefits in favour of income targeted benefits. Furthermore, the emphasis on supporting the labour market has remained a firm focus with policy primarily aimed at promoting 'welfare through work' rather than via the mechanisms of state income transfers. However, although fiscal constraint is a constant feature in reform debates, the perceived 'crisis' has been fuelled by concerns regarding policy outcomes. Persistent and high levels of poverty, evident throughout the advanced capitalist economies, has served as a stimulus for evaluating the overall structure of income maintenance programmes. With this agenda in mind the ideal opportunity exists for widespread discussion of alternative mechanisms for delivery and administration. That is, contemporary reform debates provide a more welcoming stage for radical ideas.

Social security reform is a policy arena commanding much political attention throughout Europe, which has subsequently led to a resurgence of interest in the principles elementary to the CBI concept. The issues of social justice; gender equality; the separation of work from income; the future of capitalist economic and political structures and the sustainability of the environment in view of limited resources have all been raised within the contemporary CBI literature, albeit in varying degrees. The purpose of this chapter is to identify and provide an overview of the main contributions to the current debate and locating these within an economic, political and social context. It will be concluded, however, that although it may be presented as a radical policy option, contemporary debates display a characteristic bias towards emphasising how a CBI conforms to the demands imposed by modern labour market structures. Thus the radical element is superseded by what is argued to be a productivist reform approach.

This chapter will begin by expanding on the claim made in earlier chapters regarding the perceived 'crisis' in modern arrangements for social security provision. The intention is not to revisit the already well rehearsed 'crisis in welfare hypothesis'. Rather the purpose is to emphasise that renewed interest in the CBI proposal results from an increased awareness regarding the inadequacies of current social security provision in addressing modern needs. Thus, it is argued that contemporary debates have tended to focus on the potential benefits of a CBI in sustaining the capitalist system, in view of the dynamics of modern socio-economic conditions. The remainder of the chapter will examine the various attempts made to justify reform along the lines of a CBI, which have been presented in response to concerns regarding the future of modern welfare provision. Such attempts will be categorised in terms of their 'perceived' radical nature. The conclusion will be drawn that contemporary debates demonstrate limited evidence of 'radicalism'. It will be argued that this end result is ultimately due to a continued and unyielding attachment to the principles of mainstream economic theory, in particular those related to the world of work and income. It is claimed that such a process subordinates issues of gender justice to a predefined, implicitly assumed, and unquestioned conception of economic efficiency. The CBI debate thus remains exclusive in that, similar to the economics discipline itself, it has been determined by its approach rather than its subject matter.

The turning tide: collapse of the Keynesian Welfare State Consensus and the end of full employment

In Britain, as in many other parts of Western Europe, the post-1945 era was marked by a broad social consensus based on the general commitment to "full employment in a free society" and the creation of a comprehensive welfare state. Since the late 1970s that social consensus has been shattered, and nothing has yet been put in its place. Unless a new basis for consensus does emerge, there are reasons enough to fear a steady drift towards authoritarianism, superimposed on widening inequalities and mass unemployment.

(Standing, 1992: 47)

As outlined in Chapter 4, an ideological perspective that favours *active* as opposed to *passive* state welfare arrangements has been the dominant influencing factor with respect to recent developments in British social security policy. Reforms have been framed within a context of rebuilding the system around the centrality of paid work and promoting individual responsibility. Income security is thus to be achieved by promoting the role of the labour market and ensuring that individuals are afforded the opportunity to provide for themselves and not to depend on the state as a source of income. The inadequacies of the British social security system are patently obvious whenever evidence is presented regarding incidences of poverty and social exclusion. In considering contemporary arguments for a CBI, the most pressing question to be answered is would such a policy fare any better in addressing those problems? In other words, why a CBI now?

An examination of the various cases made for a CBI indicates that, just as earlier proposals were viewed as alternatives to existing measures, topical debates have tended to focus on the proposal as a possible reform option in response to the continued attack on the system of income maintenance:

> With the apparent ineffectiveness of traditional macroeconomic policies, and with the general assault on the welfare state and big government (particularly in the United States and the United Kingdom), it may be time to consider alternative policies to address the problems of unemployment and income inequality.... A Basic Income policy (also known as Citizen's Income or Social Dividend) is a policy response to the economic maladies the developed world currently faces.
>
> (Clark and Kavanagh, 1996: 400)

As illustrated in the preceding chapter, the notion of an unconditional income due to all from the public purse is not by any means a new idea, nor should it be viewed as merely a response to the war waged on social security by the New Right. However, the result of the said war has indeed allowed the CBI debate to reach the public arena far more quickly than perhaps would have been possible if the consensus, referred to by Standing above, had not come under threat. Current proposals should thus be examined with due regard to the political, social and economic environment in which they were framed. For this purpose, before going on to critically assess the various proposals for some form of CBI that have been promoted as a means of resolving the 'crisis', it is considered essential that claims of crisis are understood in context.

The welfare state in crisis: rethinking social security policy

> Contemporary social security policy has attracted a vast amount of attention since the current depression shook the complacency with which most people viewed the future during the steady growth period of the 1960s. It would seem however that the sudden concentration of attention on social security, and in particular on the legitimacy of state protection, is above all a reaction to current economic difficulties (increasing unemployment, declining industries, monetary chaos and so forth); and, on these grounds, many people have not hesitated to accuse social security of aggravating the world-wide economic crisis.
>
> (Francis Blanchard in preface to ILO, 1984)

Blanchard, the then Director General of the International Labour Office, commissioned a study in 1983, involving a group of ten independent experts on social security policy, to analyse and report on the future development of social security in advanced industrialised countries (ibid.: 1984). The call for such a study is clear from Blanchard's opening statement (quoted above) in the final report. Social security provision was generally believed to be a main contributor to the fiscal crisis evident throughout modern welfare states and thus came under attack. The agenda became one of reforming systems in light of new demands, but more importantly, with specific reference to resource constraints. This resulted in a concentrated effort to reduce costs and to encourage, wherever possible, dependence on private means of support as opposed to reliance on the state. Although periodic attention was given to questions regarding the basis of finance and delivery, the 'so-called crisis of welfare which ensued from the international economic problems of the 1970s' resulted in an almost exclusive focus on an 'opposition between "universal" and "targeted" benefits' (Eardley *et al.*, 1996: 21). In general terms, the decades following the 1970s have witnessed a universal trend amongst welfare state governments towards absolute reductions in social policy, or at least the enactment of measures which serve to restrain the future growth of state-supported welfare provision (Hill, 1996: 293). Within this environment of restraint income transfer systems have undergone considerable changes and in particular social security policy has been characterised by a shift away from universal benefits to a greater reliance on means testing or income-targeted benefits.

The increased emphasis on selectivity has undoubtedly been driven by concerns regarding a shrinking resource base. However, it has been the question of work incentives that has tended to dominate international debates on the reform of tax and social security systems (Eardley *et al.*, 1996: 21). In fact:

> While the European Commission and many of the EU governments have resisted any wholesale reduction of insurance-based social protection, and indeed have recently emphasised the importance of the social dimension, the White Paper on Growth, Competitiveness and Employment, nevertheless recommends a range of measures aimed at increasing employment, which include reductions or restructuring of employers' non-wage costs and boosting of work incentives through income-related supplements to earnings.
>
> (ibid., 1996: 21)

Thus the principal objective behind many of the tax and social security changes occurring throughout the 1980s and 1990s has been to encourage work effort; reduce levels of welfare dependency and to cut the social costs of labour experienced by employers. This focus indicates that, on an international level, developments in social policy are being driven primarily by the perceived needs of the economy, with particular reference to changing labour markets. Although specific reforms have been directed at altering the relationship between the three 'welfare pillars' (market, state and family), or have been premised on redistributional goals, the underlying emphasis has remained strongly fixed on curbing any future growth in public expenditure. Set against this background, income maintenance measures have been subject to reforms characterised by revenue neutrality and a shift in emphasis from 'security', through employment-related insurance-based benefits to 'subsistence' through targeted income-related benefits. The trend has therefore been to view social security reform as an economic policy response to the dynamics of modern capitalist development.

Throughout the 1980s the degree to which modern welfare states followed this trend illustrated marked differences. Some countries were slower than others in responding to economic pressures, however by the 1990s the tensions between economic and social policy became universally apparent, resulting in a levelling out of the division between 'welfare leaders' and 'welfare laggards' (Hill, 1996: 293). The differences in response can be attributed to a combination of factors. The varying cultural, political and economic influences, which have informed the evolution of welfare systems, have resulted in differences in design. Thus the direct relationship between social security policy and the labour market has assumed greater importance in some countries than in others. Furthermore, historical experiences of unemployment levels have not been universal and thus the prioritising of questions of work incentives has not been a consistent common feature. Notwithstanding the effects of these factors, perhaps the most influential has been the existence of a firm political will in favour of rolling back the frontiers of the state and promoting the mixed economy of welfare. Such a political will was made explicit in Britain with the election of the Thatcher government in 1979, which marked the beginning of a definite and sustained attack on public expenditure in Britain. Furthermore, the trends towards casualisation in the labour market have been particularly strong in Britain (Hill, 1996: 312), which has had negative consequences for the effective operation of a Beveridge type social insurance model.

The British experience of concern regarding the future sustainability of income maintenance programmes is not unique:

> Globalization is believed by a majority of neoclassical economists and a large proportion of politicians and policy makers to raise the economic costs of social programmes that redistribute income and provide economic security.
>
> (Hobson *et al.*, 2002: 4)

Thus, the perceived notion that generous social security systems may operate in such a way as to limit individual economic effort, threaten labour market flexibility, and damage international competitiveness has informed the reform agenda at a global level. In Britain, however, the prolonged period of a Conservative government, primarily driven by the underlying philosophy of New Right, signified a period of dramatic changes in social security policy. (Lister, 1991; Hill, 1990, 1993; Lowe, 1993). Hill writes of the influential nature of the work of Friedman, with regard to the purpose of social security, in that benefits should be maintained at a minimum level, 'so that they serve only to prevent the more extreme cases of destitution and operate in such a way that they enforce labour market participation' (1990: 55). Hence, the actions of individuals operating freely in the labour market should be left unhindered by the effects of state income maintenance measures. Implicit in this ideological stance is the notion that the labour market remains the primary source of individual welfare. This is a crucial point when discussing the criticisms of a CBI proposal waged by the New Right and explains the predisposition of right-wing thinkers towards a form of NIT. A further related concept is the overarching aim of the New Right to reduce the role of the state in all spheres of economic, social and political life. What is advocated is the return to a 'laissez-faire' style of government with a corresponding confidence in the role of the market place to efficiently allocate resources. The principle of self-reliance emerged victorious over the notion of welfare dependency.

Prior to 1979 there had been moves to contain costs, spurred mainly by the economic crisis of 1976, which resulted in arguments relating to the goal of 'targeting' those most in need (Lowe, 1993: 314; Lister, 1991). There seemed to be a clear economic agenda for reassessing methods of income redistribution in an attempt to improve overall efficiency, defined in terms of resource allocation. The shift in emphasis from social insurance to means testing was to be justified by appealing to the fact that available resources were not in abundant supply and hence benefit payments to rich and poor alike were unaffordable luxuries. Social policy once again was destined to take a back seat to the goals of economic policy. This is a primary indication of the end of the post-war consensus where the adoption of the Keynes/Beveridge model of the mixed economy of welfare had ensured that social and economic policy were inextricably linked.

However, the Conservatives added momentum to the process by incorporating the aforementioned political considerations. The policy of favouring selective benefits over the principal of universality was to be complemented by: reductions in the real level of benefits; the implementation of harsher qualifying conditions; the replacing of grants with loans wherever possible; and a rigorous campaign to encourage individuals to appreciate the benefits of provision available within the private sector. The slogan of 'targeting those in most need', then, is most readily associated with the 18 year period of Conservative rule in Britain.

A fundamental shift occurred in policy objectives for social security and incremental reforms were designed primarily to improve the efficiency of the system by specifically addressing the problem of work incentives as opposed to the goal of reducing inequality (Barr and Coulter, 1990). The use of the term poverty disappeared altogether from government rhetoric. Preference was given to the use of 'the sanitised language of 'the most vulnerable', 'low income', 'those in greatest need' and implicit assumptions are made about the relative deservingness of different groups' (Lister, 1989: 105). In fact, the over-riding purpose of social security provision was considered to be that of relieving the worst poverty and the targeting of benefits became the central theme of state income maintenance policies. This was a marked departure from the original and more ambitious goal of eliminating 'want', and as such served to stigmatise those eligible for receipt by labelling them the worst-off in society. Furthermore, the continued emphasis on promoting the supremacy of the role of the family and community as providers of welfare, with the stated aim of promoting self reliance, merely serves to shift the realm of dependency from the public to the private sector for many individuals.

As indicated in Chapter 4, contemporary debates on the future of income transfers in Britain have not demonstrated any radical departure from the past. The early 1990s witnessed the onset of widespread political debate on future reform options. The Government embarked upon its Long Term Review and in a speech, delivered in 1993, Peter Lilley, the then Secretary of State for Social Security, appeared to be indicating that the reform agenda should not only consider the 'economic consequences' of social security policy but should also refer to its 'social purpose' (Lilley, 1993: 2). Although the emphasis on cost remained, Lilley identified the scope for political consensus regarding the objectives of policy and in recognising the need to modernise the system he welcomed the possibility of debate centred on 'radical' solutions:

> We all want to make the system <u>better</u>. We all want to safeguard, in particular, the position of the most vulnerable. We all want to ensure the system does not outstrip the nation's ability to pay. And we all agree a system designed for yesterday requires updating to reflect contemporary human needs.... So it ought to be possible to go beyond party political point scoring. And we must certainly not allow scaremongering to choke off any radical thinking. Radical ideas will often prove impractical or unattractive in themselves. But they are worth voicing since they often highlight strengths or weaknesses of the system and so help generate more modest but practical proposals.
>
> (ibid.: 15)

The potential for political agreement on objectives may exist but the question of policy outcomes is another issue. For the political right, generous social security benefits promote welfare dependency and the high levels of resources devoted to programmes negatively impact on overall economic performance. Those on the political left tend to argue from a user's point of view, claiming that means testing traps people in poverty and exacerbates the problem of social exclusion. The Commission on Social Justice (CSJ), set up by the Labour Party in 1992, examined the current social security measures employed in Britain in an attempt to develop a reform package which would modernise the system. The Commission reported the following objectives for any system of benefits, tax allowances and private provision:

1   To prevent poverty where possible and relieve it where necessary.
2   To protect people against risks, especially those that arise in the labour market and from family change.
3   To redistribute resources from richer to poorer members of society.
4   To redistribute resources of time and money over people's lifecycles.
5   To encourage personal independence.
6   To promote social cohesion.

(CSJ, 1994: 224)

Thus it would seem that in Britain, by the early 1990s, the terms of reference for the reform debate had moved beyond the limiting parameters of cost containment to encompass a broader range of social issues relating to the dynamics of modern socio-economic conditions. Furthermore, there appeared to be political commitment to at least consider policy options which represented a departure from the traditional universal vs. targeting dichotomy.

As indicated in Chapter 4, current social security measures in Britain can be criticised for failing adequately to respond to modern *needs*. As previously argued the apparent 'success' in reducing the claimant count may be as more to do with favourable economic conditions as opposed to being a direct result of government activation measures. Also, questions remain as to the future sustainability of policies placing increased emphasis on private sector *dependence* with respect to income security. Further criticisms point to the fact that the system is historically structured in such a way that it suffers from gender bias. The 'male breadwinner model' is referred to frequently in the literature focused on characterising different welfare regimes:

> The male breadwinner model was based on a set of assumptions about male and female contributions at the household level: men having the primary responsibility to earn and women to care for the young and the old. Female dependence was inscribed in the model. The male breadwinner model built into the post-war settlement assumed regular and full male employment *and* stable families in which women

would be provided for and largely via their husbands' earnings and social contributions.

(Hobson *et al.*, 2002: 5)

The design and delivery of social security policy in Britain is undeniably characteristic of a male breadwinner model. Although, as indicated in Chapter 4, more recent developments have involved measures to ensure individual entitlement, key features of the male breadwinner model remain. As previously argued, the emphasis on promoting work opportunities for all has involved redefining the target group to include a broader range of potential beneficiaries. As a consequence:

Dependants' additions to many benefits have been pared back over time, and are now rare, at least for claimants of working age, within the non-means-tested benefit system. These changes have been characterised as forming part of moves, across a range of countries, away from a "male breadwinner" model and towards an "adult worker" or "citizen worker" model.

(Bennett, 2002: 565)

However, the focus on the individual is not consistent. The practice of establishing entitlement to the principle means-tested benefits continues to use the household or couple as the unit of assessment. This has serious consequences in terms of gender inequalities, as indicated in earlier chapters. Furthermore, recent reforms, particularly in the area of child care provision and support for child care costs, indicate that the focus is clearly on improving work incentives, as opposed to representing a strategic approach to tackling gender inequalities. Social security programmes, which are linked to the formal labour market and continue to assume the traditional male-breadwinner family model, implicitly promote the citizenship rights of workers whilst denying the full inclusion of many individuals, primarily women and children, by assuming their dependency on men. As Hobson *et al.* point out:

The *new welfare contract* involves a shift from social contributions to individually defined contributions, premised on the idea that all adults are in the work-force. But this is an especially unreal assumption for women, given, first, the unequal gendered division of unpaid care work, and second, the fact that a disproportionate number of them are employed in low-paid, part-time, often care-related jobs. It is additionally the case that in the UK, where these shifts are most apparent in Europe, the means-tested nature of the whole social security system tends to run counter to individualisation.

(2002: 9)

In considering a CBI, the question now becomes one about whether or not such a reform proposal presents as a possible policy option which addresses all of the previously identified failings of current measures. However, equally important is an emphasis on establishing political acceptance for a proposal that entails a radical overhaul of existing claiming principles, methods of finance and delivery mechanisms. With this in mind, the remainder of this chapter will review the contemporary literature arguing for some form of CBI. The conclusion will be drawn that implementation remains blocked largely by questions of political expediency, as opposed to critiques regarding what a CBI can actually achieve. It is argued that not only has this served to temper the debate, but also that the focus on political will is a product of a limiting and constraining vision regarding the welfare function of modern labour markets.

First principles: integration as a radical agenda

The current direction of government policy appears to suggest that radical reform is not on the agenda. Policy seems to hinge on the primacy of *work as the best form of welfare* and, linked to this, is the idea of moving towards tax credits and away from social security benefits. Such a move reflects the growing interest and power of the Treasury in relation to this field of policy.... Tax credits are seen as the panacea for all ills but is impossible to tell at present whether they will provide the much needed solution: one scenario is that they will add yet another layer of complexity to an already confusing system.

(Rowlingson, 2003: 26)

The starting premise of any model for reform based on the CBI proposal involves full scale integration of the present systems of tax and benefits. The Conservatives opposed a move towards integration in the form of tax credits on the basis of financial considerations and rather favoured measures that would generate cost savings and increased targeting (Lilley, 1993: 17). In their search for an 'intelligent welfare state that works with rather than against the grain of change', the Labour Party considered integration of the tax and benefit systems as a possible reform strategy (CSJ, 1994: ch 6). Again, the perceived cost implications of such an approach proved to be the main stumbling block. The CSJ employed a team of independent consultants to investigate the feasibility of full-scale integration who concluded that such a structural change would not solve the current problems. Rather, what was required was a more strategic approach to ensure that that the tax and benefit systems worked in unison and reforms should centre around addressing the problems of the poverty and unemployment traps arising from the interaction of current schemes (Clinton *et al.*, 1994). The Commission subsequently reported that employing tax-benefit integration 'to try to solve the problems of the minority would be like using a sledgehammer to crack a nut'[1] (CSJ, 1994: 260).

The Commission drew attention to the differences in timescales used by the two systems, differences in units of assessment and the enormous administrative costs implied by such a large scale process of government reorganisation (ibid.: 260). However in considering a CBI package, as opposed to an NIT scheme, the Commission added weight to their objections by emphasising the political unacceptability of the 'free-rider' implications of such a policy:

> A change of this magnitude would have to be backed by a broad-based consensus, of which there is, as yet, no sign. In a society with a strong work ethic many people would oppose, as giving "something for nothing", a scheme deliberately designed to offer unconditional benefits to all. Citizen's Income does not require any *act* of citizenship; it would be paid regardless of whether someone was in a job or looking for one, caring for children or other dependants, engaged in voluntary work or not.
>
> (ibid.: 262)

In seeking a resolution to the problems associated with unconditionality, the Commission considered integration in the form of a Participation Income, but rejected this on the basis of its distributional impact, arguing that 'it would mean somewhat higher tax bills for those already paying income tax' (ibid.: 265). Furthermore, assuming it was set at a level equivalent to current personal tax allowances the Participation Income would involve extra expenditure. Thus cost considerations proved again to be a decisive factor. However, the Commission did indicate that if it were not for the presence of necessary resource restraints, there was much to commend in the idea of a Participation Income:

> If it could be afforded, particularly at a higher level than that available through abolishing tax allowances, it could go a long way towards eliminating means-testing, recognising the value of parents' and carers' unpaid work and encouraging people to take up employment, education and training.
>
> (ibid.: 265)

The third main political party in Britain, the Liberal Democrats, raised their concerns regarding a CBI in a consultation paper published in January 1994, which recommended that their previous commitment to the proposal be scrapped. (CI Bulletin, 1994: 9). The paper made clear that a full CBI had never been supported due to the excessive increase in income tax levies required to finance such a scheme. The favoured Partial Basic Income was now considered unworkable for reasons of poor targeting and expense. Furthermore, as the Partial Basic Income implied retaining some income-tested benefits to meet special needs, the benefits of integration, in terms of administrative simplicity, would not be fully realised.

Thus, in Britain in the early 1990s there appeared to be a broad-based political consensus with regard to tax-benefit integration. Common across the political spectrum was a rejection of the proposal on the grounds of costs in the short run and a clear indication that approaches involving greater targeting were to be given priority. The current Labour Government came into office stressing their commitment to reducing social security bills and addressing the social problems of poverty and exclusion through active employment measures, thereby reversing the trend in welfare dependency. As argued in earlier chapters, the promotion of employment is now understood to be a fundamental goal of both social and economic policy. Future social security reform in Britain will undoubtedly be informed, first and foremost, by the impact measures will have on the efficient functioning of the labour market.

The introduction of the various tax credits, referred to in Chapter 4, could be viewed as partial integration. However, the extent to which these truly represent 'integration' has to be considered with reference to their treatment under standard public accounting rules:

> In its preferred measure of the tax burden (net taxes and social security contributions), the government treats the working families' tax credit as negative income tax rather than benefit expenditure. International conventions state that tax credits only be counted in this way if they are an integral part of the tax system and can be used to reduce tax liability.
>
> (Brewer *et al.*, 2002b: 533)

Thus it would seem that expenditure on the WFTC will be represented as income tax foregone, despite the fact that 'around 80% of its cost represents net payment to people rather than a reduction in their tax bill' (Op. cit.). Although the new tax credits, introduced in April 2003, extend coverage to a broader client group and thus may lead to greater numbers benefiting from a reduction in reducing tax liability there will still be a significant element of 'benefit' payment. This is a crucial point of distinction when considering the political feasibility of a CBI. The accounting practice in Britain, of showing tax expenditure as negative revenue, means that the introduction of a new cash benefit, to replace all tax relief and allowances would distort the government's accounts by showing an exorbitant increase in spending. This leads Monkton to the conclusion that 'unless the Treasury is forced to mend its ways, it will always block the consideration of any universal benefit scheme, erroneously believing it to be in all circumstances unaffordable' (1993: 6). With a focus on reducing public expenditure and improving work incentives it seems a model of tax-benefit integration such as that implied by a CBI will not be embraced during the lifetime of the current political administration in Britain.

Welfare to Work or a welfare system that works?

> The obligation to do paid work is central to Labour's approach to social security reform. In the words of the Secretary of State for Social Security, Harriet Harman, we are reforming the welfare state around the work ethic.... Benefits for the unemployed have always been under-pinned by the obligation to be available for paid work, but we are now witnessing a clear shift towards the prioritising of paid work obligations over social citizenship rights. Such a shift is in the opposite direction to the principles that underpin Basic Income or Citizen's Income more generally.
>
> (Lister, 1998: 3)

The dominant view emerging, therefore, is one that places social security policy within a framework of obligations and achievements relating to the labour market (Plant, 1997: 3). That is, the main driving force behind income maintenance reform can be identified as the need to conform with the policy goals of promoting employability and supporting the operation of flexible labour markets. Social security policy thus assumes a subsidiary role in relation to employment policy and serves as a tool for furthering the principles of self-help and the work ethic. It can be argued that this particular approach to social security policy is informed by a general acceptance of the assumptions regarding human behaviour inherent within mainstream economic theory. The impact of such on the formation of social security policy was discussed at length in earlier chapters. However, it is worth reinforcing at this point the arguments as they relate to work incentives. Arguments favouring income-related benefits over universal benefits are normally presented in terms of resource savings. It is true that with a given budget constraint, the targeting of benefits to those identified as 'needy' is, in principle, cheaper than paying benefits to all regardless of need. However, in practice this may not be the case due to the very different operating structures required to administer both types of benefit. Problems arise with regard to identifying, and continually monitoring, the conditions of receipt, which in turn can prove costly. Furthermore the impact on economic activity arising from a switch to targeting may have exactly the opposite effect to that intended, thereby effectively reducing the available resource base. Aside from the financial considerations, targeted benefits tend to be promoted by those who adhere to a rather cynical view of human nature. Operating within an environment of unconditional universal benefits, the self-interested utility-maximising individual will behave in such a way as to secure receipt of those benefits. Thus the concept of moral hazard is employed to demonstrate the inevitability of over consumption and how the benefit system creates perverse incentives for individuals to engage in activities, which they would otherwise avoid, in order to meet eligibility conditions. A related argument draws upon the notion of the free-rider. Tax funded unconditional universal benefits will result in situations where the working poor are effectively subsidising those who freely choose not to work. Thus, the benefit system creates disincentives to work and has negative distributional consequences. This scenario is not only considered unfair and economically inefficient, but in the long term, politically unfeasible. Tax payers will eventually object to funding benefits at a level deemed sufficient to meet the needs of the unemployed, placing further pressures on an ever shrinking resource base. Accepting these arguments leads to a convincing case for preferring targeted benefits to universal schemes.

However, what is implied is a particular form of targeting. As previously discussed, contemporary debates on social security reform have been dominated by a targeting versus universal framework, but caution should be exercised in the use of terminology. The choice is not essentially an either/or scenario but rather involves a range of policy options (Atkinson, 1995a: 224). As indicated in Chapter 3, the concept of universalism, in its true sense, is not evident in any existing benefit structure:

> In practice virtually all existing benefits involve some degree of conditionality or are targeted in some way, either towards certain categories of people, such as those with children in the case of child benefit, by contingency in the case of disability benefits, or on the basis of contribution records for social insurance benefits.
>
> (Eardley *et al.*, 1996: 21)

What is referred to when discussing current trends towards the increased use of targeting is the practice of means testing. The operational nature of means-tested benefits was previously outlined and it has been argued that social security systems are evolving, on an ever increasing level, in line with a means-tested approach. Social security provision of this kind is that which is most commonly associated with the current use of the terms targeting or selectivity. Within a British context, the practice of targeting is clearly associated with an expansion of the 'means test'. In evaluating the quality of different systems, Yeates makes reference to a study that ranked Australia as having the 'best-designed social security system in the world' whilst the UK was ranked 37th and 'classed as a second tier system' (2003: 59,60). The issue regarding how 'targeting' operates in practice is crucial in determining this difference in 'quality':

> The main difference between the UK and Australian systems is that the former targets income need through a means test which requires

claimants to prove their poverty in order to receive benefits, while the latter does so through an "affluence test" which includes all but the highest income groups.

(ibid., 2003: 60)

The question remaining is does means testing work? Accepting that the objectives of policy have somewhat altered in recent decades in favour of prioritising labour market policy, evaluating the practice of means testing involves examining the impact it has on individual work patterns. One of the negative consequences of the increased use of means-tested benefits is indeed the effect on work incentives arising from the rapid reductions in benefits as income rises. This is compounded by increases in tax liability. The anomaly arises when individuals find themselves both in receipt of income-tested benefits and liable for income tax and national insurance deductions. A system which pays out from one government department only to recover the same via another department does not make economic sense, given the emphasis on reducing administrative costs. Furthermore, creating a situation whereby individuals find themselves no better-off in financial terms by entering the labour market, or moving to a higher paid job, is at worst immoral and at best inefficient with regard to promoting future economic growth.

Whilst these criticisms are worth detailed analysis in their own right, for the purposes of this discussion they merely add to the list of identified problems previously mentioned. Any model for reform that fails to recognise the totality of the situation and simply targets a specific issue illustrates a very narrow perception of the role public policies aimed at income redistribution play in the macroeconomy. It further demonstrates a desire to continue with existing models, adapting as the need may arise. Within this context a CBI emerges as a radical policy response. Although the contemporary literature is extensive and diverse, arguing from a range of philosophical, economic, social and environmental perspectives, the following sections will outline the main contributions as they relate to the concerns raised thus far regarding social security systems in 'crisis'. That is, the focus is directed at those arguments where issues of cost reduction, addressing poverty and social exclusion, and the functioning of modern labour markets are highlighted. The intention is to demonstrate that a CBI can be argued for convincingly on the basis that it is a system that has the potential to 'work' given the existing dominant framework, as opposed to systems that deny welfare and promote work.

The second marriage of justice and efficiency: the proactive approach

Perhaps the most prominent of theorists within the contemporary CBI literature is Phillippe Van Parijs, academic economist and co-founder of the Basic Income European Network. For Van Parijs:

(the) introduction of a basic income is not just a feasible structural improvement in the functioning of the welfare state, it is a profound reform that belongs in the same league as the abolition of slavery or the introduction of universal suffrage.

(Van Parijs, 1992b: 7)

Whilst he has made various influential contributions to the debate in a primarily philosophical sense, the analysis he develops in Chapter 13 of his edited volume *Arguing for Basic Income: Ethical Foundations for a Radical Reform* is most useful for the purposes of this particular study. Van Parijs draws upon the historical development of the CBI concept to illustrate that the concern for economic growth and the simultaneous preservation of individual rights has led many theorists in the past to make demands for an unconditional minimum income (1992c: 215). However, he begins his attempt at justifying a CBI by referring to the difficulties experienced within capitalist states in determining the criteria with which to evaluate and design redistributive social reform. Judging the political acceptability of any change in current resource allocation by estimating the amount of gainers compared to losers and implementing only those policies that are positive is flawed. This is due to ignorance on the part of voters as to whether they are, or will be, better-off or not, and because of the persuasive influence of political beliefs and ideology. Likewise, attempts to formulate social policy with reference to the legitimate functions of the capitalist state are subject to fluctuations in overall economic performance. Hence there is no direct relationship between political acceptability and the functional requirements of the capitalist state but rather social policy takes a back seat to the priority of capital accumulation. Van Parijs argues:

> ...the presence of a plausible case on the grounds of both justice and efficiency constitutes a necessary condition for any major reform in the field of social policy.
>
> (ibid.: 216)

The introduction of a CBI, for Van Parijs, can indeed meet the challenge of presenting such a plausible case in that it is a policy for reform that can be argued for convincingly in terms of promoting both social justice and economic efficiency. The caveat being, however, that the understanding of what constitutes justice and efficiency must first be re-examined, taking into account the changing socio-economic structure of modern capitalist societies.

Van Parijs rather poignantly refers to the mixed economy of welfare as representing the 'first marriage of justice and efficiency' and goes on to stress that the marriage is under immense strain due to the increasing concerns regarding the damaging effects of state activity in the area of income redistribution during periods of slow or even negative economic growth (ibid.: 215–233). Utilising tools of economic analysis and ethical theorising, Van Parijs develops an abstract framework from which he traces the relevance of the traditional considerations of 'economic value' (efficiency) and 'ethical value' (justice) to the social consensus afforded the development of the modern welfare state. Social policy was generally considered an essential ingredient in the pursuit of economic growth. However, by relating the arguments about trade-off between efficiency and equality to a variant of the Laffer curve, Van Parijs illustrates the economist's case for arguing that too much social policy actually prohibits further economic growth. This is in main due to the disincentive effects high levels of taxation, required to finance social policy, and over generous levels of transfer payments have on the supply of capital and the supply of labour respectively:

> If a rise in t (defined as the average tax rate[2]) makes people both less willing to get a job and work hard, and less willing to save and invest, how could it possibly generate a rise in average income, especially in the long run?
>
> (ibid.: 222)

This is precisely the case made by supply side economists for reducing the average tax rates for those with a higher marginal propensity to save and reducing the real level of transfer payments for those who are highly responsive to the price of labour. Thus effectively reducing the replacement ratios of income in work and income received when out of work. Such analysis was extremely influential in determining recent reforms to the social security system in Britain, particularly with regard to the unemployment trap, as well as the changes made to the tax base and reforms in the area of pension provision.

However, as Van Parijs points out, the situation in the 1930s was very different from that of today. Hence the same analysis could be utilised to argue for expansionary fiscal policy, in that increasing the overall level of transfers would:

> ...prevent minor fluctuations degenerating into full-scale slumps by stabilizing effective demand, both directly through the income guarantee and indirectly by setting a floor to wages.
>
> (ibid.: 222)

Keynes made such arguments in his General Theory and therefore the stage was set for the positive interaction of social and economic policy within advanced capitalist systems. Income redistribution would prove to be an effective policy instrument in enhancing total output and therefore social policy was attributed an economic value. Crucial to this change in policy thinking was the fact that the analysis assumes a relatively low level of t to begin with, which indeed was the case in the period of modern welfare state formation. A continued commitment to demand management techniques and expansions in social policy throughout the immediate post-war decades has led to quite considerable increases in the average rate of taxation. As national output continues to grow though, the belief is that everyone is benefiting, or at least there exists the potential for all citizens to become better-off as the size of the 'cake' has increased. However, this belief can easily be disputed. As the growth of the 'cake' is directly attributable to the increase in average transfers, some individuals will indeed be worse-off as they experience more and more of their disposable income being creamed off by the state in order to finance the expansion in social policy. This means that a further condition is necessary in proving the economic value of social policy. That is, not only must the national output grow but it must grow at a faster rate than that of t. Only then will the 'enlightened self interest' of those bearing most of the financial burden be served, at least in the long run. This leads Van Parijs to the conclusion that decisions regarding the economic value of social policy will be taken when due consideration has been given to the long run effects on average income; where this is positive the policy is said to have economic value and where this is negative the policy creates economic damage and hence will be abandoned (ibid.: 224).

Social policy formation is, therefore, traditionally determined by appealing to classical welfare economic analysis. The political will and electoral support for any reform will only ensue if long run potential Pareto improvements can be made. That is, any redistribution of current resources can only be justified if it eventually improves the welfare of all citizens. Such criteria merely provide the analytical process by which social policy is judged. The impetus for reform, however, comes from arguments concerning distributive injustice and hence the concepts of efficiency and justice become intertwined.

Questions regarding the 'ethical value' of social policy are difficult to resolve given the normative nature of the issue. The use of value judgements is extremely evident within theories of social justice. Those beholding to the libertarian view condemn any violation of the individual right to accumulate economic resources and retain ownership of these. Excessive levels of taxation threaten individual freedom, therefore social policy should not cross the boundary between what is required to ensure that at least basic needs are met and what is believed to be necessary to reduce inequality. Tax rates should hence be kept to a minimum. Conversely, egalitarian arguments promote social justice in terms of the maximum level of transfers required to ensure a more equitable distribution of resources. The average rate of taxation should be set at the maximum level determined by the financial requirements of social policy aimed at ensuring every citizen receives an income adequate to cover basic needs (ibid.: 224). Van Parijs adds two further ethical considerations. He refers to the 'Rawlsian' position, being the average rate of taxation required to maximise the level of replacement income (defined as the average expected income when income is no longer secured by employment), and the 'utilitarian' position, being the average rate of taxation which maximises total national income. The labels are used to refer to the 'boundary between economically valuable and economically damaging social policy (U) and the boundary between the normal and prohibitive range of t (R)' (ibid.: 226). The use of terminology is slightly misleading, as Van Parijs himself indicates. Rawls's maximin criteria does not apply to income alone and likewise it is the maximisation of welfare as opposed to the mere maximising of income that utilitarians are concerned with (ibid.: 225–226). These considerations are important when examining the reconceptualisation of the efficiency and justice criteria when evaluating proposals for social policy reform. However, when discussing the current criteria, social policy is said to be promoting justice when the 'Rawlsian' position is reached. That is, the level of taxation remains stable at the point where replacement incomes are maximised in terms of meeting basic needs. This is a sort of middle ground between the libertarian position and the egalitarian position:

> The conjecture is then that deliberate changes in the field of social policy can occur only if they bring us nearer to a situation in which all inequalities which do not benefit their victims, and only those have been abolished.
>
> (ibid.: 226)

Van Parijs therefore concludes that expansionary policy, which he qualifies as 'social democratic' reform, will be promoted when increases in national income can be assured, that is the policy is deemed to be economically valuable. Contractionary policy, which he qualifies as 'neo-liberal' reform, will involve deliberate reductions in the average tax rate when existing mechanisms are creating replacement incomes in excess of what is deemed socially just (Op. cit.). The problems facing contemporary capitalist societies is when the actual average rate of taxation is believed to be somewhere between these two points. Any future reform implies a trade-off between justice and efficiency, that is economic growth or increasing replacement incomes. However, a lack of confidence in the ability to secure future economic growth will inhibit expansionary reform, whilst the absence of sufficient political pressure to address the unfair distribution of wealth will prevent contractionary reform. Given this impasse any future developments in the field of social policy will require an appeal to alternative modes of justification. For Van Parijs, the current political, social and economic climate demands a second marriage of the principles of social justice and economic efficiency. The CBI concept, according to Van Parijs 'provides the foundation for a new and more progressive union by reconceptualising both of the partners to the marriage' (Manza, 1995: 887).

Considering the argument that a CBI would foster justice, Van Parijs draws on an earlier statement made that emphasis so far has been on maximising incomes. In his ensuing analysis he illustrates the often contradictory nature of anti-poverty policies. Traditionally it has been argued that the main weapon against poverty is paid employment, and as discussed earlier, this view has dominated contemporary debates on the future of social security policy. As previously stated the commitment to full employment institutionalised the right to work and as such was an effective policy instrument in combating individual poverty. Macroeconomic policy was thus perceived to be securing access to jobs for the majority of citizens hence the justice criteria should logically focus on the income side of the equation, for those individuals suffering a temporary or indeed permanent loss of such access. Further policy developments therefore secured a minimum income for the jobless poor but recent criticism has been directed at the actual level of this minimum income. The poverty lobby argues that average replacement incomes are woefully inadequate. However, by drawing on his earlier discussion, Van Parijs reminds us that:

> For reasons of both justice and efficiency ... the lowest net wages should noticeably exceed the replacement income paid to the jobless. But the higher these wages, the harder it is for the poorly skilled people to find a job. It follows, it seems, that there is a fundamental conflict between the two objectives of an effective strategy against poverty. The better it does on the income side, the worse it seems bound to do on the job side.
>
> (ibid.: 228)

By stipulating a criteria of justice which solely concentrates on maximum replacement incomes, the practice of judging the desirability or otherwise of a particular social policy is far too narrowly focused. Much more useful criteria would encapsulate not only the justice perceived to be achieved by granting a minimum income but also the questions of justice arising from individual labour market activity. With the onset of mass long term unemployment, the right to work can no longer be claimed as a product of modern capitalist development. As such, any consideration of the improvements in social justice said to result from social policy reform can no longer ignore the work element. It is in this area that Van Parijs provides a strong case for a CBI along the lines of separating work from income, whilst also demonstrating the advances to be gained from a CBI in terms of individual freedom.

The right to an income, the right to work and the right not to work are all factors worth serious consideration when appraising the fairness of social policy. All individuals by nature have different preferences for work and leisure derived mainly from their desire to consume. The ability to consume is currently determined largely by income earned or income received from state benefits. The conditional nature of those benefits means that recipients must at least demonstrate a willingness to work. Hence income is directly linked to work. Anti-poverty policies aimed at increasing the incomes of those at the lower end of the income scale, within the current economic climate, have necessitated the switch in emphasis from universal benefits to means testing; the results being that those with access to limited economic resources are categorised by society as being disadvantaged and hence deserving of public assistance. Justifying income redistribution in this manner puts pressure on recipients to make all possible efforts to secure income from alternative sources, the most obvious being the labour market. However, this becomes increasingly difficult in light of rising replacement incomes for those individuals only afforded access to traditionally low paid jobs. Correspondingly pressure is put on tax-payers to argue for value for money. The result is that only those who are willing to earn their income are viewed as deserving, whereas those individuals wishing to forgo income for more leisure time are penalised. Surely such a system is unjust in that it discriminates 'against those with a lesser taste for consumption' (ibid.: 229). The right to work combined with maximising replacement incomes can no longer be considered the appropriate criteria with which to measure justice. Income must be separated from work in order to justify the provision of economic resources to those individuals not afforded access to jobs suitable to their personal lifestyles or skill level. In doing so account will be taken of the marginalisation within the labour market of vast numbers of individuals.

Freedom on the part of the individual to choose not to engage in paid work, or indeed to refuse the offer of paid work as personal circumstances dictate, should be incorporated into any discussion of social justice. A CBI would allow for such freedom to be exercised. Those with preferences for paid work would be more able to participate in activities with little financial gain and those with preferences for leisure would not be forced into 'junk jobs'. Hence, with respect to justice, a CBI enhances both access to jobs, therefore fulfilling the primary objective of anti-poverty policies, and access to activities other than paid work, a new and more appropriate objective:

> Although it does make sense to formulate justice in terms of a maximin criterion, what is to be maximined cannot be income alone. It must, rather, be something like the real freedom (as opposed to the sheer right) to do whatever one might like to do with one's life, including consume, get a job and perform enjoyable activities. Introducing a basic income and pitching it at the highest feasible absolute level ... would precisely maximin such real freedom, and hence provide what justice demands.
>
> (ibid.: 229)

Turning to the question of the efficiency criteria, Van Parijs provides a theoretical explanation as to how a CBI could promote economic growth. If, as previously suggested, the CBI is to be pitched at the highest possible level to answer the justice criteria then the prohibitive MTRs required to finance such a policy could arguably lead to a reduction in factor supply and hence reduce the national product.[3] Any policy which permits the freedom to choose between those activities assumed to be economically productive and those activities attributed no economic value, at least within the capitalist structure, will be perceived to threaten the very survival of capitalism itself. Similar to the existing economic criticisms of minimum wage proposals, arguments against a CBI would point to the inflationary effect on wages and the subsequent effects on demand for labour. National productivity would decline and as economic profits were subject to higher and higher rates of taxation, the negative impact on investment activity would ultimately result in contractions in national output.

Focusing on the negative impact on overall economic performance of high MTRs is an indication of partial analysis. A more useful approach would be to examine the results of a CBI in terms of labour market flexibility and the resolution of economic conflict within capitalist systems (ibid.: 232). The arguments for a CBI with regard to the fostering of overall flexibility have been well documented (Standing, 1986; Van Parijs, 1996; Stroeken, 1996; Meade, 1989: part III). The granting of unconditional income guarantees provides the pre-requisite financial security required in taking 'economic risks'. Hence, a favourable environment is created for engaging in entrepreneurial activity. The opportunity costs of re-training and/or periods of study are significantly reduced, hence making them more economically attractive. In addition, the introduction of a CBI would free-up labour market practices in general as individuals would be ultimately protected by a secure, unconditional income. For Van Parijs, this would diminish the need for regulations 'such as restrictions on patterns of working time or even minimum wage legislation' (1992c: 232). In his economic analysis of a how a CBI scheme could serve to transform the nature of paid work, Purdy demonstrates how 'a BI system promotes the elusive double objective of reducing job time and redistributing waged labour' (1988: 223). Utilising indifference curve analysis, Purdy argues that the introduction of a CBI will alter the budget constraints faced by individuals and subsequently, assuming both the gross hourly wage rate and preferences between free time and income remain the same, they will now opt for shorter working hours. Purdy demonstrates that although this may lead to a welfare loss for some individual workers, it is not a necessary outcome when the overall impact on *household income* and attitudes to working time are considered. In arguing his case he differentiates between 'masculine' and 'feminine' preferences with regard to relative valuations of free time and income. Those workers illustrating 'feminine' preferences 'reveal a greater willingness to give up income in return for marginal gains of free time' (Purdy, 1988: 224). For these workers, the introduction of a CBI would create the same inducement to opt for shorter working hours as for the traditional 'masculine' defined category of workers. However as this 'feminine' group display different preferences they start from an equilibrium position where they:

> ...were overemployed: they experience the gain from shorter working hours as outweighing the loss from reduced income. Thus even if labour supply preferences are taken as given, BI may still yield static welfare gains by loosening institutional constraints on possible patterns of job time and enabling some workers to achieve a more preferred balance of their time – and income – budgets.
>
> (ibid.: 225)

Purdy adds weight to his analysis by indicating that preference orderings do not remain static and, in what he refers to as 'the transition from welfare state capitalism to basic income capitalism' it is highly likely that attitudes to working patterns will be affected by the transitional process:

> Before BI could be introduced, major changes in society's political and ideological balances would have to occur, and these would be consolidated and perhaps augmented once the new system was in place. As the work ethic retreated, "feminine" time values would gain ground over "masculine" priorities.
>
> (ibid.: 226)

Purdy, however, does point out that his case for a CBI, based on the potential such a package has for promoting shorter working hours and more jobs, depends on the gross hourly wage remaining unchanged. Reductions in the labour surplus combined with the temptation faced by workers to 'claw back' any income loss suffered as a result of reductions in working time will lead to an upward pressure on wages. For Purdy, three circumstances will enhance the risk of wage inflation (ibid.: 228). First, organised labour will find their bargaining position strengthened due to the overall increase in employment levels. Second, the introduction of a CBI will serve to restructure existing wage relationships by automatically favouring forms of 'toil reduction'. That is, in addition to promoting reductions in work time the existence of a CBI in a free market economy will result in situations where 'workers will tend to shun intrinsically unrewarding tasks, and seek out those with lower toil ratings' (ibid.: 236). Thus the CBI serves to distort equilibrium positions with regard to relative wages reflecting the relative disutilities of different jobs. In theory, wages will be forced upwards, but in the presence of segmented labour markets the converse may be true:

For it has to be remembered that the starting level of BI provides only the barest subsistence living: the purely material incentives to labour market activity remain strong. In addition the removal of the poverty, unemployment and idleness traps releases on to the market a fresh stream of workers whose endowments of skill, work experience and character are generally poor. If the labour market is segmented, and if entry into desirable, but inaccessible core jobs is denied, this increased supply of low quality labour flows into the periphery. There is, therefore, a risk that sectoral labour gluts will actually worsen pay and conditions in high toil jobs.

(ibid.: 237)

Third, due to the restructuring of existing tax and benefit transfers, necessitated by the introduction of a CBI, some individual workers may find that their actual net weekly income will fall. The likelihood of such is more probable in the case of 'higher paid, and in general better organised workers' (ibid.: 228). Thus the introduction of a CBI is directly associated with the risk of wage inflation and abating such a negative effect 'depends upon the willingness of organised workers to under-utilise their bargaining power in the interests of society as a whole' (ibid.: 229).

It is this very consideration that would explain reluctance on behalf of the trade union movement to embrace the CBI concept. That is, it serves to erode their respective bargaining power and transfers it directly to the individual. This is not to say that there is no longer a role, and indeed a very important one at that, for organised labour, but rather as Van Parijs states:

The sort of flexibility which modern technology increasingly requires could therefore acceptably be traded by the labour movement against the income security provided by basic income.

(1992c: 232)

Working conditions, health and safety practices and wage differentials remain on the agenda and the labour movement could readily afford to concentrate efforts in these areas as they would no longer have to expend resources fighting for their members' right to a minimum acceptable income. In arguing that basic social rights may be subsumed, and unjustifiably neglected, by the emphasis on income rights implied by a CBI, Deakin and Wilkinson draw attention to the importance of work-related rights:

Rights to work which are additional to the right to income involve the right to engage in productive work which improves the living standards of the community, and to have such work valued according to its worth. This raises a number of issues which have been highlighted by the European Community's Social Action initiatives – the widening of access to training and education, the right to a basic income within work through minimum wage and comparable worth legislation, the use of parental rights legislation to achieve a more even balance between the demands of paid work and non-wage caring, and the harmonisation of basic terms and conditions between the full time and "flexible" workforces.

(1992: 59)

Consideration of these factors demonstrates the continued and crucial role for organised labour in a CBI society and points to the benefits of viewing a CBI proposal as part of a package of social reform measures, rather than a policy to be implemented in isolation.

The second component (that is the reduction of conflict) of Van Parijs's argument regarding the economic value of the CBI is not as well documented and is more speculative in nature. The assignment of property rights in advanced capitalist economies is becoming increasingly difficult due to the 'spread of significant environmental externalities and the increase in the share of wealth held in the form of information, rather than material goods' (1992c: 232). The inability to rely on the market mechanism to ensure that the market price reflects the true value of a particular activity results in economic uncertainty and sharp conflicts of interest. If this trend is allowed to persist unregulated then economic chaos will ensue and the survival of market economies will be seriously questioned. For Van Parijs:

the only option open to forestall economically damaging chaos consists in reducing what is at stake in the market game – that is, in making an increasing part of material welfare depend on society's overall productivity, rather than on their individual contribution. A basic income is the most natural way of institutionalising this solution.

(ibid.: 233)

Although Van Parijs indicates in a foot note that he derives this argument mainly from a suggestion made to him by Samuel Bowles, the prominent US economist, it would appear that his line of reasoning resembles that of the some of the earlier supporters of minimum income guarantees: those who argued for social dividends, set at rates compatible with economic growth, and justified in terms of the dividend being a reflection of each individual's contribution to the national wealth.

The potential for increased flexibility and the ability to establish a direct economic link between individual welfare and the overall productivity of the economy provides a powerful rebuttal to the criticisms of a CBI based on the negative consequences of increasing MTRs. Considerations of economic efficiency have thus been redefined, taking into account the changing nature of capitalist societies. In adopting this panoramic approach a case could be made for the potential of a CBI to reduce the actual tax burden. A more flexible and less conflict-ridden market economy would be more readily equipped to efficiently deal with the demands of post-industrial development, and as such economic growth is a more likely case scenario than it is today. Output growth would increase the total income available from taxation, and hence the CBI could be financed with no changes in the overall tax rate.

The second marriage of justice and efficiency becomes a distinct possibility. However, Van Parijs, whilst providing the theoretical tools, does not imply, if his arguments are accepted, that the introduction of a CBI scheme will be secured. On the contrary, he argues that he has merely stated the case for a CBI within the traditional parameters of social policy evaluation, reworking these parameters to bring them up to date. Success will depend ultimately on political will. The confidence to implement such a radical reform can, Van Parijs believes, be gained with due regard to the economic advantages but this confidence 'is very sensitive to whether a basic income is perceived as a fair way of distributing part of the social product' (ibid.: 234). There is bound to be controversy surrounding the implementation of a policy which distributes income to individuals who are perceived to be making no contribution to the national product whatsoever. This is a crucial point and is the subject of many a discourse on what constitutes productive activity. Within this debate, the attraction to the CBI concept is evident and will be explored in the following section. However, in summing up, the contribution made by Van Parijs serves to illustrate that the tradition of attempting to justify social policy in terms of both ethical and economic value can be applied to the CBI policy proposal with positive results. He adds to his analysis though by explaining that the questions of justice and efficiency are inextricably linked when it comes to practical policy making.

The full employment fallacy: the reactive approach

> Apparently, the politico-economic system can live with mass unemployment, but it is rather more doubtful whether it can live with a social security crisis as well.
>
> (Standing, 1992: 55)

The explicit rejection of full employment and the adoption of economic policies aimed at promoting the micro-flexibility of the labour market has attracted many theorists to the CBI proposal, viewed as a mechanism of protecting individual income security in the midst of 'supply-side' economics (Standing, 1986, 1992, Gray, 1988; Deakin and Wilkinson, 1991; Meade, 1989, 1990; Manza, 1992; Block, 1990). In recent decades advances in technology and changes in consumption patterns have had quite significant effects on the level and quality of employment in all modern capitalist states. The notion of a 'post-industrial' society, emerging in the 1990s:

> portrays a new world where technicians, professionals, and managers predominate; where old-fashioned manual labour disappears; where consumers' appetites are driven towards services.
>
> (Esping-Andersen, 1991: 191)

In this new world, concern regarding the ability of the economy to adapt at a micro-level has resulted in a revival of economic doctrines devoted to improving the efficiency of individual markets. Whilst there is surplus labour in the traditional manufacturing sector, the demand for labour in the low-productivity service industries is increasing. These jobs, however, tend to be low paid with little in the way of employment rights. Rigidities existing within individual markets such as minimum wage legislation have been blamed for the failure in securing an aggregate equilibrium. The excess supply of labour in the declining trades has not been allowed to move freely into the newly expanding industries and hence emphasis has switched from aggregate demand to the supply side of the equation. Arguments favouring less government regulation in all areas of the economy and the supremacy of the free market have gained considerable ground, particularly in the US and Britain. The result is a range of policies aimed at promoting the flexibility of both labour supply and wages. However, as Standing indicates, the trend towards greater labour flexibility has in fact served to accentuate income inequality and labour market fragmentation (Standing, 1992: 54). The decline in manufacturing in recent decades has meant that not only have some individuals witnessed a marked reduction in demand for their services, but also efforts to retain income security for those still in work has often involved a trade-off between job security and pay rises. The limiting of the power of trade unions in the name of enhancing flexibility has served to further erode the employment rights of those already suffering from the adverse effects of market fluctuations. On the other hand, those believed to be benefiting from the shift in demand from manufactured goods to the services have been hindered both in terms of employment rights and income security as employment protection mechanisms disappear at precisely the same time as market forces place downward pressure on wage rates.

Hence, the free operation of the labour market, whilst providing income and job security for professionals and those with the skills appropriate to new technology, has resulted in increased experiences of joblessness and limited access to employment which is full time, regular, and which pays enough to achieve an acceptable standard of living for many individuals. The effects of such developments would not be quite so dramatic if existing systems of social security were not so heavily dependent upon the principles of full employment and social insurance:

The industrial proletariat were the backbone on which the social security system was erected, yet as industrial manual workers have been displaced from full-time jobs they have been most prone to labour-force marginalization and exposure to the 'unemployment trap'.

(Standing, 1992: 54)

Furthermore, as Deakin and Wilkinson argue:

With deregulation, the social insurance system has come under pressure from two directions: in the first place from legislation which has undermined the contributory principle; and in the second place, form the related decline in full-time, regular work, a phenomenon described by Mückenberger (1989) as the "erosion" of the standard employment relationship as the basis for wage regulation and social reproduction.

(1992: 52)

The fact that throughout Europe increasing numbers of individuals are dependent upon transfer payments, either as a sole source of income or as a means of raising their income from work, to a level deemed essential for economic survival, raises questions as to the efficiency of supply side policies when combined with an outdated system of social security. Bearing in mind the points made earlier regarding the emergence of the 'new poor' and the distinction made between exclusion and marginalisation when studying the causes of poverty it becomes clear that future anti-poverty measures must account for the inter-dependence of labour market policy and the benefit structure:

with chronic labour market surplus conditions and the spread of non-regular, non-full-time forms of employment, the contributions base has been eroded at the top (by undeclared income, by high-income earners taking pay in non-monetary terms, etc.) and at the bottom (by the loss of regular full time jobs etc.). Selective, means-tested benefits have created "poverty traps" and "unemployment traps" that have acted as disincentives to regular wage employment and contributed, almost certainly, to the growth of the "black economy" – which could be described as a perverse form of labour flexibility.

(Standing, 1992: 55)

The labour market can no longer be considered the primary source of welfare and likewise existing social security mechanisms are fundamentally flawed in that they operate as safety nets when income from work falls. Given this comment, any future reform must operate outwith the parameters of full-time paid work, supplemented by transfer payments when necessary, and rather must first redefine the relationship between social security and employment.

Acceptance of neo-classical arguments regarding the negative impact government intervention has on the operation of the labour market and the threat this entails for the future of the capitalist mode of production has been illustrated by the fervent drive to deregulate the economy. The answer to mass unemployment and resulting poverty rests within the framework of traditional micro-economic analysis. The primary rationale behind deregulation policy was to free up the workings of the market by purposefully removing any artificial obstacles:

> In practice, the fulfilment of this strategy has required the state to intervene to bring even greater coercion to bear upon the low paid and unemployed, in an attempt to make them subject to the "disciplines" of the labour market which the welfare state was said to have mitigated. In the process neo-liberal policies have in fact intensified some of the central weaknesses of the welfare state; the incomplete coverage of employment protection and social insurance legislation, and its gender bias; the over dependence on means-testing, resulting in intrusion by the state into the privacy and autonomy of benefit recipients; the inability of welfare regulation and the tax system to cope with deep structural inequalities and forms of social discrimination.
>
> (Deakin and Wilkinson, 1992: 56)

It would appear that the advances made in the immediate post-war years in terms of recognising the inter-relationship of social and economic policy were overlooked. Economic policy has since re-emerged as dominant over social policy. However, evidence exists which indicates that the free market does not operate as efficiently as traditional economists would lead us to believe, at least where the labour market is concerned. Therefore, prospects for reform involving the harmonisation of social policy with claims for economic efficiency, in particular a 'rejection of the disjunction between equity and efficiency which underlies deregulation policies' (Deakin and Wilkinson, 1992: 57), and reassessing the role of the state become more fashionable.

The recurring theme of separating income from work is to be found in the contemporary literature arguing for a CBI:

> if the labour market cannot generate income security, as presumed in the creation of the post war social consensus, then to allow the "labour market" to operate efficiently social policy should decouple income security from the labour market.
>
> (Standing, 1992: 57)

Standing is attracted to a CBI as it allows for genuine income security as a right of citizenship. He argues that the implementation of a CBI, which he likens to the 'social dividend' in that it represents a share of the national product, would encourage labour flexibility. Secure in the knowledge that an adequate income will be provided, individuals will be more willing to enter into co-operative, work and profit sharing ventures. This he argues could prove to be the basis of a new 'social consensus' in the making, in that income security is guaranteed whilst at the same time creating a favourable environment for wealth creation. Thus the basis for promoting a CBI rests on claims of promoting a more 'active society'. Although a decoupling of income from work is envisaged, citizenship rights remain inextricably linked to the traditional wage-employment relationship:

> the new argument for BI rests on its ability to better respond to and facilitate structural economic changes which have affected both the nature of work and the labour market within a social context in which (paid) work plays an increasingly important role in people's lives, individually and as members of society – as citizens.
>
> (Saunders, 1995a: 15)

The CBI therefore forms the basis of a new approach to labour market policy. If it is generally agreed that deregulation is insufficient to meet the demands imposed by modern labour market processes, an alternative approach would involve returning to the full employment model of the post-war consensus era. However:

> Within this model, social protection was linked to functions of *selection* and *integration* in the labour market; selection in the sense that only those (predominantly male) workers who satisfied the dual criteria of length and regularity of employment were protected against social and economic risks: and integration, in the sense that the standard model provided a set of hidden incentives or "constraints" to pursue continuous waged employment at the expense of (under-valued) non-waged work. Apparently full employment co-existed with deep segmentation of the labour market according to status, with particular reference to gender and marital status, age and race.
>
> (Deakin and Wilkinson, 1992: 57)

Furthermore, the scope of governments to engage in a macro-economic approach to managing employment levels has been diminished by the imposition of various external fiscal constraints, and even if this was not the case, it seems highly unlikely that such an approach would yield positive results due to structural change in labour markets. As Gray indicates:

Even to the extent that the state sector could expand, textile mill workers cannot necessarily become construction workers nor miners become nurses; there is a very real problem about re-training, gender bound occupational categories and geographical mobility.

(Gray, 1988: 122)

Gray, therefore, argues for work-sharing and in so doing advocates a form of CBI as a tool for ensuring income does not suffer drastically as a consequence of new working arrangements. Again calling for the 'need to break with the wage relation as the main source of income' (ibid.: 122).

Neo-liberal arguments regarding the role social security plays in distorting the operation of the labour market have found reasons to celebrate the CBI proposal (see for example Brittan, 1988; Brittan and Webb, 1990). Brittan states in the opening chapter to *Beyond the Welfare State: An Examination of Basic Incomes in a Market Economy* that the argument he makes, which is supported by Webb's statistical analysis, is essentially a 'pro-market and pro-capitalist' one (ibid.: 1). Concerns regarding the disincentive effects of current social security provision, increasing incidences of poverty and the mass unemployment evident since the 1980s are recurring themes which are voiced by Brittan in his attempt to illustrate the economic desirability of a CBI (1988, 1990). The need to re-examine the relationship between income and work is believed to be crucial to any discussion regarding the future direction of economic and social policy in all advanced capitalist countries. Brittan points out that so far, at least in the social security and income guarantee debate, little attention has been paid to the various sources of income other than that derived from wages and salaries:

In 1988 income derived from work, including self-employment and employers' contributions, accounted for 75 per cent of personal incomes. This still leaves a large remainder, of which 11 per cent was accounted for by rents, dividends and interest, i.e. property incomes, and 14 per cent by social security and related grants. Moreover there is very important income in kind from property, whether the value of owner occupied housing or the amenity value of land, as well as income from household and other unpaid work, not included in the personal income statistics.

(1990: 6)

Furthermore, concentration on supplementing income from work does not recognise the fact that in many instances poverty is indeed not caused by low pay. Reference is made to the fact that minimum wage measures, by way of being work related, merely serve to increase the income of the wage earner within a particular household and therefore do not address the composition of individual households and the consequent differing demands for economic resources (ibid.: 7).[4] The provision of a minimum guaranteed income independent of any work test provides the pro-marketeers with a policy instrument with which to separate pay from work and ensure that the market can operate unhindered by the necessity for jobs to provide at least sufficient income to meet individual needs. Put another way, the market clearing rate of pay may, in some cases, actually fall below what is considered essential for even the most minimalistic lifestyle. A CBI would allow workers the opportunity to 'price themselves into jobs' and 'such mass ownership would also make tolerable the distributional effects of the less drastic shift in the relative rewards of labour and capital', which is believed to be a necessary condition in the endeavour to restore full employment (ibid.: 5). The switch from contingent benefits to a CBI would result in a system that supplements the incomes of the working poor and the unemployed alike. Therefore, those who are currently marginalised in the trajectory of post-industrial employment will be able to take up offers of employment without losing benefits and subsequently being forced into abject poverty.

A CBI is justified in that it recognises the inefficiency of both the labour market and the social security system in securing incomes that are above the conventional minimum for large numbers of the populace. By removing the relationship between employment and income security, a CBI acts to provide room for activities essential to the survival of capitalism; such as engaging in low paid work, entering a retraining scheme or full-time education and engaging in ventures with no guarantee of immediate financial success. Brittan argues that:

> Classical economists who rightly argue for market rewards to factors of production usually fail to face the problems of those whose work has a low market value. The challenge for economic and social policy is to find a way of obtaining as much as we can of the benefits of an American-style labour market, without incurring the cost of American-style poverty. . . . The case for it (a basic income) is increased manifold by the practical need to find a way of re-establishing a fully functioning labour market with a market-clearing rate of pay, on a humane base which will improve the position of Rawls's "least advantaged representative person" rather than driving him or her to the wall.
>
> (Brittan, 1988: 301)

A further justification is that a CBI conforms to the ideology of the New Right in that it represents minimal state commitment to social welfare. There would no longer be the need for legislation determining minimum wage levels as the labour market would be allowed to operate freely and the administrative burden of current social security structures could be considerably reduced. Brittan and Webb find little to distinguish the CBI proposal from an NIT model, which is mainly due to their emphasis on markets and questions of efficiency. Arguing in a similar vein to Friedman, the authors illustrate their primary motivations for reform and their failure to consider issues of social justice. Minimum income guarantees are praised for their ability to guide the economy towards full employment and hence reinstate the traditional relationship between work and income. Although providing insight into the ability of a CBI to appeal to a diverse political audience, the limited analysis serves to present the concept in such a way that benefits to be achieved in terms of promoting individual autonomy are denied.

In conclusion then, the separation of income from work is an inherent feature of the arguments in support of a CBI discussed above. In this sense such a strategy can arguably be viewed as representing a radical approach to social security policy, but it is worthwhile noting that the separation envisaged is assumed to be a limited one. The aim is ultimately to provide individuals with an alternative source of income to paid employment. However, although this will serve to offset the damaging economic effects witnessed by the decline in traditional forms of employment, in terms of both equity and efficiency, an equally, if not more important purpose is to promote a wider range of options for forms of work (Deakin and Wilkinson, 1992: 58). Thus the emphasis is on addressing structural change in the labour market and the CBI proposal emerges as an appropriate policy tool.

Independence versus dependence: the radical approach

> The intriguing consequence of the basic income is that it would put the worker in the same position as the capitalist: it gives him/her independent means.
>
> (Walter, 1989: 108)

Given the 'new world' of post-industrial production and the resulting changes in patterns of employment it follows that systems of income distribution are radically altered from that which existed in the post-war era of mass production and mass consumption; with the returns to capital outweighing the returns to labour-owners of capital profit, at the expense of owners of labour. The gap between rich and poor widens to a point that threatens the very survival of the capitalist structure. Attempts to redesign modern capitalist societies in light of this change have followed two main courses of action (Jordan, 1986: 265). The first is that adopted by the social democratic governments of the industrial world. Efforts to sustain full employment and industrial production have been pursued with the traditional relationship between work and incomes in mind. Economic policy has largely been concerned with controlling wages (both in work and out of work), investment and prices so as to protect the real levels of income and investment from the effects of worldwide reductions in demand and increased competition from abroad. Social policy, on the other hand, has served to expand the state sector as an employer and provider of services in order to counteract the effects of tight monetary controls on private sector incomes and investment:

> Those societies in turn have experienced difficulties associated with the attempt to maintain full employment and industrial production, resulting in wasteful investment and declining productivity, falling rates of growth per capita disposable incomes, and in some cases (e.g. Poland) an actual fall in real standards of living.
>
> (ibid.: 265)

In terms of income distribution, then, as there is less to distribute, modern capitalist states slide further into recession and citizens suffer correspondingly from reduced access to economic resources. The second strategy has been to go down the market-oriented route. Prices and incomes would be determined by the unfettered operation of the free market wherever possible, whereas the public sector was characterised by low wages, minimal benefits and policies directed at promoting the work ethic and traditional 'family lifestyles'. The interaction of economic and social policy serves to contradict the overall goals of free market ideology in that low wages coupled with means-tested benefits erode work incentives whilst emphasis on the role of the family as a provider of welfare promotes private dependency rather than individual liberty. Distribution of national income remains highly unequal and in fact the growing divide is exacerbated by free market policies. For Jordan, neither system of distribution can claim to adequately secure individual freedom in an era witnessing significant changes in employment patterns and individual lifestyles. He is thus drawn to a CBI, arguing:

> that there is a third alternative to these two strategies, and one which could be tried under either major economic system. It rests on the notion of distributing the basic income which individuals need for subsistence, and a new definition of the rights and duties of citizenship. It thus transcends both the market and central planning as fundamental distributive principles, and substitutes a notion of individual autonomy, around which designs for both market-orientated and planned societies could be developed.
>
> (ibid.: 266)

Although Jordan is driven by the notion that post-industrial society will not provide sufficient jobs for those who want them and that flexibility in the labour market is paramount to the objective of economic efficiency, he views a CBI as a mechanism by which 'free and equal citizenship for all' can be secured (ibid.: 226). Free choice about whether to work or not would be granted to all citizens. More importantly, the provision of an independent income for all would allow for free and equal choices in terms of living arrangements and the division of domestic duties. A CBI would 'thus abolish both the dependence of women on men, and also the conditions surrounding dependence of citizens on the state' (ibid.: 226). Jordan reiterates the theme of economic efficiency combined with the rights of citizenship throughout his work when discussing the CBI proposal (1987, 1988). However he is not alone in his claims.

The prospects for a CBI to fulfil the dual objective of economic efficiency and the preservation of individual freedom in a rapidly changing socio-economic climate has been expressed by many social theorists in recent years (Galbraith, 1994; Purdy, 1988, 1989; Walter, 1989; Parker, 1993; Miller, 1983). Advocates of a CBI who stress the potential of unconditional, universal income guarantees in securing individual autonomy, raise not only the issue of crisis in current social security systems, but also the need to reconceptualise the relationship between individual and society to meet the demands of substantial social, political and economic change. Modern democratic states claim equal freedom for all citizens but such claims are open to criticism when many individuals are denied the economic means with which to enjoy their 'equal freedom'. Furthermore, the concentration on paid employment as the primary source of independent economic resources has led to policies aimed at promoting the right to work and subsequently has placed emphasis on the route to freedom being secured through formal labour markets. This has denied the right of citizens to determine and shape the course of their own lives particularly those normally occupied in unpaid activities. The welfare of vast numbers of citizens depends to a large extent on the care provided informally by relatives or friends within the domestic domain. Such caring activities are normally undertaken by women. By providing freedom from want for all citizens and further ensuring financial independence throughout the lifecycle, a CBI secures the equal freedom for all but also recognises unpaid caring work as economically valuable. This not only addresses the 'wages for housework' debate but more importantly provides all men and women with the financial independence crucial to the goal of promoting gender justice. The role of women and a CBI has been raised in the contemporary literature and attention drawn to the positive advantages in terms of recognising the duties and responsibilities of women as mothers, wives and carers (Parker, 1993; Miller, 1983; Walter, 1989; Jordan, 1988; Withorn, 1990). Thus, the CBI proposal has an important part to play in discussing a feminist critique of social policy. In particular, the disadvantaged position women currently experience in the labour market and in existing social security arrangements has provided the spur for renewed interested in the minimum income guarantee proposal.

However, the need to formulate social policy, which explicitly recognises the value of unpaid work, and provides for a more flexible approach to be taken towards participation in the labour market, can undoubtedly be perceived as representative of a continuum. That is, arguing for a CBI on the basis that it provides a framework for formally recognising non-waged work is reflective of a view that citizenship rights remain tied to participation in, rather than independence from, the labour market. For Shaver, the emphasis on participation in the reform process is indicative of 'social policy developments adapting citizenship to its post-industrial context' (1995: 8). Although the boundaries may be extended to include non-traditional forms of employment, such as unpaid caring or voluntary work, which are now recognised as important contributory factors in the promotion of social welfare, the obligations and rights of citizenship are still determined by individual demonstrations of productive capacity. An indication of the implicit focus on active participation is given when Chamberlayne talks of the Green/SDP response in Germany to the perceived crisis in welfare:

> In the Green/SDP debate it was argued that a generous social wage would promote flexibility and human creativity and further gender equality by providing a secure economic base for all, including home carers. It would facilitate the end of "work for work's sake" and "dead jobs", freeing more human resources for caring activities and linking citizenship with social usefulness rather than paid employment. Not that social usefulness would be a condition of the social wage; advocates of the social wage argued that it was "natural" to be socially useful, as was shown by the performance of housework by women, without the external discipline of the labour market.
>
> (Chamberlayne, 1992: 10)

Thus, social security policy in the post-industrial welfare state serves to promote a wider range of work options, and although explicit forms of conditionality may be removed, the basis of receipt does not represent a radical rethinking of the rights of citizenship. The implied notion that provision of income security is based on the 'natural' obligation of citizens to pursue 'socially useful activities' merely serves to transform the conditional basis of benefits from one based on paid employment to one based on *legitimate* participation.

Arguing for a CBI within this framework serves to detract from one of the principal defining features of the proposal, the notion of unconditionality, and fails to recognise the moral and ethical benefits to be gained from such a proposal in promoting real freedom of choice in how people live their lives. Whilst there are gains to be made in terms of social policy development by formally recognising the social welfare value of unpaid work, the practice of equating citizenship with participation is limiting in that:

(it) still defines worth through work. Citizenship is supposed to mean something more than this, to signal the social and moral equality of all persons as members of the social community. It is not meant to be conditional upon performance. Citizenship is meant to be more than simply welfare rights. It is also supposed to be a foundation for participation in democratic government, in parents' and citizens' associations, in local council affairs, in parliamentary politics and in social movements, including the women's and environmental movements.

(Shaver, 1995: 11)

Furthermore, as Shaver indicates, basing entitlement to income maintenance payments on 'participation, defined as work, whether for love or money, involves an intensification of social control exercised by the welfare state' (ibid.: 10). The practice of having to categorise and continually reassess those activities deemed to be 'socially useful' would bestow a great deal of power, not to mention administrative difficulties, on the state. It would also entail a degree of intrusion into the private lives of individuals for the purposes of determining eligibility thus acting to threaten the respective levels of personal autonomy individuals are able to exercise in their life choices. The CBI is cited precisely for its potential in minimising these factors. However, the contemporary debate has increasingly focused on the issue of participation, alongside questions concerning the actual levels of payment, for purposes of political expediency. Thus the radical nature of the policy becomes subsumed by the practice of appealing to the *rational* taxpayer.

Modified versions: the practical approach

As discussed earlier, the main objections to the CBI proposal are the prohibitive costs involved in implementing the scheme and the negative effects on work incentives within the traditional labour market. In an attempt to address these concerns supporters have advocated various modified schemes that incorporate either work tests or cost controls. It is argued that in the process of doing so the proposal becomes neither a 'citizens'' nor a 'basic' income and thus the focus on reform switches from a progressive radical approach to a conformist practical one.

After conducting extensive research into the costing of a full CBI scheme in Britain, Parker (1989) concluded that the costs involved were too expensive both politically and financially. Parker proceeded to cost a modified scheme which entailed a partial CBI (half the current IS rate) due unconditionally to each adult, supplemented with various income-tested benefits to provide for special needs and housing costs. Further envisaged in the Parker scheme is a reformed Social Fund which would pay grants instead of loans and would be viewed as a 'safety net of last resort' (Parker, 1994). For Parker, the only condition for receipt of the partial CBI would be legal residence but a work test would be incorporated into the scheme for housing benefit and the new Social Fund. The Parker proposal, therefore, in attempting to make a CBI more politically and financially feasible given the current political and economic climate, departs from the main advantages of a true CBI. The amount paid would have to be supplemented by means-tested benefits for the majority and receipt is not granted as of a right of citizenship due to the fact that a work test still prevails. Within such a scheme, complexity of administration, the stigmatisation of those in receipt of the necessary supplements, and an increasing reliance on mean-tested benefits could not be avoided, thus departing from the main advantages of a CBI.

Professor Tony Atkinson of the London School of Economics is an active supporter of a CBI scheme (Atkinson, 1989c; 1993c). However, like Parker, he too remains concerned about the cost and in particular the high tax rates required in financing a full CBI. In a paper jointly written with Holly Sutherland, Atkinson analysed the distributional consequences of the tax-benefit integration with a partial CBI (Atkinson and Sutherland, 1988). They conclude that the results from their analysis illustrate that a partial CBI could be introduced in Britain without having major distributional consequences. That is, there would be 'relatively few families who would experience a large gain or loss, and for a quarter there would be no change' (ibid.: 17). This is obviously an advantage for purposes of electoral support, given that appeal to as wide a base as possible is essential and wide-scale redistribution would lose many votes from the middle- and upper-income voters. Atkinson and Sutherland argue that a partial CBI:

> may be seen as a compromise solution or as the first stage along the route to a full basic income. The latter takes account of the important consideration, that, in terms of practical policy making, what is relevant is not just the destination of reform but the process of transition by which a full scheme could be approached.
>
> (ibid.: 7)

Atkinson and Sutherland therefore provide justification for a partial CBI in terms of a necessary precursor to a full CBI. In his later work Atkinson goes on to examine the unconditional nature of a CBI and the possibility of gaining political support for such a scheme given the institutionalisation of social insurance in Britain (Atkinson, 1993a, 1995a: ch 15). Atkinson maintains that the reason a full CBI has not yet been seriously considered by policy makers as a workable reform solution is due to the widespread public support for the existing system of social insurance, and the absence of any work test as a condition for receipt of a CBI. He goes on to draw comparisons with the political support gained in France for the *Revenue Minimum d'Insertion* (RMI). This scheme, intended as a form of safety net provision, involves targeting benefits to those claimants eligible and who enter into negotiation with the state in establishing a contract, which will ensure the claimant's obligation and efforts to re-enter the labour market (Whitton, 1993). For Atkinson, then, the necessary political support could be achieved by compromising on the issue of unconditional entitlement and by developing a two-tier system in the sense that the CBI would supplement rather than replace existing social insurance schemes. His proposed solution is a Participation Income that would replace means-tested social assistance. Payment would be dependent upon acknowledgement by the beneficiary that receipt bestows upon the individual a duty to make all possible efforts to contribute to the production of the nation's wealth. Atkinson does not limit the obligation to 'contribute to wealth creation' to paid work but rather speaks of a 'social contribution' (1993a). It is in this sense that he borrows from the Social Contract as proposed by Rhys Williams. However, as discussed earlier, the Social Contract gave way to the widely acclaimed Beveridge plan, which set the agenda for social security provision in post-war Britain. Atkinson may believe that his scheme would perhaps be more attractive in today's political climate and indeed he refers to the importance of continuity throughout Europe (ibid.). However, as Euzéby (1994) points out, the French experience with this form of contract has not been at all successful. For Euzéby, prevailing socio-economic conditions have rendered the RMI inefficient, in that the right to work can no longer be guaranteed in a labour market witnessing the growth of computerisation and the 'transfer of labour intensive activities overseas' (ibid.: 16).

Furthermore, Atkinson's proposed Participation Income is subject to similar criticisms to those identified above. That is, the scheme implies an administrative burden being imposed upon the state, and the operation of this represents a strong element of social control creeping back into the system. As previously indicated, one of the main purposes of a CBI is to avoid such characteristics of state income maintenance schemes. Therefore, viewing Atkinson's Participation Income as an acceptable route to a full CBI is problematic in that it represents a policy proposal which institutionalises some of the worst aspects of existing systems, particularly those with a gender bias. That is, the types of activities that would be subject to examination for purposes of determining their social usefulness, such as informal unpaid work, are primarily conducted by women (Jordan, 1988: 119; Hantrais and Letablier, 1996: 110–111; Lewenhak, 1992, Human Development Report, 1995; Lister, 1997: 130–133).

Anne Gray views her modified version of a full CBI, mentioned above, to be an appropriate mechanism for defending the introduction of 'workfare' and for securing an acceptable level of income for the majority in light of mass unemployment and the weakened power of the trade unions (Gray, 1988). The unconditional universal benefit (UUB) proposed by Gray is to be paid to each individual over the age of 16 'regardless of employment status or position within a household' at a rate sufficient to ensure that no individual is financially worse off than under existing income maintenance measures (ibid.: 130). In arguing for a UUB, Gray's analysis relies heavily on the potential of an increased monetary social wage to empower labour in the sense that low paid work could be more readily refused. However, she does make reference to the effects her proposal would have on the position of women in the household by stating that a 'UUB facilitates the re-appropriation of non-wage labour as useful time, in place of the wasted and stigmatised time of unemployment' (ibid.: 132). This valuable insight into how a CBI could serve to promote gender equality is disappointingly overlooked in the search for a model which would safeguard against unscrupulous employers taking advantage of the CBI to reduce wage levels. Gray advocates a gradual implementation process by introducing what she refers to as a Universal Hourly Benefit (UHB) (Gray, 1993). This benefit would represent a retainer in that a certain percentage of social security entitlement would not be lost when an individual took up employment and would be paid alongside wages. Gray argues that this amount could be increased over the years, eventually becoming a full CBI. The UHB, therefore, acts on the supply side by building 'incentives to seek high hourly wages into the income maintenance system, rather than accept low wages backed up by benefits' (ibid.: 15). This type of reasoning reflects an awareness of the dangers inherent with any form of state support which effectively subsidises low wages and hence draws upon the historical experience of schemes such as the Speenhamland system of poor relief. This is a crucial point when considering the actual operation of a CBI scheme. It demonstrates the need to view the reform process as encompassing a range of complementary measures, such as national minimum wage legislation, rather than accepting the CBI as an isolated tool for remedying all of the perceived problems of existing income maintenance schemes. However, Gray's arguments follow from an exclusive focus on the impact a CBI would have on the operation of traditional labour markets and as such represents a partial analysis.

The contributions to the contemporary debate made by Bill Jordan, a sociologist and long time advocate of the CBI proposal, are particularly enlightening for the purpose of this study in that he vocalises issues relating to gender and emphasises social citizenship rights (Jordan, 1986, 1987, 1998). However, in discussing the implementation of a CBI, he draws upon Hermione Parker's work in analysing the costs involved, and agrees with her conclusions. That is, he argues that the high tax rates required to finance a full CBI 'would not be considered a politically feasible level of taxation in a strongly liberal and market-orientated society like Britain' (Jordan, 1987: 163). He further points to the problem of predicting the effects on work incentives and the subsequent consequences for labour supply if a full CBI were to be implemented immediately (ibid.: 163). Jordan therefore supports Parker's compromise solution and

regards such as a 'practical proposal for transitional reform, which introduces a radical new principle but stays within the parameters of traditional
policy constraints' (ibid.: 164). He reiterates his position on transitional
schemes by referring to attempts that have been made to cost an adequate
CBI. In doing so he specifies the possible positive distributional aspects of
a transitional scheme:

> The most careful and responsible calculations have been made by
> Hermoine Parker and Holly Sutherland,[5] based on detailed study of
> household budgets and the real costs of various needs (unlike actual
> social welfare provision) and the attempt to minimise sudden gains
> and losses in a transitional period between the final provision of basic
> incomes and the present system. Parker and Sutherland aim to set out
> various options for transition to a basic income scheme that improve
> incentives for those at present excluded from labour markets, but do
> not leave individuals and households suddenly exposed to new risks,
> or significantly worse off than they are at present. Their proposals are
> broadly revenue-neutral in the short to medium term, though obvi-
> ously there are gainers (single-earner households with children, and
> women generally) and losers (mainly higher-income households, and
> men).... These distributive consequences stem from their assump-
> tions (for instance, about the need to retain a means-tested housing
> benefit as a residual feature of the system, for a small minority of
> households with low earnings and high housing costs) rather than
> from intrinsic features of the basic income principle itself.
>
> (Jordan, 1998: 179–181)

It would appear then that Jordan is advocating a process of reform which
would draw on variations of the CBI model in accordance with the relative
weightings attached to meeting the demands of different groups of
gainers or losers. The type of scheme introduced would therefore depend
upon how policy makers prioritise the distributional impact on taxpayers
and beneficiaries. However, the problems associated with means testing,
contingency-based entitlement and inadequate levels of benefit remain
inherent within such transitional schemes and as such the broader range
of benefits associated with a CBI model are not realised. For Jordan,
though, the plan offers real scope for moving towards a society in which
the social rights of citizenship could be granted to each individual and is
one that does not radically conflict with existing attitudes towards work
nor does it require a profound transformation of traditional economic
orthodoxies.

In considering the prospect of a CBI society, Jordan maintains that, as a
proposal for income maintenance reform, a CBI can be justified by
appealing to its capacity for promoting equal autonomy for all citizens.
Whether or not the policy is desirable when work incentives are con-

sidered is another question. In fact Jordan agrees with the criticism that a CBI, operating in isolation:

> ...cannot supply the motivating factors that would lead them [citizens] to do the work that is necessary for social reproduction, or provide them with the opportunities to contribute to the common good in the ways required for human flourishing.
>
> (1998: 181)

This does not imply a rejection of the CBI proposal. First, as a means of promoting distributional justice it is to be applauded, and as indicated, the implementation process can be designed to ensure flexibility in terms of redistributional impacts. Furthermore, any negative views expressed with regard to costs, framed in terms of the prohibitive burdens being imposed on the taxpayer, are based on restricted perceptions and thus prove misleading:

> The basic income is a pure transfer, and involves less expenditure of resources – staff time, buildings, material – than any other conceivable system of income transfers. It is not like a redistribution of goods and services, or a collective infrastuctural good. Hence it does not reduce the total volume of resources available for the production of goods and services, as taxes raised for those kinds of public expenditures, do.
>
> (ibid.: 179)

Second, although a CBI may not be a 'sufficient' condition for social justice, it is a 'necessary' one (ibid.: 181). In this sense Jordan appears to continue with the tradition of emphasising the operational effects on the labour market by arguing that complementary measures are needed to 'motivate active contribution and participation, and provide opportunities for fulfilling work.' (ibid.: 179). However, upon further reading of Jordan it is apparent that he adopts a much broader view of 'active contribution and participation' than that associated with the more traditional method of defining 'worth through work'. In developing his 'radical' agenda for a policy programme directed at addressing social exclusion, Jordan identifies the CBI as a crucial component. In doing so, Jordan stresses the relevance of economic activity in the 'social economy' and provides a valuable insight into how a CBI could form an integral part of localised economic regeneration strategies (ibid.: 181–188). It is with respect to this particular line of argument that Jordan's analysis proves conducive in developing a feminist economics perspective on the CBI concept, which is the subject of the following chapter.

Conclusion

The exploration of the literature contained within this chapter, and Chapter 6 has demonstrated the wide range of support voiced in favour of a CBI and the diverse range of perspectives employed in justifying the proposal. Whilst the aforementioned analysis should not be considered an exhaustive review of the existing literature, the main components of both historical and contemporary debates, focusing on a minimum income guarantee, have been discussed with a view to demonstrating the prevalence of a biased and limiting analytical framework. Whether the policy has been proposed as an alternative to existing strategies, or as a response to demands imposed by the onset of capitalist development or indeed, the future sustainability of capitalist structures given the dynamics of modern socioeconomic conditions, the case has been made that 'radicalism' has given way to 'reformism'. Furthermore, the concern for political acceptability and the tendency to operate within the limits of traditional models of full-time male waged labour, with the subsequent emphasis on the superiority of the labour market in providing welfare for the majority, has resulted in a situation whereby the real benefits of a CBI are being overlooked. It would appear that the current political and economic climate dictates a continued emphasis on reducing expenditure with a renewed commitment to enacting social security reforms that act to support contemporary labour market processes. This narrow approach to the reform agenda can only be assumed to bring with it more of the same rather than embracing a radical rethinking of income maintenance policy overall.

Purdy, in his 'radical approach to labour economics' provides a comprehensive account of the benefits to be gained from a CBI:

> Specifically basic income would help nudge society gently along four new evolutionary paths; 1) personal income would be decoupled from employment; 2) the total amount of time the collective labourer devotes to waged work would be reduced and redivided; 3) the economy would be re-organised around the concept of ecological sustainability; and 4) dependent and alienated forms of production and consumption would be phased out in favour of independent and emancipated patterns of working and living.
>
> (Purdy, 1988: 201)

Repeated reference to paths one and two are to be found in the existing literature and although path three is relegated to the periphery in terms of mainstream debates (Fitzpatrick, 1999: ch 9), increasing interest in environmental and green issues may serve to redress this imbalance. However, path four has not yet been fully appreciated and it is in this area that questions of gender inequality are most relevant. It follows then that for the debate to progress it is essential that these issues are explored.

8 Commodification versus non-commodification

A feminist economics perspective in support of a Citizens' Basic Income

Introduction

The preceding chapter provided evidence of how a CBI proposal has emerged in recent decades as a radical proposal for state welfare reform. However, despite the wide and varied base of support for the proposal, which has produced a range of convincing arguments in favour a CBI, to date no government has yet adopted it. The apparent lack of political will to implement a CBI has been considered against a background of 'crisis' in state welfare provision, in particular the perceived problems associated with the funding and operation of social security systems. Implementing a CBI entails radical reform of existing patterns of welfare delivery. The institutionalised relationship between work and welfare, upon which modern welfare states are premised, is brought into question. Thus, a central focus amongst the most prominent CBI theorists has been identified as a need to reassess the foundations of modern welfare capitalism in light of the apparent unsustainabilty of full employment. Evidence has been presented of the ineffectiveness of existing social security measures designed in accordance with the functioning of traditional labour markets. A CBI is proposed as a model for reform of income maintenance policy that effectively dissolves the formal relationship between work and income. Thus the model, it is claimed, provides policy makers with a tool to support contemporary labour market structures as well as fulfilling a necessary welfare function of the state. This crucial integration of economic and social policy is one of the main attractions of a CBI scheme leading advocates to commend it as a means of promoting both social justice and economic efficiency.

However, the tendency to emphasise the effects on labour markets following the introduction of a CBI, evident within the existing literature, is indicative of an androcentric bias. Although the role of women in society is central to social policy reform, the existing literature is disturbingly devoid of any comprehensive treatment of women. No genuine discussion has taken place regarding the valuing and nature of women's lives and work. It is argued that the neglect of this crucial aspect of the reform agenda follows from a tacit acceptance of the leverage of traditional economic practices in the research process. Social policy reform must take account of gender inequalities and not just those relating to the traditional labour market. However, as long as the principles associated with conventional economic theory dominate the method of approach, the nature of such inequalities will never be fully understood. The analytical framework must therefore be adapted to ensure that, rather than focusing on a predetermined set of issues, welfare reform debates are deemed to be more inclusive, in that all relevant issues are incorporated.

The purpose of this chapter, then, is to draw further attention to the bias inherent within the current debate and subsequently to develop a feminist economics perspective on the CBI proposal. It is argued that such a perspective makes a positive contribution to the literature and debates on a CBI in two ways. First, the case is made that issues of gender justice are subordinated to those concerning economic efficiency. Providing evidence of this fact serves to negate the arguments made thus far with regard to social citizenship rights and the CBI. That is, the process of prioritising efficiency goals, which are based on a particular concept of economic efficiency, leads to an exclusive notion of social citizenship rights. Within that context, arguing for a CBI on the grounds of its potential to promote social justice is misleading in that it is the citizenship rights of a specific category of individuals, those who are considered in terms of their quantifiable productive outputs, which are promoted. Second, in developing a feminist economics perspective, attention is drawn to the opportunity provided by a CBI to redefine work. It is argued that attempts to justify a state-supported unconditional minimum income guarantee can follow one of two possible routes. Paying people in exchange for *nothing* can be justified on the grounds that much economic activity remains invisible, and therefore what appears to be 'free-riding' may actually turn out to be examples of productive activity. Overcoming this problem normally involves assigning appropriate market values in cases where they are not immediately apparent. This can be referred to as the 'commodification' route, and much of the literature so far can be classified in terms of this approach. This further demonstrates the prevalence of an androcentric bias akin to that found in neo-classical economic theory. An alternative approach would be to justify the CBI as a mechanism for formally recognising those activities with a welfare-enhancing function, but which are not produced or consumed within a market-determined framework. Rather than attempting to indicate the worth of such activities by computing their respective market values, the practice associated with the application of mainstream economic analysis, this approach allows for the inclusion of all socially valuable activities without having to categorise them in terms of a work/non-work dichotomy. This route can be referred to as the 'non-commodification' route and it is claimed that it strengthens existing arguments in support of a CBI by allowing for a better understanding of the nature of women's lives and work.

In developing a 'non-commodification' argument in favour of a CBI scheme the purpose is not to engage in further debate on the possible advantages and disadvantages of the proposal as a tool for social security reform. The intention is rather to contribute to existing debates in a positive way by reconceptualising notions of work in modern capitalist societies and demonstrating how this could impact on gender roles within the economy. It is claimed that adopting this particular perspective facilitates a richer awareness of the potential a CBI has for promoting both economic efficiency and gender neutral social citizenship rights. Although economic considerations remain a crucial feature, by shifting the focus away from narrowly-defined concepts of efficiency, as defined by traditional economic theorising, a more realistic vision of the nature of economic and social interaction emerges. Furthermore, the role a CBI could play in 'nudging society gently along' Purdy's fourth evolutionary path is demonstrated in practical terms. That is, reforming state welfare systems in accordance with a CBI scheme creates a favourable environment for the future development and sustainability of 'independent and emancipated patterns of working and living'. This would have particular advantages for women and therefore a CBI is to be applauded for the contribution it makes in the promotion of gender equality. However, the creation of such an environment is also considered to be a crucial feature of effective strategies designed to combat the problem of social exclusion. It is therefore argued that a CBI scheme presents as a welfare reform strategy that is appropriate in addressing a range of modern social problems. Thus, the insights to be gained from developing a feminist economics perspective, in the study of the CBI proposal, serve to reinforce existing supporting arguments.

This chapter will begin by setting out a feminist perspective on the relationship between work and income in societies where production and consumption exchanges are predominately determined by market-based structures. Attention will be drawn to the nature of 'work' in such societies and how, traditionally, there has been a tendency to attach 'value' to those activities demonstrating a productive and tangible output. Subsequently, activities producing output that is not easily measurable are assigned a lesser value. Categorising work in this way leads indirectly to gender inequalities in that much of the work women perform falls within the 'lesser value' category. This will lead to discussion focusing on the nature of women's lives and work and the structures of constraint that serve to inform their choices. A further section will outline, in practical policy terms, drawing upon an exemplary local economic regeneration strategy, how current restrictive definitions of 'work' could be broadened to include a wider range of activities. It will be argued that the Intermediate Labour Market (ILM) model presents an opportunity to engage in debate on the reconceptualisation of work in modern capitalist society. A further section will link the experience of the ILM model in operation with the

CBI proposal, claiming that a common framework can be identified for separating work from income. That is, the ILM model could serve as a mechanism for supporting the case made for a CBI in that it provides real evidence of the economic and social value of work undertaken outside the confines of traditional market-based exchanges. Thus, there exists a practical strategy that demonstrates the relevance of the non-commodification route in tackling the problem of social exclusion. However, a final section will indicate that, similar to the debate focusing on the CBI proposal, the ILM model has been subsumed by an approach which emphasises the formal labour market. That is, the ILM model has been viewed first and foremost as an active labour market strategy rather than a radical approach to local economic regeneration. The conclusion will be drawn that the separation of income from work envisaged within the literature on both CBI and the ILM model is a temporary one, and thus the full advantages to be gained from either strategy in promoting gender justice are not realised.

Reconceptualising work and income: a feminist perspective

Conceptually, work is usually distinguished from leisure. The implication is that the cost of time spent engaging in activities clearly defined as work can be measured in terms of the associated sacrifice of leisure time. This is not to say that all of those activities we deem enjoyable are categorised as leisure, and activities involving pain, toil or a sacrifice of enjoyment as work. Work may be something we enjoy but it is distinct from leisure in that it is not done solely for its own sake but must also be purposeful. Any activity which displays 'the characteristic of using up time and energy for an extrinsic purpose' can be defined as work, in that desirable end results are created through a process of working which involves an opportunity cost of lost leisure time (Himmelweit, 1995: 3). These end results are not only produced for the enjoyment or satisfaction of the individual carrying out the activity but also have a use value which can be shared by others. It is therefore the productive, purposeful aspect of any activity that defines it as work.

For André Gorz, conceptualising work in this way is a feature of modern industrial capitalism:

> So long as commodity production remained marginal and the great majority of needs were covered by domestic production and the village economy, the notion of "work" as such ... could not take hold. People "produced", "constructed" and "prepared" things; they "laboured", "toiled", "drudged" and "attended to" a wide variety of specific "occupations" which had no common measure between them within the framework of the domestic community. And responsibility for the various *activities* was assumed by the husband, the wife, the

children or the older members of the family according to an immutable division of labour. These activities were gendered ... and thus there was no common denominator between them. They were not interchangeable, and could not be compared and evaluated in terms of a single yardstick. The term "work" referred not to a creative or productive act but to the activity in so far as it entailed pain, annoyance and fatigue.

(1994: 53)

The dominance of commodity production and consumption over subsistence production brought about by the development of capitalist modes of production results in the depersonalisation of work activities. This leads Gorz to assert that the modern notion of work refers to:

the name of an activity fundamentally different from the activities of subsistence, reproduction, maintenance and care performed within the household. This is not so much because "work" is a paid activity, but because it is done in the public domain and appears there as a *measurable, exchangeable and interchangeable performance*, as a performance which possesses a use-value for others, not simply for the members of the household community carrying it out; *for others in general*, without distinction or restriction, not for a particular, private person.

(ibid.: 53)

This socialisation of productive activities means that the worker becomes separable from the resulting output. Producing goods and services for exchange in the public domain renders the direct relationship between the person carrying out the task and the actual output irrelevant. Activities are interchangeable between workers, and outputs become measurable in terms of their use value to others. In modern terms, the concept of work is associated with any impersonal activity which results in output that can be measured and presented as a commodity for sale or exchange in an impersonal public market place.

Many of the activities frequently performed by women are 'invisible', in the sense that there is no tangible output. Consequently, these activities do not meet the criteria which would allow them to be labelled 'work'. Although much progress has been made in the valuing of domestic work which subsequently illustrates the significance of women's productive contribution to the economy (see for example, the Human Development Report published for the United Nations Development Programme, 1995) little has been done to quantify 'provisioning' functions within the family. Many non-physical exchanges or services performed in the household contribute positively to individual welfare. Examples include the transfer of knowledge or skills; providing a safe and loving environment; expressing and acting on concern for the health and emotional needs of family members, and organising the distribution and allocation of resources within the family unit. Many of these activities are essential for human survival, particularly when considering the care of children (Nelson, 1993: 32). Non-material sources of human satisfaction influence intra-family power structures and directly impact on the economic position of women. The fact that they remain in the periphery of the economics discipline is possibly because quantifying them would be a technically difficult thing to do. However, it is more likely due to the fact that such activities are not viewed as 'important' simply because they are performed by women:

> Humans are born of women, nurtured and cared for as dependent children, socialised into family and community groups, and are perpetually dependent on nourishment and shelter to sustain their lives. These aspects of human life, whose neglect is often justified by the argument that they are unimportant or intellectually uninteresting or merely "natural", are, not just coincidentally, the areas of life thought of as "women's work".
>
> (Nelson, 1996: 31)

The 'provisioning' aspects of human life that Nelson talks of are fundamental in influencing the behaviour of women. Furthermore, the dichotomy of work/non-work has had detrimental effects on inequalities within households.

Market-based economies have an inherent tendency to value productive activities by the notion of opportunity cost. The increased participation of women in the formal labour market has resulted in attempts to measure lost production in the home in terms of the equivalent market wage and vice versa. The process of commodifying domestic work has resulted in the production of substitute goods, which can be purchased in the market place. This can be achieved with relative ease when the producer and consumer are impersonal agents, performing their respective roles separately and autonomously. The same can not be said about provisioning activities. This fact is further demonstrated when considering the needs that are satisfied by work/non-work activities:

> As marketed substitutes become available for more and more of those domestic activities that count as "work", the apparent importance of the needs they satisfy increase relative to those remaining needs which are not perceived to be so readily met by the market. These tend to be the needs whose satisfaction requires activities which are inseparable from the person performing them, including caring and self-fulfilling activities. These are the needs that remain invisible, of apparent marginal significance to the economy, and thus their importance to the actors within it easily ignored.
>
> (Himmelweit, 1995: 10)

The redistribution of work from the domestic realm to the market has indirectly resulted in the devaluing of the time and efforts women spend fulfilling both their own and others' affiliation needs, that is, 'the need of human beings to belong and to be loved' (Nelson, 1996: 73). Individual needs and desires are therefore socially constructed via the process of commodification. The principles of production and consumption dominate, and those activities which do not fit neatly into the model become undervalued by society in general. Individuals who exhibit a preference for pursuing non-marketable provisioning activities are labelled as non-workers or 'idlers' suffering from the negative connotations this implies. A witty but illustrative retort would draw upon the old adage 'relationships are hard work'!

As Nelson suggests in her observations on the provisioning aspects of human life, quoted above, it is clear that the undervaluing of 'un-commodifiable' needs does not render them less important in terms of their contribution to individual welfare. However in a male-work-dominated society women continue to shoulder a disproportionate share of these 'non-work' activities and the process of commodification has undermined their position. The choices that women make are influenced by this process and hence the preference is to perform 'work' that is socially valued. This social construction of needs has obvious consequences in terms of the sharing of domestic responsibilities between men and women. Policies aimed at promoting equal sharing, which ignore the social constraints imposed on choice, will ultimately fail.

A CBI scheme that incorporates the recognition of equal rights of citizenship has the potential to re-orientate socially constructed preferences. This potential, however, will remain concealed unless the scheme is accompanied by a reconceptualisation of work and a better understanding of the sexual division of labour in determining the distribution of family duties. Insights can be gained from the current work of feminist economists to incorporate theories of the social construction of gender into their, traditionally male-dominated and defined, discipline:

> Feminist theory suggests that the definition focusing on choice, which looks at human decisions as radically separated from physical and social constraints, and the definition stressing material well-being, which ignores non-physical sources of satisfaction, are not the only alternatives. What is needed is a definition of economics that considers humans in relation to the world.
>
> (Nelson, 1993: 32)

By considering humans in relation to the world and not just the world of work, gender-specific constraints that inform and influence choice can be identified. The tendency to polarise the analysis between work and 'non-work' results in a failure to fully understand and recognise the contributions women make to family life.

Nancy Folbre, a prominent feminist economist, defines constraint as the 'assets, rules, norms and preference that delimit what people want and how they can go about getting what they want' (1994: 54). She goes further to explain that distinctive sets of constraints can help shape collective identities and subsequent collective action. Women, a group defined by gender:

> ...have some similar assets (their reproductive and sexual endowments), are subject to similar rules (many rights and responsibilities are gender specific), are governed by similar norms (such as ideals of femininity), and express some similar preferences (such as enjoyment of caring relationships).
>
> (ibid.: 55)

This is not to say that all women share these similarities. The point Folbre makes is that socially constructed collective structures of constraint fosters 'group identity and creates common group interests' which in turn provide natural allegiances conducive to powerful forms of collective action (ibid.: 57–58). All four categories of constraint work together to form this collective action. Therefore, the removal of one would not necessarily eliminate the constraints imposed by the others on a particular group. Granting a CBI to men and women effectively removes basic economic constraints. However, to assume that the removal of asset constraints would result in equal outcomes ignores the influence of rules, norms and preferences in the processes of co-operation and conflict between genders.

The emphasis on viewing a CBI as a tool for supporting more flexible forms of working implicitly encourages women to enter the realm of paid work. Constraints on choice in this area are effectively removed by providing independent income security. As women gain in terms of rights and increasingly enter the labour market, their jobs become an important source of identity. Furthermore, the continual process of substituting unpaid work, normally performed by women in the home, with goods and services which can now be purchased externally suggests that cultural identifications associated with family labour diminish in importance. The existence in the market place of relatively cheap substitute goods, produced and consumed impersonally, further devalues the work that women continue to do within the family. All of this assumes that women have suddenly switched from a preference for affiliation, that is, the need to be part of a collective loving family unit and to take on all of the rights and obligations that entails, to one for promoting their own autonomous self-interested needs. This begs the question of who now should shoulder the responsibilities of caring for children and families?

Much research (e.g. reviewed in Bergman, 1986) suggests the stylized fact that wives' increased agency has been permitted, not so much by husbands taking on affiliative work, but by decreases in wives standards of living, particularly in regard to time for rest and recreation.

(Nelson, 1996: 74)

If work is associated with productive outputs then surely affiliative work is productive, measurable by the positive contributions it makes to individual welfare. However the personal nature of such activities renders them difficult if not impossible to measure. If such activities are continually devalued within market-based economies it is unrealistic to assume that by removing or altering one aspect of the social constraints imposed upon women, that is access to economic resources, the result will automatically be equal sharing between men and women of affiliative work. Individual preferences within market-based economies will be influenced directly by the value attached to activities producing identifiable and exchangeable output. Individuals may therefore demonstrate a preference for 'valued work' over 'non-work' activities. There is therefore no reason to assume that men will alter their preferences and whilst women may be influenced to pursue 'socially valued' activities there is no reason to assume that they will do so at the expense of sacrificing their existing preference for affiliation. Men will continue to engage in 'valued work' and women will now engage in both work and 'non-work' activities. The tendency to commodify and subsequently value all human activity results in unduly restrictive social citizenship rights, particularly those related to income security. Thus policies aiming to achieve gender equality must take account of gender-based social structures of constraint and explicitly recognise the positive welfare contribution of 'non-work' activities. The question remaining is how can this technically be achieved?

A possible solution: intermediate labour markets

Attempts to resolve this question may benefit from examining a particular local economic development strategy, the 'intermediate labour market' model. The creation of ILM programmes provides useful insights into the value of 'non-work' activities in sustaining local economies. Broadly defined, these programmes provide temporary jobs, offering a combination of training and employment, for long-term unemployed people. Participants are remunerated at a level between state benefits and the current market-determined rate for the job. The main purpose of such programmes is to combat social exclusion by providing the long-term unemployed with a link to the formal labour market. However, an equal emphasis is placed on the nature of the work. It is this aspect of the ILM model that proves interesting in developing a gender sensitive case for a CBI, in that it provides a framework for reconceptualising work.

Within the ILM model, the product of the work undertaken must have 'either a direct social purpose or is trading for a social purpose where that work or trading would not normally be undertaken' (Finn, 1996: 25). ILMs are related to the notion of a 'social economy' by attempting to:

> build capacity and stimulate the activities of not for profit organisations (community businesses; voluntary organisations; co-ops; friendly societies) to help them identify and organise jobs with a social purpose as well as develop new markets in which the private sector would not invest.
>
> (ibid.: 26)

Local economic activity which is organised around principles of community ownership and control; production and exchange for social gain; and the promotion of social entrepreneurship, is an important, if not the main, source of job creation in deprived neighbourhoods. Defining such activity as part of a 'social economy' takes account of the fact that the economic relationships evolving in this sector are very different in nature from those which exist in the mainstream economy. It follows that the nature of work in the social economy is distinct from traditional employment patterns as it is organised and structured within a different economic system:

> Work within the social economy is varied and should not be idealised, but can serve to illustrate work for a social gain, through more inclusive and participative models of organisation, greater recognition of the contribution of volunteering, explicit value-led motivation, and beneficial social or environmental impact.
>
> (Mayo, 1996: 151)

The distinguishing features of work created and organised at a local level, in communities where the market economy has failed to produce sufficient jobs, are made explicit within the ILM model. ILMs should therefore not be confused with compulsory 'work-fare' programmes where participants are required to work for their benefits. Although entry into employment is a desired end result, equal emphasis is placed on creating quality jobs, which promote self-reliance and have a community-based function. The ILM is primarily a model for encouraging local economic activity and contributing to the urban regeneration process. Furthermore, it is a model which demonstrates the personal and social benefits to be derived from alternative ways of organising and doing work.

The principle of ILMs has been put into practice by the Wise Group of companies in Glasgow, a city in Scotland recognised by European funding bodies as experiencing widespread areas of multiple urban deprivation, and more recently the 'Glasgow Works' programme. Both organisations, through a series of local partnerships and the creative use of existing resources, have acted to promote and support job creation projects which meet community needs (Finn, 1996: 25). The Wise Group initially provided training and employment for unemployed people in insulating the homes of elderly, disabled and low-income households within Glasgow. Projects now include local environmental improvements, the provision of energy conservation advice and the installation of home security devices. Glasgow Works, a pilot scheme, which builds on the ILM model, supports a number of projects which have been identified as significant in improving the quality of life in Glasgow. Projects supported fall within the following broad themes:

> working in a beautiful city; growing up in safety – "a child friendly city"; health and well being – "promoting healthy lifestyles"; and culture and heritage – "a City with a great past and a great future".
>
> (ibid.: 31)

Many of the project activities are non-marketable, mainly because people are too poor to pay for them, and can be categorised within the provisioning functions, discussed above, primarily undertaken by women in the household economy. Examples include the provision of after-school childcare; the employment of community health workers to advise on diet and fitness; and a theatre group developing productions for schools on young peoples issues, such as sex education and drugs.

The experience of these projects indicates that goods and services previously provided in the 'invisible' household or community economy are crucial elements in the urban regeneration process. Many 'non-work' activities, not normally associated with monetary gain, can be identified as fundamental ingredients in the daily functioning of local economies. The motivation to engage in these activities must therefore be driven by considerations other than financial reward. In this instance Folbre's argument, detailed above, regarding the role played by distinctive sets of constraints in determining collective identities and collective action, are pertinent. Individuals, or groups of individuals, living in areas deprived of economic resources experience a set of common constraints which are determined by the environment in which they live. Communities where most, if not all, individuals are experiencing poverty can become united by a sense of shared deprivation. This is particularly the case if that poverty has been the result of a common experience such as the closure of a factory, coal mine or steel works which represents the removal of the major employer in the area. When the economic base of a community is dominated by a particular industrial production process, residents sharing daily work and life experiences, which are similar, become bound by a common 'occupational culture'. This common culture in turn forms the basis for collective identities. The removal of that economic base does not necessarily imply that collective identities are also removed. Rather, it can be argued that the structural unemployment associated with the demise of traditional industries, occurring in concentrated local areas, can reinforce the collective identities experienced by individuals residing in those areas. Similar to the case made by Folbre about women, these individuals find themselves governed by a set of similar assets (limited economic resources and employment opportunities); rules (the rights and responsibilities associated with the traditional 'male bread-winner model' of family forms); norms (ideals of community and working class 'solidarity') and preferences (the enjoyment of 'belonging' to an area with a shared cultural heritage) which 'delimits' what they want and influences how they go about getting what they want. As previously argued, these socially-constructed collective structures of constraint promote common group interests which in turn form the basis for collective action. Many 'non-work' activities may therefore be the result of this collective action in operation.

What the ILM model does then is provide a valuable insight into the role played by community and family relationships in sustaining the welfare of individuals living in areas deprived of economic resources. Shared experience as members of a community leads people to engage in activities which are certainly productive, even though their output is not easy to measure, and which offer rewards not associated with traditional forms of work and pay. The ILM framework provides a basis for formally recognising these activities and taking account of the contribution they make in promoting economic and social welfare. It therefore proves a useful tool in developing a more inclusive definition of work that includes voluntary and community-based activities. It is for this reason that the ILM model supports the case for a CBI. Linking arguments for a CBI with the experience of ILMs could be a mechanism for curbing the tendency to commodify wherever possible. However, in practice this has not been the case in that the focus has been on assigning 'non-work' activities with market values.

Work and income separated: a reprieve?

The process of commodifying 'non-work' activities means transforming these functions into activities which are directly associated with the receipt of payment, commensurate with the task undertaken. These activities then become a 'means to an end' rather than being undertaken for the utility value to be derived from performing the activity itself. The values attached to 'non-work' activities are now determined by the amount of spending power allowed by the rate of payment. By re-emphasising the value of paid work, the commodification process means that the receipt and spending of money becomes the prominent factor informing daily activities. This effectively serves to transform social relations in communities where prolonged periods of limited access to the formal labour market has led to the emergence of alternative patterns of production, consumption, and distribution. The balance between different modes of production and distribution is tipped in favour of the traditional work-and-pay relationship. Thus the focus switches from issues of promoting a sense of belonging, caring, and collective responsibility, to issues of market-based values and transactions in the resource allocation process. Commodification, therefore, forces alternative forms of social formation into an inferior position relative to modern capitalist relationships. This is similar to the processes inherent within neo-classical economic theory. That is, the practice of analysing, and understanding, issues is primarily determined by a process of exploring how they are located within the dominant theoretical framework. If necessary, the analytical process then evolves to ensure that that this direct link can be made. The Glasgow experience with the ILM model has illustrated that this would appear to be the desired result, in that the focus is on formalising 'non-work' activities within a traditional labour market framework.

The Glasgow ILM model was analysed by the Commission on Social Justice (CSJ), the independent review body set up by the British Labour Party in 1992, referred to in Chapter 7. The overall task of the Commission was to examine the dynamics of socio-economic relationships in Britain in an attempt to develop a package of public policy reforms which would 'enable every individual to live free from want and to enjoy the fullest possible social and economic opportunities' (Commission on Social Justice, 1994: 412). The CSJ reported that the Government should actively encourage the development of ILMs in areas of urban deprivation as part of a 'new strategy to help the long-term unemployed *earn* their way out of poverty' (ibid.: 172). For the CSJ, the ILM model is first and foremost an active labour market measure, which effectively provides a stepping stone to the formal labour market for unemployed people living in areas with very few jobs. However, the CSJ also reported that organisations like the Wise Group can:

> overcome a real market failure where the private sector cannot translate needs into economic demand or where potential customers simply cannot afford to pay for private services.

> (ibid.: 179)

Therefore, ILMs provide 'enormous potential for the creation of *new* markets in which social economy organisations are the main participants' (Op. cit.). The emphasis is on encouraging market-based transactions for previously non-marketed goods and services. This will provide direct access to paid work in disadvantaged areas and indirectly contribute to a 'multiplier' effect by increasing the spending power of previously unemployed people. The process of commodifying and imposing market values on 'non-work' activities continues. With regard to the ILM experience, the bias in favour of commodification also serves the purpose of ensuring that the formal labour market and paid work command supreme, and indeed almost exclusive, positions within the urban regeneration process.

A similar process of privileging paid work has taken place within the current confines of the CBI debate. Paid work remains the prominent source of income for most individuals in a market economy. Income is derived either directly from employment or indirectly from state welfare payments representing compensation for loss of income via the formal labour market. As discussed in earlier chapters, contemporary social security schemes have been designed with the primary purpose of supporting the labour market by remedying market failure. The analysis of formal labour market processes is therefore essential to any debate centred on social security reform. However, radical shifts in socio-economic conditions call for radical redirections in policy. The dynamics of modern labour markets have served to limit the effectiveness of benefit structures that act to support, and indeed encourage, paid work.

The success of employment strategies based on a policy goal of full employment, or rather the goal of ensuring equal rights for every citizen to a meaningful 'paid' job, will largely depend on the degree of control national governments can demonstrate in managing the macro-economy. The process of economic globalisation has curtailed this level of control. Combating unemployment requires a rethinking of policies premised on the traditional model of market-determined work-and-pay arrangements and a belief in the positive relationship between economic growth and employment. Attempts to transform social and economic relationships in deprived neighbourhoods by imposing a set of market-based values on those relationships effectively serves to privilege the worker with a 'job' over the unpaid worker. Regeneration strategies which emphasise the benefits of employment fail to take account of the social benefits to be derived from community-based initiatives which promote both alternative approaches to work, and alternative mechanisms for rewarding socially valued activities. Rather than acting exclusively as a prescription for remedying particular market failures, policy should be directed at supporting and promoting a diverse range of community-based economic activities which could operate alongside traditional employment arrangements. An opportunity exists to reconceptualise work in view of modern socio-economic conditions. A CBI is a radical policy option in that it provides the framework to do so by challenging the traditional relationship between work and income.

Work and income: a possible divorce?

A CBI would effectively displace the economic necessity to enter into employment for many individuals. The question of work incentives has therefore been a central focus amongst CBI theorists. However, the debate thus far can be criticised for remaining firmly grounded within a traditional productivist model. Although within the existing CBI literature reference is frequently made to the potential the policy has for separating work from income, the implication is that such a separation is partial or indeed temporary (Van Parijs, 1996: 64). As indicated in Chapter 5, to justify a CBI solely or mainly by reference to the need for a flexible labour market is to ignore or discount the characteristic social experience of women. The introduction of a CBI may or may not improve work incentives but this issue becomes less crucial in attempts to justify the policy if the focus was switched to issues of recognising and valuing 'non-work' activities.

In addressing the criticisms of a CBI for exacerbating the 'free-rider' problem, attempts have been made to justify the policy by recognising the value of productive leisure activities:

> a society in which those living quietly on their citizen's income included not only those who would find it difficult to get a paid job, but also a lot of people who have the ability to get such a job but choose not to – the budding poet, the passionate bonsai-grower, the hyper-political activist.
>
> (Dore, 1996: 62)

Such arguments draw attention to the implicit distinction drawn between 'idleness' and leisure in modern capitalist society. The activities Dore mentions can be classed as leisure activities in that they are not paid and it is assumed that those engaging in such activities do so because they derive enjoyment from the activity. However such activities are also productive, both for those who perform them and for the wider community. They are not undertaken for pecuniary gain, but they nevertheless contribute to individual and social well-being. The point is that leisure activities themselves have been categorised to 'fit' with the modern notion of 'work':

> One can be said to be working in a garden or on a piece of knitting or on a painting or perhaps even on a stamp-collection or an ant farm. But we can almost never work at taking a stroll or carousing with friends in a bar (as Oscar Wilde observed, "Work is the curse of the drinking classes"). American society has perhaps internalised the productivist ethic of political economy more fully than any other, and hence to the extent that these latter activities are describable as exercises in idleness, they are more or less deplored.
>
> (Gagnier and Dupré, 1995: 106–107)

Personal leisure activities which are not related to others and display a tangible output are being 'socially valued' in the same way as paid work. Whilst a separation is made between income and traditional employment, justifying a CBI within this framework serves to reinforce the notion that all sources of income derive from engaging in 'productive' activities. Idleness per se is condemned and it would prove extremely difficult to justify any policy that promoted idleness given the importance modern society attaches to the 'work ethic'. Thus, the influence of neo-classical economic analysis in the research process is further demonstrated in that leisure activities are considered in terms of their possible economic value and thus are understood with reference to how they 'fit' within a model of market-based exchange.

Furthermore, the gender bias, indicated by the focus on paid employment with reference to the 'free-riding' argument, is very clearly demonstrated by Carole Pateman who draws attention to 'massive free-riding in the household – by husbands' (2004: 99). As Pateman so cogently argues:

> The private and public sexual division of labor,... continues to be structured so that men monopolize full-time, higher paying and more prestigious paid employment, and wives do a disproportionate share of unpaid work in the home. Given the structure of institutions and social beliefs, this appears as a "rational" arrangement. The mutual reinforcement of marriage and employment explains why husbands can take advantage of the unpaid work of wives and avoid doing their fair share of the caring work.
>
> (Op. cit.)

Thus, men, as husbands, can be viewed as guilty of 'free-riding' on a regular and sustainable basis. This however goes unrecognised in contemporary discussions of a CBI 'because marriage and the household rarely enter the argument' (Op. cit.). For Patemen this is the direct result of a continued adherence to mainstream economic theorising:

> The narrow parameters of discussion and the influence of the assumptions of neo-classical economics preclude attention to institutional structures and their inter-relationships. Van Parijs is an exception in recognizing that a problem of free-riding exists in households, but his neo-classical theoretical apparatus leaves him unable to acknowledge that the problem is one of men (husbands) and the work of caring for household members. ... His theoretical approach in *Real Freedom for All* precludes analysis of the structure of relations between the sexes, and a crucial area of debate is, therefore, removed from the discussion of basic income.
>
> (Op. cit.)

Thus, addressing the 'free-rider' argument by justifying a CBI as recognition of 'socially valued' activities is limited in the sense that many activities normally performed by women are invisible. Furthermore, the continued emphasis on commodification and computing market values for many 'non-work' activities serves to inform future income maintenance policy within the traditional confines of work and pay. For policy to address gender bias inherent within current income maintenance mechanisms it is essential that the rationale for implementation divorces itself from the polarisation of work/non-work activities. Any future social policy reform that accepts and recognises the worth of those invisible activities predominantly performed by women, without requiring the formal measurement of outcomes, will facilitate a gender neutral conception of citizenship.

Conclusion

It has long been recognised that the source of independent income in a market economy is an important if not crucial role of the formal labour market. The continued reliance on paid employment as the predominant source of individual welfare narrows the range of policy options and produces restrictive definitions of justice and efficiency. State-supported income maintenance schemes are based upon a framework of rewards and punishments and carry an obligation to work, or at least to engage in, activities deemed to be socially valuable. By pursuing their affiliative needs, which are intangible and often invisible to even the most direct beneficiaries, women are forced into the realms of 'non-workers' with negative consequences for their rights to an independent income. In support of his vision of a society which 'provides access to income and to meaningful work, paid or unpaid for all citizens', Mayo argues that:

> there is a pressing social and economic need to reverse the low status and conditions of unpaid work, given the increasing stress and personal cost to those doing it. Unpaid work is an essential base on which the rest of our lives rest.
>
> (1996: 146–147)

A fuller understanding of the effects of gender divisions, both in constraining women's options and in shaping their preferences, reinforces the case for a CBI as a right of social citizenship and strengthens the case for decoupling income from work, however defined. At the same time, it counters the androcentric bias of conventional arguments for a CBI and offers a more balanced and attractive vision of the prospective marriage between justice and efficiency in which flourishing households and resilient communities are safeguarded from the capitalist commodification process.

9 Conclusion

The way forward?

Introduction: challenging the existing analytical framework

> Sorry, who is this "Market" bloke? Who elected him then? Listen the
> market is something we have created for our own purposes, not some
> law of physics as unchangeable as the ebbing of the tides or the
> waning of the moon. . . . The market is our servant, something we have
> created – if it is causing poverty and destitution then we must inter-
> fere to stop it doing those things.
>
> (O'Farrell, 1998: 78)

A CBI scheme is often perceived as a panacea for the failings of current
social security systems. However, arguments in favour of a CBI have
traditionally been contrived within a fixed set of parameters associated
with a particular view of the principles of economic organisation. That is,
a CBI is considered a model for social security reform that conforms to
market-based structures of exchange and as such contributes positively to
the efficient functioning of capitalist economies. Accepting the supremacy
of the market in determining the nature of modern socio-economic relationships has resulted in convincing theoretical arguments in support of a
CBI. However, such arguments are limited in that the emphasis remains
centred on possible labour market effects following the introduction of a
CBI. The first purpose of this book was to demonstrate the confining
nature of the current debate. The second purpose was to examine the CBI
proposal from a different perspective. This involved initially identifying,
and subsequently questioning, the existing dominant approach employed
in the analysis of income maintenance policy. The process of doing so has
provided the background for the development of a feminist economics
perspective on the CBI proposal. By casting doubt on the notion that *all*
interactions can be explained, and thus predicted, by appealing to a
model of the economy which is premised on the dominance of market-
based structures, a feminist economics perspective allows for a more inclusive conception of human relationships. Thus, the capitalist model of
economic organisation is identified as comprising part, albeit an import-

ant one, of a bigger picture. However, the tendency to privilege the economic structures associated with capitalism, in the analytical process, is central to neo-classical economic theory. It has been argued that this particular and limiting view of the world serves to constrain policy debates. In order to break free from such constraints, and thus move the welfare reform debate forward, it is essential that existing barriers are identified and deconstructed. That is, rather than accept the dominant analytical framework *'as unchangeable as the ebbing of the tides or the waning of the moon'*, a more informative approach would be to accept that it is *'something we have created'* and thus can be *'interfered'* with. The challenge therefore, in arguing for a CBI, is to identify the limiting nature of traditional approaches in the study of income maintenance policy, and to present an alternative approach that incorporates more inclusive and realistic observations on the nature of human relationships.

Understanding income maintenance policy

The relevance of neo-classical economic theory in the study of income transfer schemes is undeniable. Based on the notion of competitive markets, populated by rational, autonomous, utility-maximising actors, neo-classical theory provides a positive analytical framework for justifying the transfer of income between individuals, and within groups of individuals. Within this framework, income maintenance policy is viewed as a necessary component of state activity in the promotion of economic efficiency. However, while the application of this particular theoretical stance provides a rationale for income maintenance policy, it also serves to inform the actual design of policy. That is, income maintenance measures are understood in terms of the impact they have on the workings of the market economy, in particular the world of paid work. It has been argued that the focus on neo-classical theory leads to limited conceptions of the nature and functions of income maintenance policy.

The emphasis placed on promoting economic efficiency and the subsequent prioritising of this objective above all else is an inherent feature of the neo-classical approach to policy analysis. It is claimed that this represents a biased and exclusive theoretical perspective. Following from this critique of the subjective nature of the neo-classical approach, the treatment of income maintenance policy within this framework is exposed to the influence of value judgements. Policy is therefore understood, and evaluated, in terms of the role it performs in an assumed economic world, rather than in the real economy. This approach to policy is restrictive in that it fails to adequately account for the multiplicity of objectives associated with the provision of income maintenance in modern capitalist economies. Thus, the orthodox economic approach to the study of income maintenance policy tends to obscure our vision of the broader picture. In order to develop a more inclusive understanding of income maintenance policy it is considered essential that standard economic practice embraces a feminist economic perspective.

Feminist economics seeks to identify the prejudices central to neo-classical theory and to remove them where possible or desirable. This leads feminist economists to question the basic features of economic method and to re-evaluate the models and tools of analysis employed in the application of neo-classical theory. The first step, therefore, in developing a feminist economics perspective in the study of income transfer systems is to provide evidence of how inherent biases, entrenched in mainstream economics, act in determining the nature of policy. This is not always immediately obvious in that the assumptions and axioms which form the basis of neo-classical economic theory 'seem so obvious and natural to most economists that they are not considered values' (Kuiper and Sap, 1995: 5). That is, the existence of bias is rendered invisible by the dominant value structure. Therefore, the claim made by traditional economists that their discipline is a positive value-free science is to be treated with caution. The mainstream economic approach is itself defined by a set of value positions on what is worthy of study and on the methods to be employed. Subsequently these positions inform policy debates, which implies a 'hidden' agenda. Understanding policy within this framework means that there will be a continual privileging of the ideals associated with neo-classical economic theory. It follows that the process of opening up debates, to include a more representative range of perspectives on the purpose and design of policy, involves separating the dominant theoretical framework from real world phenomena. Thus, it is argued that the approach to study should begin by exploring the actual nature of policy, alongside an examination of the problems such policy is intended to address. Equipped with a better understanding of the functions and range of objectives associated with income maintenance measure, policy makers are better served by theoretical perspectives as opposed to being dominated by such.

In order to distinguish theory from policy, the initial chapters provided an outline of the prevailing influence of neo-classical economics in the design of income maintenance policy, combined with an inquiry into the modern social problems of poverty and social exclusion. This served to illustrate the ineffectiveness of current measures in meeting modern demands. The case was made that the reform agenda continues to be driven by an assumed acceptance of the neo-classical construct. That is, income maintenance policy, both in an historical and contemporary sense, is understood primarily in terms of its direct relationship to the workings of a market-oriented economic system. Such a specific and limited approach subsequently influences our understanding of possible reform options. The contribution of theory to the understanding of the purpose and nature of policy is not denied. However, what is in question is the appropriateness, and indeed usefulness, of the continued and exclusive application of a particular theory, which in itself is representative of a value-based paradigm.

Introducing a CBI within this exclusive theoretical framework points to the possible benefits to be derived from such a reform proposal. However, it only provides part of the picture in that the issues traditionally ignored within mainstream economic theory are subsequently neglected in the policy analysis process. Situating the position of women in society within a neo-classical analytical framework fails to account for the significant role played by gender differences in determining the outcomes of policy. Thus, gender as a variable is effectively discounted and policy is considered with regard to is impact on what is assumed to be an homogeneous population. It is claimed that as long as this particular approach dominates in the process of understanding income maintenance policy, the full potential benefits, particularly those relating to women, of a CBI will remain peripheral to the debate. Thus, in demonstrating an androcentric bias, the favoured analytical framework imposes on reform debates a particular set of ideals and beliefs regarding the purpose of policy. Moving the debate beyond such confining parameters necessitates that an alternative approach to study is adopted.

Why feminist economics and the CBI proposal?

The changing nature of socio-economic relationships is a crucial feature of welfare reform debates. Poverty and the related concept of social exclusion can no longer be explained, if indeed they ever could be, in terms of limited incomes. The causes and consequences of material deprivation in advanced capitalist societies are varied and wide-ranging. The process of analysing such draws attention to the prevalence of gender inequalities. Men and women have very different experiences of deprivation, which can be attributed mainly to gender divisions of labour both within the household and the workplace. A central focus of feminist economic theory has been to comprehend and to subsequently promote an awareness of the causes and consequence of gender inequalities. It follows then that adopting a feminist economics approach in the analysis of social security provision will aid in understanding the functions and outcomes associated with any particular policy. That is, the approach to study does not set out with a predetermined set of objectives in mind, but rather the focus is on exploring real world economic phenomena and then assessing policy in terms of its impact on such.

Unless we can adapt the theory, policy will remain static and thus ineffective in adapting to the changing needs of modern capitalist society. That is, if the way we interpret and understand the world remains driven by an attachment to neo-classical economic theory, we will never fully understand the true nature of deprivation. In considering the CBI proposal, much can be gained from employing a feminist economics perspective. Feminist economists criticise those traditional economists who attempt to research the family without changing the tools of analysis. Within such attempts it is generally assumed that gender divisions are somehow 'natural' rather than socially constructed. Such assumptions stem from an unyielding attachment to the principles of self-interested, rational, utility-maximising individuals, which serve to define the neo-classical approach. In analysing the CBI debate the feminist economist critique proves relevant. Arguments in favour of a CBI have been dominated by an exclusive focus on the operational nature of modern labour markets. Similar to neo-classical approaches in analysing the family, assumptions are being made about the nature of social and economic exchange in contemporary society. The welfare function of paid work is emphasised and thus any policy which may be construed as representing a possible threat to that function will be implicitly rejected. Assuming that choices made with regard to the world of work are somehow 'natural', in that they are primarily determined by financial considerations, follows from an adherence to the neo-classical construct. Considering that such choices may be 'socially constructed' gives way to a broader conceptual understanding of the role income maintenance performs in a modern socio-economic environment.

Feminist economic theory encompasses the notion of socially-constructed preferences. The neo-classical construct proves problematic in this sense in that the stylised notion of the 'individual' fails adequately to account for the influence of a whole range of social relations and institutions. In terms of welfare reform debates then, it is considered crucial that feminist economic analysis is embraced given that many of the problems welfare policy is intended to address results from socially-constructed inequalities. Considering a CBI in terms of its wider remit, that is, the provision of social security rather than income maintenance is indicative of an approach that moves beyond traditional economic analysis regarding the role of policy. Thus, the application of feminist economic theory in this particular area proves enlightening in that it allows for a richer awareness of both the function of policy and the true nature of the problems policy is designed to address. Developing a feminist economic perspective on the CBI proposal makes a positive contribution to the debate that serves to demonstrate the potential a CBI has in promoting gender neutral citizenship rights.

Gender blind or gender neutral: the relevance of a CBI to the welfare reform agenda

Many regard the fight for gender equality as largely a "women's affair" requiring perhaps some concessions here and there. If women are emerging as a key axial principle in the new socio-economic equilibrium, it follows that the quality of our future society hinges on how we respond to their new claims on men, the welfare state, and on society at large. For good or bad, gender equality becomes therefore a "societal affair", a precondition for making the clockwork of post-industrial societies tick. Gender equality is one of the key ingredients that must go into our blueprints for a workable new welfare architecture.

(Esping-Andersen, 2002: 69)

It has been argued that a CBI presents a radical approach to income maintenance policy in the sense that it provides the foundations for 'a workable new welfare architecture'. Thinking about welfare reform along the lines of a CBI provides scope to conceptualise state welfare arrangements outside the constricting parameters associated with traditional neoclassical economics. However, thinking outside the 'box' is not yet a reality in that discussion has remained constrained by the traditional economics approach. This in turn has resulted in a failure adequately to recognise and address the relevance of gender differences.

As previously argued the structures and norms associated with advanced capitalist economic systems embody a range of social and cultural norms that serve to influence and determine individual behaviour. Such norms are 'gendered' in the sense that they have differential *versus* consequences for men and women. The individual choices of 'rational' economic agents are effectively constrained by a given set of socially-determined roles, responsibilities and expectations. Gender, therefore, *matters* in determining outcomes and impacts across the range of public policy interventions. However, issues relating to gender are too often presented as 'add-ons' within the context of the policy process. This implies an approach focused on 'acting' upon gender inequalities as they are identified, or arise, rather than one that sets out to understand and subsequently *transform* the processes and structures that create and sustain such inequalities. As indicated in the introductory chapter, the gender mainstreaming agenda, which refers to the systematic integration of gender equality into all areas of public policy, is now considered a defining feature of the policy making process. The continued and future operation of the European Union's Structural Funds will be strongly influenced by the EU's policy of mainstreaming and the UK government have on several occasions stated their firm commitment to mainstreaming, specifically with reference to spending decisions (Rees, 2000, Rake, 2000). The political will to promote gender equality has thus been demonstrated on both an international and national level but the issue yet to be resolved is how best to put this will into practice.

A CBI could provide a possible solution, at least with reference to welfare reform, in that it would act in promoting *gender neutral* rights of citizenship. However, this potential will never be fully realised as long as reform debates remain focused on preserving a traditional work-and-pay relationship. That is, the underlying assumption is that income *should* derive from work, however that work is defined. A CBI explicitly incorporates the notion that income *should* be derived from rights of citizenship. Such an approach to policy provides for an account of the different social experiences of men and women in a market-based economy. A CBI therefore, has the potential to shift the focus away from a 'gender blind' approach to social security provision and to promote more gender equitable outcomes.

The practice of arguing for reform based on a CBI would be greatly enhanced by incorporating a feminist economics perspective. Indeed, it is only when such a perspective is included that a CBI can be considered a truly comprehensive and 'workable' alternative for *all* citizens. Rather than 'add CBI and stir' the preceding analysis has set out to adapt the analytical framework employed in the policy process to incorporate a feminist economics perspective. In doing so it is argued that the stage is now set for 'thinking the unthinkable' and giving serious consideration to a proposal that would effectively *transform* modern welfare states in such a way as to promote real freedom for all.

Notes

2 Justifying income transfers

1 MV represents marginal value.
2 That is the supplier.

3 Social security or income maintenance policy?

1 'Social Protection in the sense of the State assuming ultimate responsibility for the health and welfare of its citizens is very much a European invention.... Beginning in Germany in the 1870s, governments throughout Europe, accepting the principle – and indeed necessity – of state intervention to tackle these problems, gradually took action to alleviate the poverty and hardship caused when workers, deprived of access to the land, became incapable of working and earning a wage.... All Member States provide their citizens with income support during old-age, sickness, invalidity, maternity and unemployment, as well as when caring for children, and provide access to free, or highly subsidised health care' (Commission of European Communities, 1993: 15).
2 This type of accounting practice is crucial when considering the political acceptability of reform proposals, particularly the Citizens' Basic Income model, due to the implications such a policy has for distorting the government's accounts by showing an exorbitant increase in spending (see for example Monkton, 1993).
3 The Bismarkian model of social insurance refers to one of the earliest schemes of compulsory insurance established in Germany by Chancellor Bismark between the years 1883 and 1889 (ILO, 1984: 3). Bismark's scheme for social insurance was financed by contributions which were graduated with reference to wage levels and likewise benefit payments were linked to previous earnings (Wilson and Wilson, 1993: 358).
4 This model is generally identified as forming the basis of the post-war scheme for social security provision in Britain.
5 For the Wilsons, the simplicity inherent within the Beveridge proposals in terms of uniformity and universal coverage is what distinguished the British system of social insurance from those of other countries and the belief that a single contribution covering all risks would effectively prevent poverty is what 'attracted so much interest and support' (1993: 58).

5 Why a Citizens' Basic Income?

1 It is worth noting that no system of state-supported cash transfer scheme can be defined literally as unconditional. With a CBI scheme, eligibility would be based on the recipients' citizenship status. This gives rise to questions of 'who is a

citizen?' and 'what are the establishing criteria?' Such questions imply conditionality and therefore merit further investigation when examining the actual implementation of a CBI. However, for the purpose of this analysis it is assumed that the unconditional and universal nature of a CBI implies that eligibility is dependent upon residency and requires no further action by the individual.

2 There has been no detailed discussion on the treatment of children within the current literature. However, it is generally assumed that the actual amount payable for children would be less than that paid to adults. Passing reference has been made to flat rate as opposed to age-related grants for children and the possibility of granting supplements to expectant mothers (see Parker, 1993: 22). These issues, alongside related questions of additional supplements for the elderly, the disabled, and housing costs are all important considerations when discussing the actual form policy should take and further analysis in these areas is therefore essential prior to the implementation of a CBI.

6 Arguing for a universal income guarantee

1 It is interesting to note that Paine himself was dismissed in 1765 from one of his earlier jobs in the excise office for passing some goods without a full inspection.

2 Activism on his own part was demonstrated by his ability to organise fellow socialists, such as Bertrand Russell, Sidney and Beartrice Webb and George Bernard Shaw, by encouraging them to engage in regular debating sessions of which he was of course a central figure. One such debating session became known within the academic community as the famous 'Cole group' where participants engaged in a form of role playing where they took on the responsibilities of members of a future Labour government (Van Trier, 1989). Cole, himself, was therefore an inspirational figure in that he engendered active debate and a conducive atmosphere for the formation of new policy amongst a prominent community of middle class intellectuals committed to social reform.

3 Cole specifically mentions: beer, tobacco, cinemas and theatres as goods which are viewed by some as necessary to secure an acceptable standard of living and further maintains that as society benefits from economic growth the range of such 'second class' necessaries grows (ibid.: 224–225). Cole therefore shows foresight in considering the dynamics of poverty.

4 See Appendix B in Cole (1947) *Money: Its Present and Future*

5 Parker explains in a footnote on p. 420 that Jaques Duboin's writing, which included *La grande revolution qui vient* (1934); *En route vers l'abondance* (1935) and *Liberation* (1936) are now out of print.

6 For example, Bismark's pioneering scheme of social insurance implemented in Germany between 1883 and 1889, and in New Zealand non-contributory pensions were introduced in 1898 (Barr, 1993: 19,22).

7 Citizens Income Bulletin No. 17, January 1994, p. 32, draws attention to the fact that an earlier version of *Something to Look Forward To* was published and circulated privately three months prior to the Beveridge Report of December 1942, but that this publication is not widely available. As Rhys Williams states in the foreword to her 1943 publication she has 'elaborated' on the proposals contained within the earlier publication in light of the Beveridge Report. However, when considering the Rhys Williams doctrine in terms of an alternative to the Beveridge plan the existence of this earlier publication is an important factor.

8 Family Income Supplement (FIS), introduced in 1971, displayed characteristics similar to an NIT scheme (Creedy and Disney, 1985: 155)

9 The authors refer to the New Jersey Income Guarantee Experiments conducted in 1972.

7 Arguing for a CBI – a radical policy response?

1 Reference to the 'minority' is worthy of note when considering gender issues in arguing for a CBI. The practice of examining the impact a particular policy has on women is often identified within an 'equality' agenda and as such is presented as a positive step in addressing the needs of 'minorities'. Considering the policy evaluation process in these terms is misleading as women are clearly not a minority group. More importantly, engaging in a gender impact assessment should not be viewed as 'doing women' but rather, more accurately as an approach which takes account of any possible differential effects a policy has for men and women. The point being made is that if the 'minority' position is dominant in the literature arguing for a CBI, it serves to hinder the development of debates focusing on the potential the proposal has for promoting gender equality.

2 Van Parijs actually defines t as 'an average rate, as the ratio of what is collected for the sake of transfers to disposable income' (1992c: 219). He further distinguishes between different levels of responsiveness of Y (national income) depending on how the tax is levied. The effects will be determined by the degrees of elasticity illustrated by the supply of labour and the supply of capital.

3 This is of course in relation to declared factor supply and taxable national product as Van Parijs points out. Many critics of a CBI scheme point to the effects such a policy would have on activity in the 'underground economy', thereby seriously eroding public revenue from taxation. Such arguments are grounded in a belief in the disincentive effects of high MTRs and therefore demonstrate an analytical bias. That is, no account is taken of the balancing effect of incentives to participate in the labour market arising from the institutionalisation of a minimum income guarantee.

4 On a similar note, a case could be argued for a CBI in terms of addressing individual poverty which arises from an unequal distribution of resources within households. This issue is of particular relevance when discussing the potential a CBI has in promoting gender equality. However, it is unlikely that Brittan is referring specifically to this, nor would he be concerned with such issues given his explicit emphasis on market mechanisms and promoting the efficiency of the capitalist system. He merely wants to ensure that families receive a means of subsistence equivalent to their particular needs. How that income is then distributed is another matter.

5 Jordan refers to their article in Citizen's Income Bulletin No. 19, 1995, 'Why a £20 CI is better than Lowering Income Tax to 20%'.

Bibliography

Abel-Smith, B. (1985) 'The Major Problems of the Welfare State: Defining the Issues', in Eisenstadt, S.N. and Ahimer, O. (eds) *The Welfare State and Its Aftermath*, London and Sydney: Croom Helm.

Abel-Smith, B. (1992) *The Beveridge Report: Its Origins and Outcomes*, Proceedings of the International Conference 'Social Security: 50 Years After Beveridge', University of York, 27–30 September 1992.

Alcock, P. (1987) *Poverty and State Support*, London and New York: Longman.

Alcock, P. (1989) 'Unconditional benefits: misplaced optimism in income maintenance', *Capital and Class*, 37: 117–132.

Atkinson, A.B. (1989a) 'Poverty', in J.M. Eatwell, M. Milgate and P. Newman (eds) *The New Palgrave Social Economics*, London and New York: Macmillan.

Atkinson, A.B. (1989b) *Poverty and Social Security*, London and New York: Harvester Wheatsheaf.

Atkinson, A.B. (1989c) 'Basic Income Schemes and the Lessons from Public Economics: Taxation, Incentives and the Distribution of Income Programme (TIDI)', discussion paper TIDI/136, London School of Economics: STICERD.

Atkinson, A.B. (1991) 'A National Minimum? A History of Ambiguity in the Determination of Benefit Scales in Britain', in Wilson, D. and Wilson, T. (eds) *The State and Social Welfare: The Objectives of Policy*, Essex: Longman.

Atkinson, A.B. (1992) *Towards a European Social Safety Net*, The Welfare State Programme Suntory-Toyota International Centre for Economics and Related Disciplines (WSP/STICERD), Discussion Paper WSP/78, London School of Economics: STICERD.

Atkinson, A.B. (1993a) *Participation Income. Citizen's Income Bulletin*, No. 16.

Atkinson, A.B. (1993b) *Beveridge, the National Minimum, and its Future in a European Context*, The Welfare State Programme Suntory-Toyota International Centre for Economics and Related Disciplines (WSP/STICERD), Discussion Paper WSP/85, London School of Economics: STICERD.

Atkinson, A.B. (1995a) *Incomes and The Welfare State: Essays on Britain and Europe*, Cambridge: Cambridge University Press.

Atkinson, A.B. (1995b) *Public Economics in Action*, Oxford: Clarendon Press.

Atkinson, A.B. (1996) 'Seeking to Explain the Distribution of Income', in Hills, J. (ed.) *New Inequalities: The Changing Distribution of Income and Wealth in the United Kingdom*, Cambridge: Cambridge University Press.

Atkinson, A.B. (1998) 'Social Exclusion, Poverty and Unemployment', in Atkinson, A.B. and Hills, J. (eds) *Exclusion, Employment and Opportunity*. Centre for Analysis of Social Exclusion (CASE), CASE Paper 4, London School of Economics: STICERD.

Atkinson, A.B. and Sutherland, H. (1988) *Integrating Income Taxation and Social Security: Analysis of a Partial Basic Income*, Taxation, Incentives and the Distribution of Income Programme (TIDI) Discussion paper TIDI/123, London School of Economics: STICERD.

Barr, N. (1993) *The Economics of the Welfare State*, London: Weidenfeld and Nicolson.

Barr, N. and Coulter, F. (1990) 'Social Security: Solution or Problem', in Hills, J. (ed.) *The State of Welfare: The Welfare State in Britain Since 1974*, Oxford: Clarendon Press.

Becker, S. (2003) 'Security for Those who Cannot: Labour's Neglected Welfare Principle', in Millar, J. (ed.) *Understanding Social Security Issues for Policy and Practice*, Bristol: The Policy Press.

Bennett, F. (2002) 'Gender implications of social security reforms', *Fiscal Studies*, 23(4): 559–584.

Berthoud, R. and Kempson, E. (1990) *Credit and Debt in Britain*, London: Policy Studies Institute.

Blake, T. (1996) 'Including the excluded – where next for EU social policy?' *European Information Service*, 167: 6–8.

Block, F. (1990) *Post Industrial Possibilities: A Critique of Economic Discourse*, Berkeley, Los Angeles and Oxford: University of California Press.

Bradshaw, J. (1993) 'Developments in Social Security Policy', in Jones, C. (ed.) *New Perspectives on the Welfare State in Europe*, London and New York: Routledge.

Brewer, M., Clark, T. and Wakefield, M. (2002a) Five Years of Social Security Reform, Institute for Fiscal Studies, July 2002 WP02/12.

Brewer, M., Clark, T. and Wakefield M. (2002b) 'Social security in the UK under new Labour: what did the third way mean for welfare reform?' *Fiscal Studies*, 23(4): 505–537.

Brittan, S. (1988) *A Restatement of Economic Liberalism*, Basingstoke and London: Macmillan.

Brittan, S. (1990) 'The Case for Basic Incomes', in Brittan, S. and Webb, S. (eds) *Beyond the Welfare State: An Examination of Basic Incomes in a Market Economy*, Aberdeen: AUP Hume Paper 17.

Brittan, S. and Webb, S. (1990) *Beyond the Welfare State: An Examination of Basic Incomes in a Market Economy*, Aberdeen: AUP Hume Paper 17.

Brown, J.C. (1984a) 'Introduction: The Oxford Working Party', in Brown, J.C. (ed.) *Anti-Poverty Policy in the European Community*, London: Policy Studies Institute.

Brown, J.C. (1984b) 'The Nature of Anti-Poverty Policy in the United Kingdom', in Brown, J.C. (ed.) *Anti-Poverty Policy in the European Community*, London: Policy Studies Institute.

Brown, M. and Payne, S. (1994) *Introduction to Social Administration in Britain*, London and New York: Routledge.

Brunsdon, E. and May, M. (2002) 'Evaluating New Labour's Approach to Independent Welfare Provision', in Powell, M. (ed.) *Evaluating New Labour's Welfare Reforms*, Bristol: The Policy Press.

Burkitt, B. (1984) *Radical Political Economy: An Introduction to the Alternative Economics*, London and New York: New York University Press.

Burkitt, B. and Hutchinson, F. (1994) 'Major Douglas' proposals for a national dividend: a logical successor to the wage', *International Journal of Social Economics*, 21(1): 19–28.

Buti, M., Franco, D. and Pench, L.R. (1998) 'Reconciling the Welfare State with Sound Public Finances and High Employment', in Directorate-General for Economic and Financial Affairs (ed.) *European Economy Reports and Studies Number 4, 1997: The Welfare State in Europe Challenges and Reforms*, Brussels: Directorate-General for Economic and Financial Affairs of the European Commission.

Byrne, D. (1985) 'Social Security and Taxation – the Need for Parallel Reform', in Silburn, R. (ed.) *The Future of Social Security: A Response to the Social Security Green Paper*, London: Fabian Society.

Carmel, E. and Papadopoulos, T. (2003) 'The New Governance of Social Security in Britain', in Millar, J. (ed.) *Understanding Social Security: Issues for Policy and Practice*, Bristol: The Policy Press.

Chamberlayne, P. (1992) 'New directions in welfare? France, West Germany, Italy and Britain in the 1980s', *Critical Social Policy*, 11 (3(33)): 5–21.

Citizens' Income Research Group (CIRG) (1994) Citizens Income Bulletin No. 17, January 1994.

CIRG (1994) Citizens Income Bulletin No. 18, July 1994.

Claeys, G. (1989) *Thomas Paine: Social and Political Thought*, Boston, London, Sydney and Wellington: Unwin Hyman Inc.

Clark, C. (1977) *Poverty Before Politics: A Proposal for a Reverse Income Tax*, London: Institute of Economic Affairs.

Clark, C.M.A. and Kavanagh, C. (1996) 'Basic Income, Inequality, and Unemployment: Rethinking the Linkage between Work and Welfare', *Journal of Economic Issues* 30(2): 399–406.

Clinton, D., Yates, M. and Kang, D. (1994) *Integrating Taxes and Benefits?*, The Commission on Social Justice Report 8, London: Institute for Public Policy Research.

Cole, G.D.H. (1935) *Principles of Economic Planning*, London: MacMillan and Co, Ltd.

Cole, G.D.H. (1947) *Money: Its Present and Future*, London, Toronto and Melbourne, Sydney: Cassell.

Commission of European Communities (1993) *European Social Policy Options for the Union Green Paper Com(93)551*. Luxembourg Office for Official Publications of the European Communities: Directorate-General for Employment, Industrial Relations and Social Affairs of the European Commission.

Commission on Social Justice (CJS) (1993) *Making Sense of Benefits*, London: Institute for Public Policy Research.

Commission on Social Justice (CJS) (1994) *Social Justice: Strategies for Social Renewal – The Report of the Commission on Social Justice*, London: Vintage.

Creedy, J. and Disney, R. (1985) *Social Insurance in Transition: An Economic Analysis*, Oxford: Oxford University Press.

Cross, M. (1993) 'Generating the "New Poverty": a European Comparison', in Simpson, R. and Walker, R. (eds) *Europe: For Richer or Poorer*, London: CPAG.

Culyer, A.J. (1983) *The Political Economy of Social Policy*, Oxford: Martin Robertson.

Cutler, T., Williams., K. and Williams, J. (1986) *Keynes, Beveridge and Beyond*, London and New York: Routledge and Kegan Paul.

Daly, M. (1992) 'Europe's poor women? Gender in research on poverty', *European Sociological Review*, 8(1): 1–12.

Deacon, A. (1995) 'Spending More to Achieve Less? Social Security Since 1945', in

Gladstone, D. (ed.) *British Social Welfare: Past, Present and Future*, London: UCL Press Limited.

Deacon, A. (2003) 'Social Security Policy', in Ellison, N. and Pierson, C. (eds) *Developments in British Social Policy 2*, Hampshire and New York: Palgrave Macmillan.

Deakin, S. and Wilkinson, F. (1992) 'Social policy and economic efficiency: the deregulation of the labour market in Britain', *Critical Social Policy*, 11 (3(33)): 40–61.

Dean, H. (1991) *Social Security and Social Control*, London: Routledge.

Dean, H. and Shah, A. (2002) 'Insecure families and low-paying labour markets: comments on the British experience', *Journal of Social Policy*, 31(1): 61–80.

Department of Social Security (1993a) *The Growth of Social Security*, London: HMSO.

Department of Social Security (1993b) *Containing the Cost of Social Security*, London: HMSO.

Department of Social Security (1995) *Social Security Departmental Report – The Government's Expenditure Plans 1995–96 to 1997–98*, London: HMSO.

Department of Social Security (2000) *The Changing Welfare State: Social Security Spending*, London: HMSO.

Dilnot, A. and Kell, M. (1989) 'Male Unemployment and Women's Work', in Dilnot, A. and Walker, I. (eds) *The Economics of Social Security*, Oxford: Oxford University Press.

Dilnot, A. and Walker, I. (1989) *The Economics of Social Security*, Oxford: Oxford University Press.

Dilnot, A., Kay, J. and Morris, C. (1984) *The Reform of Social Security*, Oxford: Clarendon Press.

Dore, R. (1996) 'A feasible Jerusalem?' *The Political Quarterly*, 67(1): 58–63.

Douglas, C.H. (1920) *Credit Power and Democracy*, London: Cecil Palmer.

Douglas, C.H. (1924) *Social Credit*, London: Cecil Palmer.

Douglas, C.H. (1935) *Social Credit*, London: Eyre and Spottiswoode.

Doyal, L. and Gough, I. (1991) *A Theory of Human Need*, Basingstoke and London: Macmillan.

Eardley, T., Bradshaw, J., Ditch, J., Gough, I. and Whiteford, P. (1996) *Social Assistance in OECD Countries: Synthesis Report*, London: HMSO.

Ekins, P. (1986) *The Living Economy: A New Economics in the Making*, London and New York: Routledge and Kegan Paul.

Esping-Anderson, G. (1991) *The Three Worlds of Welfare Capitalism*, Princeton, New Jersey: Princeton University Press.

Esping-Andersen, G. (2002) 'Foreword: Sustainable Social Justice and "Open Co-ordination" in Europe' and 'A New Gender Contract', in Gaillie, D., Memerijck, A. and Myles, J. (eds) *Why We Need a Welfare State*, Oxford: Oxford University Press.

European Commission (1999) 'Improving the socio-economic knowledge base', *RTD Info Fifth Framework Programmes 23 Key Actions*, 21(28): (Supplement February 1999).

Euzéby, C. (1994) 'From "insertion" income to "existence" income', *Citizens Income Bulletin*, 17 January 1994: 14–18.

Evans, M., Paugam, S. and Prélis, J. (1995) *Chunnel Vision: Poverty, Social Exclusion and the Debate on Social Welfare in France and Britain*, The Welfare State Programme Suntory-Toyota International Centre for Economics and Related Disciplines (WSP/STICERD), Discussion Paper WSP/115, London School of Economics: STICERD.

Ferber, M. and Nelson, J. (1993) 'Introduction: The Social Construction of Economics and the Social Construction of Gender', in Ferber, M. and Nelson, J. (eds) *Beyond Economic Man: Feminist Theory and Economics*, Chicago: Chicago University Press.

Finlay, J.L. (1972) *Social Credit: The English Origins*, Montreal and London: McGill–Queen's University Press.

Finn, D. (1996) *Making Benefits Work: Employment Programmes and Job Creation Measures*, Manchester: Centre for Local Economic Strategies (CLES).

Finn, D. (2003) 'Employment Policy', in Ellison, N. and Pierson, C. (eds) *Developments in British Social Policy 2*, Hampshire and New York: Palgrave Macmillan.

Fitzpatrick, T. (1999) *Freedom and Security: An Introduction to the Basic Income Debate*, Basingstoke: Macmillan.

Folbre, N. (1994) *Who Pays for the Kids: Gender and the Structures of Constraint*, London and New York: Routledge.

Ford, J. (1991) *Consuming Credit, Debt and Poverty in the UK*, London: CPAG.

Friedman, M. (1982) *Capitalism and Freedom*, Chicago: University of Chicago Press.

Friedman, M. and Friedman, R. (1980) *Free to Choose A Personal Statement*, New York and London: Harcourt Brace Jovanovich.

Gagnier, R. and Dupré, J. (1995) 'On work and idleness', *Feminist Economics*, 1(3): 96–107.

Galbraith, J.K. (1994) 'The good life beckons', *New Statesman and Society*, No 287, 28th January 1994.

Gardiner, K. (1997) *Bridges From Benefit to Work: A Review*, York: Joseph Rowntree Foundation.

Garfinkel, I. and Kesselman, J. (1978) 'Professor Friedman, meet Lady Rhys Williams: NIT vs CIT', *Journal of Public Economics*, 10: 179–216.

George, H. (1913) *Progress and Poverty*, London: J.M. Dent and Sons, Ltd.

Gibson-Graham, J.K. (1996) *The End of Capitalism (As We Knew It): A Feminist Critique of Political Economy*, Oxford and Cambridge: Blackwell.

Gillespie, M. and Scott, G. (2004) *Advice Services and Transitions to Work for Disadvantaged Groups: A Literature Review*, Report of work programme of the Equal Access Development Partnership supported under Theme A of the European Commission's Equal Community Initiative GB Programme, Glasgow: Scottish Executive, North Lanarkshire Council and Glasgow Caledonian University.

Ginsburg, N. (1992) *Divisions of Welfare: A Critical Introduction to Comparative Social Policy*, London, Newbury Park and New Delhi: Sage.

Glendinning, C. and Millar, J. (1992) *Women and Poverty in Britain: The 1990s*, London: Harvester Wheatsheaf.

Glyn, A. and Miliband, D. (1994) 'Introduction', in Glyn, A. and Miliband, D. (eds) *Paying for Inequality: The Economic Cost of Social Injustice*, London: IPPR/Rivers Oram Press.

Gordon, M.S. (1988) *Social Security Policies in Industrial Countries*, Cambridge: Cambridge University Press.

Gorz, A. (1994) *Capitalism, Socialism, Ecology*, London and New York: Verso.

Gough, I. (1979) *The Political Economy of the Welfare State*, Basingstoke and London: Macmillan.

Graham, H. (1992) 'Budgeting for Health: Mothers in Low-income Households', in Glendinning, C. and Millar, J. (eds) (1992) *Women and Poverty in Britain, the 1990s*, Hemel Hempstead: Harvester Wheatsheaf.

Gray, A. (1988) 'Resisting economic conscription', *Capital and Class*, 34: 119–146.

Gray, A. (1993) *Citizen's Income, Minimum Wages and Work Sharing*, BIRG/CIRG, Citizen's Income Bulletin No. 16, July 1993: 14–18.

Green, A. (1996) 'Aspects of the Changing Geography of Poverty and Wealth', in Hills, J. (ed.) *New Inequalities: The Changing Distribution of Income and Wealth in the United Kingdom*, Cambridge: Cambridge University Press.

Green, C. (1967) *Negative Taxes and the Poverty Problem*, Washington: Brookings Institution.

Gregg, P. (1965) *A Social and Economic History of Britain 1760–1965*, London: George Harrap and Co.

Hantrais, L. (1995) *Social Policy in the European Union*, London: Macmillan.

Hantrais, L. and Letablier, M. (1996) *Families and Family Policies in Europe*, New York: Longman.

Harding, S. (1991) *Whose Science? Whose Knowledge?*. Milton Keynes: OUP.

Harkness, S., Machin, S. and Waldfogel, J. (1996) 'Women's Pay and Family Incomes in Britain, 1979–91', in Hills, J. (ed.) *New Inequalities: The Changing Distribution of Income and Wealth in the United Kingdom*, Cambridge: Cambridge University Press.

Heilbroner, R. (1980) *The Worldly Philosophers: The Lives, Times and Ideas of the Great Economic Thinkers*, New York: Simon and Schuster.

Hemming, R. (1984) *Poverty and Incentives. The Economics of Social Security*, Oxford: Oxford University Press.

Hewitson, G. (1999) *Feminist Economics: Interrogating the Masculinity of Rational Economic Man*, Cheltenham: Edward Elgar.

Hewitt, M. (2002) 'New Labour and the Redefinition of Social Security', in Powell, M. (ed.) *Evaluating New Labour's Welfare Reforms*, Bristol: The Policy Press.

Hill, M. (1990) *Social Security Policy in Britain*, Aldershot: Edward Elgar.

Hill, M. (1993) *The Welfare State in Britain: A Political History since 1945*, Aldershot: Edward Elgar.

Hill, M. (1996) *Social Policy: A Comparative Analysis*, London: Prentice Hall and Harvester Wheatsheaf.

Hills, J. (1995) *Joseph Rowntree Foundation Inquiry into Income and Wealth*, York: Joseph Rowntree Foundation.

Hills, J. (1996) *New Inequalities: The Changing Distribution of Income and Wealth in the United Kingdom*, Cambridge: Cambridge University Press.

Hills, J. with the LSE Welfare State Programme (1993) *The Future of Welfare, A Guide to the Debate*, York: Joseph Rowntree Foundation.

Himmelweit, S. (1995) 'The discovery of "unpaid work": the social consequences of the expansion of work', *Feminist Economics*, 1(2): 1–19.

Hobson, B., Lewis, J. and Siim, B. (2002) 'Introduction: Contested Concepts in Gender and Social Politics', in Hobson, B., Lewis, J. and Siim, B. (eds) *Contested Concepts in Gender and Social Politics*, Cheltenham: Edward Elgar.

Hutchinson, F. (1995) 'A Heretical View of Economic Growth and Income Distribution', in Kuiper, E. and Sap, J. with Feiner, S., Notburga, O. and Tzannatos, Z. (eds) *Out of the Margin: A Feminist Perspective on Economics*, London and New York: Routledge.

International Labour Organisation (ILO) (1984) *Into the Twenty-First Century: The Development of Social Security*, Geneva: ILO.

Jacobs, J. (1992) *Beveridge 1942–1992: Papers to Mark the 50th Anniversary of the Beveridge Report*, London: Whiting and Birch.

Jacobs, J. (1992) 'An Introduction to the Beveridge Report', in Jacobs, J. (ed.) *Beveridge 1942–1992: Papers to Mark the 50th Anniversary of the Beveridge Report*, London: Whiting and Birch.

Jenkins, S. and Millar, J. (1989) 'Income Risk and Income Maintenance: Implicatins for Incentives to Work', in Dilnot, A. and Walker, I. (eds) *The Economics of Social Security*, Oxford: Oxford University Press.

Johnson, P. (1994) 'Taxes and Benefits, Equality and Efficient', in Glyn, A. and Miliband, D. (eds) *Paying for Inequality: The Economic Cost of Social Injustice*, London: IPPR/Rivers Oram Press.

Jordan, B. (1986) *The State: Authority and Autonomy*, Oxford and New York: Basil Blackwell.

Jordan, B. (1987) *Rethinking Welfare*, Oxford: Basil Blackwell.

Jordan, B. (1988) 'The prospects for basic income', *Social Policy and Administration*, 22(2):116–122.

Jordan, B. (1989) *The Common Good*, Oxford: Basil Blackwell.

Jordan, B. (1992) 'Basic Income and the Common Good', in Van Parijs, P. (ed.) *Arguing for a Basic Income: Ethical Foundations for a Radical Reform*, London: Verso.

Jordan, B. (1996) *A Theory of Poverty and Social Exclusion*, Cambridge: Polity Press.

Jordan, B. (1998) *The New Politics of Welfare*, London: Sage.

Joshi, H. (1992) 'The Cost of Caring', in Glendinning, C. and Millar, J. (eds) *Women and Poverty in Britain in the 1990s*, London: Harvester Wheatsheaf.

Keithley, J. (1991) 'Social Security in a Single European Market', in Room, G. (ed.) *Towards a European Welfare State?* Bristol: SAUS.

Keynes, J.M. (1936) *The General Theory of Employment Interest and Money*, London: Macmillan and Co. Ltd.

Keynes, J.M. (1951) *The General Theory of Employment Interest and Money*, London: Macmillan.

Kofman, E. and Sales R. (1996) 'The Geography of Gender and Welfare in Europe', in Garcia-Ramon, M.D. and Monk, J. (eds) *Women of the European Union: The Politics of Work and Daily Life*, London and New York: Routledge.

Kuiper, E. and Sap, J. (1995) 'Introduction', in Kuiper, E. and Sap, J. with Fiener, S., Ott, N. and Tzannatos, Z. (eds) *Out of the Margin: Feminist Perspectives on Economics*, London and New York: Routledge.

Lange, O. and Taylor, F.M. (1964) *On the Economic Theory of Socialism*, New York, Toronto and London: McGraw-Hill Paperbacks and University of Minnesota Press.

Lerner, A.P. (1970) *The Economics of Control*, New York: Augustus M. Kelly.

Lewenhak, S. (1992) *The Revaluation of Women's Work, Revised Edition*, London: Earthscan Publications.

Lilley, P. (1993) *Benefits and Costs: Securing the Future of Social Security*, MAIS Lecture delivered on 23rd June 1993.

Lister, R. (1989) 'Social Security', in McCarthy, M. (ed.) *The New Politics of Welfare: An Agenda for the 1990s*, Chicago: Lyceum Books.

Lister, R. (1991) 'Social security in the 1980s', *Social Policy and Administration*, 25(2): 91–107.

Lister, R. (1992) *Women' Economic Dependency and Social Security*, EOC Research Discussion Series No 2, Manchester: EOC.

Lister, R. (1997) *Citizenship: Feminist Perspectives*, Basingstoke and London: Macmillan.

Lister, R. (1998) 'New Labour, Old Times?', *Citizen's Income Bulletin*, 25: 2–4.

Lonsdale, S. (1992) 'Patterns of Paid Work', in Glendinning, C. and Millar, J. (eds) *Women and Poverty in Britain the 1990s*, London: Harvester Wheatsheaf.

Lovenstein, M. (1966) 'Guaranteed Income and Traditional Economics', in Theobald, R. (ed.) *The Guaranteed Income: Next Step in Economic Evolution*, New York: Doubleday.

Lowe, R. (1993) *The Welfare State in Britain since 1945*, Basingstoke: Macmillan.

Lutz, M and Lux, K. (1988) *Humanistic Economics: The New Challenge*, New York: Bootstrap Press.

MacDonald, M. (1998) 'Gender and social security policy: pitfalls and possibilities', *Feminist Economics*, 4(1): 1–25.

Manza, J. (1992) 'Post industrial capitalism, the state and the prospects for economic democracy', *Journal of Political and Military Sociology*, 20(2): 209–241.

Manza, J. (1995) 'Book Review: *Arguing for Basic Income* by Philippe Van Parijs', *Theory and Society*, 25: 881–889.

Massey, D. and Allen, J. (1995) 'High-Tech Places: Poverty in the Midst of Growth', in Philio, C. (ed.) *Off the Map: The Social Geography of Poverty in the UK*, London: CPAG.

Mayo, E. (1996) 'Dreaming of Work', in Meadows, P. (ed.) *Work Out – Or Work In? Contributions to the Debate on the Future of Work*, York: Joseph Rowntree Foundation.

McKay, A. and Scott, G. (1999) *What Can We Afford? A Woman's Role Considering the Welfare Implications of Money Management*, Proceedings of the first Scottish Trade Union Research Network Conference, Glasgow, University of Paisley.

McKay, S. (2003) 'Reforming Pensions: Investing in the Future', in Millar, J. (ed.) *Understanding Social Security Issues for Policy and Practice*, Bristol: The Policy Press.

McLaughlin, E. (1994) 'Employment, Unemployment and Social Security', in Glynn, A. and Miliband, D. (eds) *Paying for Inequality The Economic Cost of Social Injustice*, London: IPPR/Rivers Oram Press.

Meade, J. (1990) 'Can We Learn a "Third Way" from the Agathatopians?', *The Royal Bank of Scotland Review*, 167, September 1990: 15–28.

Meade, J.E. (1989) *Agathotopia: The Economics of Partnership*, Aberdeen: Aberdeen University Press, The David Hume Institute.

Meadows, P. (1998) 'The working families tax credit', *National Institute Economic Review*, 74–77.

Millar, J. (2003a) *Understanding Social Security Issues for Policy and Practice*, Bristol: The Policy Press.

Millar, J. (2003b) 'Social Security: Means and Ends', in Millar, J. (ed.) *Understanding Social Security Issues for Policy and Practice*, Bristol: The Policy Press.

Millar, J. and Glendinning, C. (1989) 'Survey article: gender and poverty', *Journal of Social Policy*, 18(3): 363–381.

Miller, A. (1983) *In Praise of Social Dividends*, Edinburgh: Department of Economics, Heriot-Watt University, Edinburgh.

Miller, A. and Chapman, D. (1986) 'Taxation, Benefits and the Basic Income', in Ekins, P. (ed.) *The Living Economy: A New Economics in the Making*, London and New York: Routledge and Kegan Paul.

Mishra, R. (1990) *The Welfare State in Capitalist Society*, London: Harvester Wheatsheaf.

Mitchell, D. (1991) *Income Transfers in Ten Welfare States*, Aldershot: Avebury.

Monkton, C. (1993) *Basic Income Research Group (BRIG)*, Bulletin 16.

Morris, L. (1990) *The Workings of the Household*, Cambridge: Polity Press.

Morris, L. and Llewellyn, T. (1991) *Social Security Provision for the Unemployed: Report for the Social Security Advisory Committee*, London: HMSO.

Needham, R. (1994) *A Justification and Defence of Basic Income: Freedom, Work Incentives and the Labour Market*, Paper Presented at Basic Income European Network Annual Conference, London: Sept. 1994.

Nelson, J. (1993) 'The Study of Choice or the Study of Provisioning? Gender and the Definition of Economics', in Ferber, M. and Nelson, J. (eds) *Beyond Economic Man: Feminist Theory and Economics*, Chicago and London: University of Chicago Press.

Nelson, J. (1996) *Feminism, Objectivity and Economics*, London and New York: Routledge.

Nixon, J. and Williamson, V. (1993) 'Returner and Retainer Policies for Women', in Jones C. (ed.) *New Perspectives on the Welfare State in Europe*, London: Routledge.

O'Farrell, J. (1998) *Things Can Only Get Better*, London: Doubleday.

Oppenheim, C. (1993) *Poverty: the Facts*, London: CPAG.

Oppenheim, C. (1994) *The Welfare State: Putting The Record Straight*, London: CPAG.

Orloff, A. (1990) *Comment on Ann Withorn 'Is One Man's Ceiling Another Woman's Floor? Women and BIG'*, Unpublished conference paper presented at conference 'Basic Income Guarantees: A New Welfare Strategy?' University of Wisconsin-Madison, USA April 6–8, 1990.

Oser, J. and Blanchfield, W. (1975) *The Evolution of Economic Thought, 3rd Edition*, New York: Harcourt Brace Jovanovich.

Pahl, J. (1989) *Money and Marriage*, Basingstoke and London: Macmillan.

Paine, T. (1796) 'Agrarian Justice', in Foner, P.F. (ed.) *The Life and Major Writings of Thomas Paine*, New Jersey: Citadel Press.

Palmer, A.J. (1995) *The Gender of Economics and The Economics of Gender: An Analysis of Undergraduate Courses and Textbooks in the U.K.*, Bristol: Department of Economics, University of West of England.

Palmer, G. North, J., Carr, J. and Kenway, P. (2003) *Monitoring Poverty and Social Exclusion 2003*, York: New Policy Institute and Joseph Rowntree Foundation.

Parker, G. (1992) 'Making Ends Meet: Women, Credit and Debt', in Glendinning, C. and Millar, J. (eds) *Women and Poverty in Britain: The 1990s*, London: Harvester Wheatsheaf.

Parker, H. (1989) *Instead of the Dole; An Enquiry into the Integration of the Tax and Benefit System*, London: Routledge.

Parker, H. (1991) *Basic Income and the Labour Market*, London: Citizens Income.

Parker, H. (1993) *Citizen's Income and Women*, London: Citizens Income.

Parker, H. (1994) 'Citizens' Income', *Citizens' Income Research Group Bulletin*, 17, January 1994: 4–12.

Parker, H. (1998) *Low Cost but Acceptable: A Minimum Income Standard for the UK; Families with Young Children*, Bristol: The Policy Press and the Zacchaeus 2000 Trust.

Pateman, C. (2004) 'Democratizing citizenship: some advantages of a basic income', *Politics and Society*, 23 (1): 89–105.

Payne, S. (1991) *Women, Health and Poverty: An Introduction*, London: Harvester Wheatsheaf.

Pierson, C. (1991) *Beyond the Welfare State? The New Political Economy of Welfare*, Cambridge: Polity Press.

Piven, F.F. and Cloward, R. (1993) *Regulating the Poor: The Functions of Public Welfare (Updated Edition)*, New York: Vintage.

Plant, R. (1997) 'Citizenship, employability and the labour market', *Citizens Income Bulletin*, 24: 2–3.

Polanyi, K. (1968) *The Great Transformation*, Boston: Beacon Press.

Purdy, D. (1988) *Social Power and the Labour Market: A Radical Approach to Labour Economics*, Hampshire, London: MacMillan.

Purdy, D. (1989) 'Incomes Policy, Citizenship and Basic Income', in Alcock, P., Gamble, A., Gough, I., Walker, A. and the Sheffield Group (eds) *The Social Economy and the Democratic State (A New Policy Agenda for the 1990s)*, London: Lawrence and Wishart.

Purdy, D. (1994) 'Citizenship, Basic Income and the State', *New Left Review*, 208: 30–48.

Rainwater, L., Rein, M. and Schwartz, J. (1986) *Income Packaging in the Welfare State A Comparative Study of Family Income*, Oxford: Clarendon Press Oxford.

Rake, K. (2000) 'Into the Mainstream? Why Gender Audit is an Essential Tool for Policymakers', *New Economy*, 7(2): 107–110.

Rees, T. (2000) 'The learning region? Integrating gender equality into economic development', *Policy and Politics*, 28(2): 179–191.

Regan, S. (2003) 'Paying for Welfare in the 21st Century', in Ellison, N. and Pierson C. (eds) *Developments in British Social Policy 2*, Hampshire and New York: Palgrave Macmillan.

Rhys-Williams, J. (1943) *Something to Look Forward To: A Suggestion for a New Social Contract*, London: MacDonald and Co. Ltd.

Rhys-Williams, J. (1953) *Taxation and Incentives*, London, Edinburgh and Glasgow: William Hodge and Company Ltd.

Roche, M. (1992) *Rethinking Citizenship: Welfare, Ideology and Change in Modern Society*, Cambridge: Polity Press.

Roll, J. (1992) *Understanding Poverty: A Guide to the Concepts and Measures*, Family Policy Studies Centre (Occasional Paper 15): Joseph Rowntree Foundation.

Rowlingson, K. (2003) 'From Cradle to Grave: Social Security Over the Life Cycle', in Millar, J. (ed.) *Understanding Social Security Issues for Policy and Practice*, Bristol: The Policy Press.

Russell, B. (1918) *Roads to Freedom*, London: George Allen and Unwin.

Sanderson, C.R. (1936) *Social Credit*, Toronto: Mclelland and Stewart, Ltd.

Saunders, P. (1995a) 'Conditionality and Transition as Issues in the Basic Income Debate', *Two Papers on Citizenship and Basic Income by Sheila Shaver and Peter Saunders*, Social Policy Research Centre Discussion Papers, 55, The University of New South Wales, Australia.

Saunders, P. (1995b) 'Improving work incentives in a means-tested welfare system: the 1994 Australian social security reforms', *Fiscal Studies*, 16(2): 45–70.

Schulte, B. (1993) 'Guaranteed Minimum Resources and the European Community', in Walker, R. and Simpson, R. (eds) *Europe – For Richer Or Poorer?*, London: CPAG Ltd.

Scottish Office (1998) *Social Exclusion in Scotland: A Consultation Paper*, produced on behalf of the Scottish Office by The Stationery Office J16477 2/98.

Sen, A.K. (1995) 'Varieties of Deprivatin: Comments on Chapters by Pujol and

Hutchinson', in Kuiper, E., Sap, J. with Feiner, S., Notburga, O. and Tzannatos, Z. (eds) *Out of the Margin: A Feminist Perspective on Economics*, London and New York: Routledge.

Shaver, S. (1995) 'Wage Earners or Citizens: Participation and Welfare', *Two Papers on Citizenship and Basic Income by Sheila Shaver and Peter Saunders*, Social Policy Research Centre Discussion Papers, 55, The University of New South Wales, Australia.

Silburn, R. (1985) *The Future of Social Security: A Response to the Social Security Green Paper*, London: The Fabian Society.

Simpson, R. and Walker, R. (1993) *Europe: For Richer or Poorer*, London: CPAG.

Spicker, P. (1993) *Poverty and Social Security: Concepts and Principles*. London and New York: Routledge.

Standing, G. (1986) 'Meshing labour flexibility with security: an answer to British Unemployment?', *International Labour Review*, 125(1): 87–106.

Standing, G. (1992) 'The Need for a New Social Consensus', in Van Parijs, P. (ed.) *Arguing for Basic Income*, London and New York: Verso.

Strachey, J. (1936) *Social Credit: An Economic Analysis*, London: Victor Gollancz Ltd and The Workers' Bookshop Ltd.

Strassman, D. (1995) 'Editorial: Creating a Forum for Feminist Economics Inquiry', *Feminist Economics*, 1: 1-5.

Stroeken, J. (1996) 'A case for Basic Income: the Dutch social security debate is hotting up', *New Economy*, 3(3): 187–191.

Thane, P. (1996) *Foundations of the Welfare State*, London and New York: Longman.

Theobald, R. (1966) 'The background to the guaranteed income concept', in Theobald, R. (ed.) *The Guaranteed Income: Next Step in Economic Evolution*, New York: Doubleday and Co. Inc.

Theobald, R. (1966) *The Guaranteed Income: Next Step in Economic Evolution*, New York: Doubleday and Co. Inc.

H.M. Treasury (August 1995) *Work Incentives*, London: HMSO.

H.M. Treasury (News Release) (29th March 1999) *Tackling Poverty and Extending Opportunity*, London: HMSO.

United Nations Development Programme (1995) *Human Development Report*, Oxford: Oxford University Press.

Van Der Veen, R. and Van Parijs, P. (1986) 'A capitalist road to communism', *Theory and Society*, 15(5): 635–756.

Van Parijs, P. (1991) 'Why surfers should be fed: the liberal case for an unconditional basic income', *Philosophy and Public Affairs*, 20(2): 101–131.

Van Parijs, P. (ed.) (1992a) *Arguing for Basic Income: Ethical Foundations for a Radical Reform*, London: Verso.

Van Parijs, P. (1992b) 'Competing Justifications of Basic Income', in Van Parijs, P. (ed.) *Arguing for Basic Income: Ethical Foundations for a Radical Reform*, London: Verso.

Van Parijs, P. (1992c) 'The Second Marriage of Justice and Efficiency', in Van Parijs, P. (ed.) *Arguing for Basic Income: Ethical Foundations for a Radical Reform*, London: Verso.

Van Parijs, P. (1992d) 'Basic income capitalism', *Ethics*, 102: 465–484.

Van Parijs, P. (1996) 'Basic income and the two dilemmas of the welfare state', *The Political Quarterly*, 67(1): 63–66.

Van Parijs, P. (2004) 'Basic Income: A Simple and Powerful Idea for the Twenty-first Century', *Politics and Society*, 32(1): 7–39.

Van Trier, W.E. (1989) *Who Framed Social Dividend? A Tale of the Unexpected*, Belgium Research Unit on Labour Economics, SESO – UFSIA University of Antwerp Prinsstraat 13 B-2018 Antwerpen.

Walker, C. (1987) 'Reforming Social Security – Despite the Claimant', in Walker, C. and Walker, A. (eds) *The Growing Divide*, London: CPAG.

Walker, C. (1993) *Managing Poverty: The Limits of Social Assistance*, London: Routledge.

Walker, C. and Walker, A. (1987) *The Growing Divide*, London: CPAG.

Walter, T. (1989) *Basic Income: Freedom from Poverty, Freedom to Work*, London and New York: Marion Boyars.

Whitton, T. (1993) 'Does "insertion" work? France's minimum income', *Citizens Income Bulletin*, 16, July 1993.

Whynes, D. (1993) 'The Poverty Trap', in Barr, N. and Whynes, D. (eds) *Current Issues in the Economics of Welfare*, Basingstoke and London: Macmillan.

Williams, F., Popay, J. and Oakley, A. (1999) *Welfare Research: A Critical Review*, London: UCL Press.

Wilson, T. and Wilson, D. (1982) *The Political Economy of the Welfare State*, London: George Allen and Unwin.

Wilson, T. and Wilson, D. (eds) (1991) *The State and Social Welfare: The Objectives of Policy*, London and New York, Longman.

Wilson, T. and Wilson D. (1993) 'Beveridge and the reform of social security – then and now', *Government and Opposition*, 28(3): 353–371.

Wiseman, J. (1991) 'The Welfare State: A Public Choice Perspective', in Wilson, T. and Wilson, D. (eds) *The State and Social Welfare: The Objectives of Policy*, London and New York: Longman.

Withorn, A. (1990) 'Is One Man's Ceiling another Woman's Floor? Women and BIG', paper presented at the conference 'Basic Income Guarantees: A New Welfare Strategy', University of Wisconsin, Madison, April 6–8, 1990.

Yeates, N. (2003) 'Social Security in a Global Context', in Millar, J. (ed.) *Understanding Social Security Issues for Policy and Practice*, Bristol: Policy Press.

Index

Lightning Source UK Ltd.
Milton Keynes UK
UKOW04f0426220814

237369UK00006B/51/P